The Criminal Lifestyle

To Patti, Christopher, and Tara

The Criminal Lifestyle

Patterns of Serious Criminal Conduct

Glenn D. Walters

SAGE PUBLICATIONS
The International Professional Publishers
Newbury Park   London   New Delhi

For information address:

SAGE Publications, Inc.
2111 West Hillcrest Drive
Newbury Park, California 91320

SAGE Publications Ltd.
28 Banner Street
London EC1Y 8QE
England

SAGE Publications India Pvt. Ltd.
M-32 Market
Greater Kailash I
New Delhi 110 048 India

Printed in the United States of America

Library of Congress Cataloging-in-Publication Data

Walters, Glenn D.
    The criminal lifestyle : patterns of serious criminal conduct / by
Glenn D. Walters
        p.   cm.
    Includes bibliographical references and indexes.
    ISBN 0-8039-3840-3
    1. Criminal behavior.   I. Title.
HV6115.W35   1990
364.3--dc20
                                                                    90-37509
                                                                    CIP

FIRST PRINTING, 1990

Sage Production Editor: Kimberley A. Clark

Contents

Preface

I have been sitting at my typewriter for some time now, wondering how I should proceed with this Preface. To say my feelings are mixed would be a major understatement. On the one hand, I want to develop a theme capable of carrying this book to a meaningful conclusion. On the other hand, I don't want to invest a significant amount of time in a section most readers (the present author included) rarely peruse. In what I hope is not too roundabout a way of dealing with my ambivalence, I would like to point out that a book on crime is not unlike a mystery novel. I offer this analogy cognizant of the fact that both entail a multitude of unknowns and, as any aficionado of the genre knows, the core of any good mystery is the what, why (or who), when, and how of the crime. With this in mind, I invite the reader to join me on a short excursion into an area normally reserved for the likes of Dashiell Hammett, Agatha Christie, and Mickey Spillane.

In considering the "what" of this book, it is important to understand that just about every one of us has committed a crime at one time or another. Most of these crimes are relatively minor in nature—such as traveling five miles over the speed limit or taking a pen home from work—but crimes nonetheless. In this book, however, we will be focusing our attention on persons who engage in serious criminality as part of a wider lifestyle. As such, we not only avoid the problem of triviality but also enhance the future universality of our results. This is because research clearly suggests that while lifestyle criminals are small in number, they account for a decisive majority of the serious crimes committed in this country (see Hamparian, Schuster, Dinitz, & Conrad, 1978; Shannon, 1982; Wolfgang, Figlio, & Sellin, 1972).

My principal motivation in writing this book was to contribute something of value to what I have come to call the field of criminal science. The "why" or "who" of this book is therefore grounded in my years of clinical experience working with groups of criminal offenders. This is a perspective I find to be invaluable for someone attempting to produce a book on criminals. Too often, authors of criminology and criminal science texts have had limited personal contact with real-life criminals. I mention this, not out of arrogance, but in an effort to point out that it is difficult to draw a consummate picture of

7

something one has rarely seen in operation. Consequently, research results and theoretical speculation might be more meaningful if tempered with clinical observation and direct contact with the subjects of one's investigation. The question of "when" may be more appropriately phrased, "why now?" After all, there have been numerous books written on the subject of crime, some of which have been published relatively recently (e.g., Wilson & Herrnstein, 1985). I respond to this query by referencing an old adage: "There's no time like the present." In addition to my seven years of clinical experience working daily with various groups of criminal offenders, I have been concatenating this information with selected research findings in an effort to devise a model of criminal behavior that is both meaningful and useful. Although I do not offer this model as definitive, I do believe that it has been sufficiently developed to serve as a hypothesis for others to review, examine, contemplate, and criticize.

In addressing the question of "how," I believe it is important for the reader to understand that I approach my work with lifestyle criminals as a sort of working hypothesis that is continually in the process of revision (although the foundation of this approach—conditions, choice, and cognition—has remained stable throughout my investigation). In fact, this is exactly how I approached the writing of this book. With only minor exceptions, the chapters appear in the order in which they were written. In this way, the reader can see for him- or herself how research and clinical observation can serve as a basis for a theory of lifestyle criminality and personal change.

Though this book may not be received with open arms by everyone in the criminology/criminal justice community, it does offer a fresh perspective on issues which, while central to criminal science investigation, have too often been overlooked by a majority of theorists in the field. Predominant among these is the fact that despite the influence of internal and external conditions, the individual makes certain choices. In understanding serious and reoccurring patterns of criminal conduct, it is therefore essential that we appreciate the kinds of choices the criminal makes and the belief system upon which these choices are based. With this in mind, we proceed through a maze of research, theoretical, and clinical findings—a trek, which, it is hoped, by journey's end should shed light on the what, why, when, and how of serious criminality.

Acknowledgments

I would like to thank Miriam Boyle and Joan Walters for their assistance in locating several of the newspaper articles referenced in this book.

The assertions contained in this book are the private views of the author and should not be construed as official or as reflecting the views of the Department of Justice or the Federal Bureau of Prisons.

1. A Working Hypothesis

Shortly after accepting employment as a clinical psychologist with the federal prison system, I was approached by a middle-aged inmate with a question that has served to stimulate my subsequent interest in the criminal lifestyle. In explaining how he had spent much of his adult life incarcerated in one correctional facility or another, this individual asserted that he had grown weary of confinement even before being released "the last time." He was puzzled because this sentiment did not seem to deter him from violating the law once he returned to the streets. Consequently, he found himself confined after only several months in the community. In my own mind, I had problems reconciling the obvious discrepancy between this individual's stated desires and his overt behavior. I also had difficulty discerning how a reasonably intelligent individual, as this inmate truly was, could engage in behavior that was so plainly self-destructive. What I failed to appreciate at the time, but am much more aware of today, is that criminality has less to do with intellectual ability or stated desires, and a great deal more to do with how a person structures his or her experience into specific cognitive patterns.

Taking a ground-roots approach to the question of crime, I scanned the literature for clues that might be useful in my effort to understand criminal behavior. I read the works of Cleckley (1976), Hare (1970), Quay (1977), and Yochelson and Samenow (1976), but still there was something missing. Then in 1987, I began supplementing my clinical work with a series of research investigations and theoretical position papers. In the first of a series of six articles written in reference to lifestyle criminality, Tom White and I examined the beliefs of prison inmates, college students, and criminal justice experts about the causes of crime (Walters & White, 1988). A wide assortment of different causal factors were mentioned, poverty and family influences being relatively popular among the subjects in all of the three groups. There were, nevertheless, several notable dissimilarities between the criminal justice experts, on the one hand, and subjects in the inmate and student conditions on the other. The experts, for instance, tended to place much less emphasis on personal choice as a cause of crime than did subjects in the student and inmate conditions. We interpreted this finding as reflecting the demise of choice and personal responsibility as viable explanations of crime in the minds of individuals society considers to be its experts in the field.

The Classical-Positivist Debate

A review of the literature published in the criminal justice/criminology field over the past several years shows a similar movement away from personal responsibility in favor of a more deterministic view of man. Thus the classical school of criminological thought, which posits that criminals choose to engage in various forms of lawbreaking behavior, is popular with only a minority of criminologic scholars, but still holds favor with those working in the U.S. criminal justice system. With its roots in the early teachings of Jeremy Bentham (1748-1832) and Cesare Beccaria (1738-1794), traditional classicism hypothesized that a person engages in a particular criminal act when the pleasure associated with that act exceeds the anticipated pain. In their work on the criminal personality, Samuel Yochelson and Stanton Samenow (1976, 1985, 1986) provide a modern version of the classical perspective.

Appreciably more popular than the classical viewpoint is the positivist school of thought. Grounded in the philosophical writings of Auguste Comte (1798-1857), a French mathematician and philosopher, the positivist position dismissed free will and argued that behavior was a function of various biologic and environmental factors. The positivist approach was first applied to criminal behavior by Cesare Lombroso, an Italian physician, who, along with several colleagues, focused on the physical characteristics of a group of hard-core felons. Lombroso claimed that criminality was an inherited trait that could be identified by means of certain physical traits (e.g., large, protruding jaw; sloping forehead) and hypothesized that the criminal was a throwback to a more primitive stage of human development. Although Lombroso's approach to criminality no longer guides the thinking of researchers in the field, two current biologically oriented theories of crime (i.e., Hare, 1970; Mednick, 1987) seem to have been influenced by Lombroso's brand of biological positivism.

Perhaps the most abounding school of criminologic thought is the one established by sociologically minded positivists. This group of theorists have argued that crime is caused by various environmental conditions over which the individual has minimal control. There is little room for choice, free will, and personal responsibility in an approach such as this. Asserting that criminal behavior is learned within the context of certain social interactions—peer relationships in particular—Edwin Sutherland (Sutherland & Cressey, 1978) advanced the deterministic notion that criminal behavior is principally a function of having been exposed to definitions favorable to violations of societal laws and rules. Other popular sociological positivist theories of criminal behavior include negative labeling theory (Schur, 1971), Merton's (1957) strain theory, and the Marxist approach to crime (Spitzer, 1975). Though scholars like David Matza (1964) have pointed out the limitations associated with overreliance on the deterministic predilections of positivism, this field of thought continues to exert a major impact on contemporary criminologic theory.

Where research and/or clinical support can be found for both the classical and positivist approaches to criminology, each explanation is seriously incomplete. The classical perspective, for instance, provides for the prospect of personal choice in human behavior, something which seems to make good intuitive sense. However, this approach seems to overlook a wealth of empirical data that suggest biological and environmental factors are moderately predictive of certain types of behavior. Further, this model's heavy reliance on free will and hedonism as explanatory concepts seems almost archaic by modern standards (see Peterson, 1984). Positivism, on the other hand, has the advantage of being based on verifiable fact and solid research findings. Unfortunately, it fails to explain why some persons exposed to sundry "criminogenic" conditions never engage in a single serious criminal act. It would seem that the classical and positivist explanations of criminality are at opposite ends of the spectrum, with differences that are irreconcilable. This disharmony may be more apparent than real, however.

Before discussing the potential compatibility of the classical and positivist viewpoints, it may be helpful to examine the individual proponents of each. Experience has taught us that court officials, clinical practitioners, and other professionals entrusted with the responsibility of making decisions about individual offenders are often drawn to the classical philosophy that people are accountable for their actions. This idiographic approach contrasts sharply with the nomothetic leanings of most empirically oriented scholars. Positivism, on the other hand, satisfies the academician's interest in research/statistical control and group data. What needs to be realized is that these two positions are not as incongruous as they may at first appear. In fact, if integrated properly, these two explanations may actually complement one

another. The classical and positivist schools are much like two sides of the
same coin, their value being interdependent and principally a function of how
they are paired rather than how they are contrasted.

In forging a link between the classical and positivist interpretations of
criminal behavior, there are three characteristics that should be considered.
These three characteristics form a system of interacting influences relative
to the criminal lifestyle, a system I have come to call the three Cs: conditions,
be they internal or external; choice or the human decision-making process;
and cognition, or better yet, thinking. In reviewing these three characteristics,
I hope to demonstrate how each can be useful in reconciling the classical-
positivist controversy in a manner that facilities our appreciation of the
criminal lifestyle.

Conditions

Research has clearly established that we are born with certain biological
characteristics and into a specific environmental situation. Certain of these
characteristics and conditions have been found to correlate with subsequent
delinquent behavior and adult criminality. An individual who is born with a
difficult temperament, raised in an environment where pimps and drug
dealers are seen as heroes, and exposed to inconsistent or abusive discipline,
for instance, is placed at increased risk for later criminality (Wilson &
Herrnstein, 1985). Conditions such as these would appear to lay the groundwork for later involvement in serious criminal activity.

I would submit that conditions can be grouped into two general categories:
person variables and situation variables. Person variables are characteristics
of the individual that are correlated with subsequent criminal behavior.
Heredity (Walters & White, 1989a), intelligence (Hirschi & Hindelang,
1977), temperament (Kellam, Adams, Brown, & Ensminger, 1982), and age
(Hirschi & Gottfredson, 1983) are among the person characteristics thought
to be linked with recidivistic lawbreaking behavior. Situation variables, on
the other hand, are characteristics of the environment or situation that have
been investigated as part of the criminal science effort. The list of situation
variables that have been studied relative to the issue of crime is legion,
although some of the more popular environmental antecedents include social
class (Braithwaite, 1981), drugs (Anglin & Speckart, 1988), media violence
(Leftkowitz, Eron, Walder, & Huesmann, 1977), and family relationships
(Loeber & Dishion, 1983).

As vital as individual person and situation variables may be to the development of the criminal lifestyle, the person by situation (hereinafter referred to as person×situation) interaction is of even greater importance. Though some theorists argue that the person and situation are so tightly intertwined as to defy meaningful analysis (see Magnusson & Allen, 1983), others maintain that through the use of interactional designs and multivariate statistics some of these effects can be teased out and studied (Rowe, 1987). Bem and Funder (1978) even offer a methodology through which this might be accomplished. The concerns of theorists like Magnusson and Allen notwithstanding, I would contend that the person×situation interaction can be studied and that it takes place in three primary domains: the physical, the social, and the psychological. This, in fact, provides the structure for our discussion of developmental issues in Chapter 5.

Choice

That conditions exert an undeniable impact on behavior does not preclude the possibility of choice. As the existential philosopher Ludwig Binswanger (1963) once noted, we need to be responsible for the choices we make within the boundaries established by certain biologic and environmental conditions. Even though the choice process itself may be influenced by certain factors, to include cognitive maturity, sphere of information, and one's reinforcement history, the individual still chooses to engage in particular actions. In the final analysis, our options may be limited for certain personal and situational factors, but these factors or conditions do not determine our choices.

A young child, by virtue of its limited intellectual understanding and restricted range of prior information, is much less capable of making informed decisions than is the average adult. However, as this child's brain matures, so does his or her ability to think, reason, and rationalize. As a result, the child becomes increasingly more capable of making informed decisions as he or she grows older. Although our reinforcement histories influence our conduct regardless of how old we are (i.e., we tend to engage in those behaviors for which we are reinforced), it is how we interpret a particular reinforcing condition, and not the condition itself, that determines how we behave. Moreover, research conducted with groups of criminal offenders has demonstrated that they do, in fact, make decisions and choices concerning the crimes they commit (see Cornish & Clarke, 1986).

Cognition

Cognition is the final link in the chain I am drawing between the classical and positivist schools of criminology. The thinking style we develop in response to the early conditions to which we are exposed and the early choices we make relative to these conditions are at the root of all behavior, criminal as well as noncriminal. Likewise, I believe it is essential for the reader to understand that this book will be examining criminality as a way of life—crime as a lifestyle. Isolated episodes of illegality and criminal actions that do not satisfy our definition of lifestyle criminality (see Chapter 4) will not be discussed at any length here. It is hypothesized, then, that the lifestyle criminal constructs a belief system grounded in various early conditions and associated choices that serve to justify, support, and rationalize his subsequent criminal actions. We must therefore understand criminal thinking if we are to comprehend criminal behavior.

Crime in Perspective

The Criminal Lifestyle will treat crime as a multidimensional concept. This contrasts sharply with the more typical practice of approaching crime unitarily. However, if we can assume that choice is important in the criminal development process, then it would stand to reason that there are variegated reasons why people engage in criminal action. The field of psychology has realized for some time now that general theories of human behavior are too global to be of much use, and there is now movement away from omnibus theories of human personality in favor of models that describe a circumscribed subset of behavior. This book will remain faithful to this trend by focusing on a group of individuals who, while they may not be the most prevalent group of offenders in terms of numbers, account for the majority of serious, predatory-type crimes committed in the United States (Hamparian, Schuster, Dinitz, & Conrad, 1978; Shannon, 1982; Wolfgang, Figlio, & Sellin, 1972)—if not the world. Because these individuals approach crime as a way of life, we will enlist the term lifestyle criminality[1] to describe their behavior.

In examining this issue of lifestyle criminality, the question that quite logically comes to mind is why propose a new lexicon when more established terms like career criminal (Petersilia, Greenwood, & Lavin, 1978) and criminal personality (Yochelson & Samenow, 1976) are available? In order to answer this query, we need to examine the logic that guided the initial development of the theory of lifestyle criminality. When the term lifestyle criminal was first coined, the intent was to capture the inveterate nature of the behavior being observed as well as to place this behavior within a developmental context. It was further reasoned that neither the career criminality nor the criminal personality conceptualizations adequately addressed both issues. Lifestyle criminality may overlap with the career criminal concept, an issue that will be discussed further in Chapter 3, but it is also possible for one to be a career criminal without being a lifestyle criminal and vice versa. Consequently, these terms are not interchangeable, though they are related.

In a similar vein, this book will focus on adult criminality rather than delinquency or juvenile crime. Research suggests that while nearly all career criminals began offending at a relatively early age (Greenwood, 1983), not all juvenile offenders carry this pattern with them into adulthood (see also Greenwood & Zimring, 1985). It is therefore likely that the correlates of juvenile delinquency and adult criminality differ enough to justify separate treatment. Consequently, this book will consider aspects of juvenile delinquency only to the extent that doing so will facilitate our understanding of the criminal lifestyle. It should be noted, however, that there are many issues central to the theory of lifestyle criminality that have only been addressed by research carried out on adolescents. Therefore, while delinquency will not be the focal point of our discussion, research using juvenile subjects will receive a considerable amount of attention when we examine several of the more prominent theories of criminal conduct and explore the issue of behavioral change.

The Criminal Lifestyle will attempt to confront a methodological conundrum that has existed for many years and for which there is no easy answer. Researchers have been debating for some time now the most appropriate source of data for criminal science research. Some investigators swear by self-report data, while others would not even consider conducting a study without having access to official police records. This situation is complicated further by the relatively recent introduction of a third data source, victimization surveys. Research comparing these three sources of criminal science information has found a general lack of correlation between these various measures of criminality except in the case of several isolated crime categories like homicide (see Messner, 1984). Hence, the approach taken in developing the theory of lifestyle criminality has been to examine as many different sources of data as possible. The method used to develop this theory consisted not only of self-report, official, and victimization data, but clinical and observational information as well.

Having been trained as a psychologist under the scientist-practitioner model, I firmly believe in the value of both research and clinical experience. Both are capable of providing us with insight into human behavior, although both also have their individual blind spots and inherent limitations. As with the classical and positivist schools of criminology, research and clinical practice complement one another, although finding a workable integration has not always been easy. In the field of psychology, for instance, scientists and practitioners have been at odds for many years now, each side threatening to secede from the American Psychological Association unless the other makes certain concessions. This is the kind of polarized thinking I have taken pains to avoid in the present publication. Consequently, a relatively novel approach taken in this book concerns the use of both research and clinical data in formulating a theory of lifestyle criminality.

The Working Hypothesis Approach to Theory Building

In developing our ideas on criminality, my colleagues and I have treated this evolving theory of lifestyle criminality as a kind of working hypothesis. The ideas of such research-oriented scholars as Quay (1977), Cleckley (1976), and Sutherland (Sutherland & Cressey, 1978) and the writings of such clinically oriented theorists as Yochelson and Samenow (1976) originally served as the impetus for many of our early hypotheses on crime and criminals. These early hypotheses were then compared with what we observed in our clinical contacts with prison inmates and other groups of offenders. The newly formed working hypotheses this procedure engendered were subsequently examined empirically by means of various research paradigms and additional clinical findings. The theory of lifestyle criminality presented in this book is simply the most recent version of this working hypothesis. Even though new information is continually being incorporated into the framework of this theory, the primary tenets—namely conditions, choice, and cognition—have remained remarkably stable over the course of several revisions.

Since a theory of human behavior is no better than the data upon which it rests, research and clinical findings must be an integral part of the theory-building enterprise. Research provides a theory with its foundation and practice provides its utility. This notion will be developed further in a later chapter. In closing this present chapter, I would like to say that I had several goals in mind when writing this text. Of prime importance, however, was my desire to provide a perspective that integrated aspects of the classical and positivist schools of thought; capitalized on the contributions of scholars from several different academic disciplines; and promoted an understanding of crime as a lifestyle. I leave it to the reader to decide whether my efforts serve to shed light on the relevant issues in a manner that not only furthers our understanding of habitual and serious forms of criminal conduct, but also addresses the question posed to me by that middle-aged inmate nearly six years ago.

NOTE

1. The terms *lifestyle criminality*, *criminal lifestyle*, and *(lifestyle, habitual, high-rate, recidivistic, repeat) criminal/offender* will be used interchangeably throughout this book.

2. Criminologic Theory

Having available to us a wealth of research findings is no guarantee that we will make effective use of these data. Consequently, research results need to be considered within a wider theoretical framework if they are to prove useful. Frank P. Williams (1984), for one, asserts that the field of criminology has sacrificed theoretical creativity in the name of operationality and empirical scientism. In order to produce outcomes that are meaningful, Williams recommends that we make a concerted effort to integrate or blend creativity into our empirical investigations and avoid the implicit dualism that seems to have characterized much of our thinking on crime and criminals. A good theory advances knowledge by organizing disparate bits of information into a meaningful whole and by providing testable hypotheses that serve to direct future research investigation. A poor theory, on the other hand, often muddies the waters by diverting our attention from important, verifiable issues to ones that are trivial, superfluous, or untestable.

Integration is often a primary goal of theory. Divergent bits of data may be integrated into a single theory, or several different theories might be consolidated to form an integrated model. Two recent attempts at integration, one by Pearson and Weiner (1985), the other by Thornberry (1987), seem worthy of at least a brief review. In surveying 12 of the more popular theories of criminology, Pearson and Weiner uncovered three general integrating variables: internal antecedents, external antecedents, and consequences. The internal antecedents would include utility demands (motivation), behavioral skill (acquired actions directed toward securing utilities), rules of expedience (cognitive patterns that orient behavior toward maximizing the acquisition of utilities), and rules of morality (cognitive patterns that orient behavior along the lines of right versus wrong). Of the external antecedent variables examined by Pearson and Weiner, opportunities (contextual stimuli that signal whether a utility can reasonably be anticipated) and behavioral resources (vehicles by which utilities are obtained) are among the most important. Utility reception (rewards and punishments emanating from specific behaviors) and information acquisition (knowledge about the pattern of reinforcement under specific environmental contingencies) constitute the primary consequences studied by Pearson and Weiner within the context of this integrative model.

Two years after Pearson and Weiner introduced their social learning integration of criminology theory, Terence Thornberry (1987) proposed a social-developmental perspective that also encompassed an integration of ideas from a number of different criminologic theories. In advancing this model, Thornberry contends that delinquency is as much a cause as it is an effect of various social variables and conditions. Causal relationships are said to form a mutually dependent network of interlocking forces that vary as a function of developmental changes taking place in the individual. Consequently, attachment to one's parents may be crucial to the crime-social variable relationship during childhood, but the focus shifts to peer and school attachment with the advent of puberty. Thornberry maintains that during early adulthood, additional changes take place in the crime-social variable nexus. During this life stage attachments formed within the context of marriage, college, employment, and military life assume increasing prominence.

Integrative schemes, such as those offered by Pearson and Weiner (1985) and Thornberry (1987), are a vital step in theory building. First, however, we must understand the basic theories themselves. To this end, we find ourselves probing eight theories of criminal behavior. So as to achieve a balanced review, all eight theories will be examined using a common set of criteria. These criteria were initially developed by Salvatore Maddi (1976) in his review of various theories of personality, although they are appropriate for the present purposes as well. According to Maddi, a good theory should be important, operational, precise, parsimonious, stimulating, and empirically valid. Before entering the review portion of this chapter, it may be useful to briefly define each of the six criteria of a good theory.

The criterion of importance asks whether the theory is more concerned with essential, meaningful, and clinically relevant relationships than trivial detail. Operationality considers whether the conceptualizations one employs are accurate, tangible, and have empirical referents that demonstrate the attributes of a robust measure (i.e., reliability and validity). Maddi's third criterion, precision, holds that a theory should avoid ambiguous, figurative, or analogical wording, striving instead to be clear, concise, and succinct. The goal of parsimony, our fourth criterion, is simplicity in theorizing: A parsimonious theory is one that can explain a set of phenomenon using a minimal number of assumptions and concepts. Maddi also considers whether a theory stimulates or provokes others to action, whether this response be positive or negative, theoretical or empirical. The essence of empirical validity, the sixth and final criterion, involves exploring whether predictions derived from the theory hold true when scrutinized experimentally.

Differential Association

The French scholar Gabriel Tarde (1912) was one of the first persons to propose that patterns of delinquency and crime are learned in much the same manner as any occupation, primarily through imitation of and association with others. Edwin H. Sutherland (1939) took this basic idea and developed it into a theory of criminal behavior. Sutherland hypothesized that criminal behavior is learned through associations established with those who violate society's norms. The learning process involves not only the actual techniques of crime, but also the motives, drive, attitudes, and rationalizations favorable to the commission of antisocial acts (Sutherland & Cressey, 1978). According to the theory of differential association, then, a person becomes delinquent because of the presence of an "excess of definitions favorable to violations of the law over definitions unfavorable to violations of the law" (Cohen, Lindesmith, & Schuessler, 1956, p. 9).

Sutherland's (1939) differential association theory of criminality asserts that: (1) criminal behavior, like any behavior, is learned; (2) criminal behavior is learned in intimate association with those who commit crimes; (3) criminality is determined by the frequency, duration, intensity, and priority of these associations; (4) cultural conflict underlies the differential association process; (5) individual differences are only important to the extent that they effect differential association. Ronald Akers (1977) recently expanded the learning base of differential association theory by integrating it with Skinner's (1953) operant theory of behavior. Since the initial publication of his theory of differential association in 1939, Sutherland had always taken a learning approach to the question of crime, although Akers's contributions would appear to make this theory even more compatible with behavioral and social learning formulations.

In an early study on differential association theory, James F. Short (1957) found results that were generally supportive of the theory. He did note, however, that delinquency was more strongly linked to the intensity, than either the frequency, duration, or priority, of the association. In a subsequent replication study, Harwin Voss (1964) found much the same relationship: Individuals who associated with delinquent friends tended to engage in significantly more delinquent behavior than individuals whose contact with delinquent peers was minimal. Enyon and Reckless (1961) also observed that companionship with antisocial peers often preceded the onset of both self-reported and officially recorded delinquency.

The province of research that has been most damaging to Sutherland's formulations on differential association is that which has considered the issue of crime specialization. Thus, while Sutherland predicts specificity in criminal and delinquent behavior based on the associations one makes, research tends to support neither Sutherland's predictions concerning specificity nor crime specialization in general (see Farrington, 1982; Smith, Smith, & Noma, 1984; Wolfgang et al., 1972). There are, however, other postulates advanced by Sutherland that do stand up under empirical scrutiny.

Reiss and Rhodes (1964) examined differential association theory using a stratified sample of 378 12- to 16-year-old boys enrolled in public, private, and parochial schools in Davidson County, Tennessee. The boys were grouped in triads, each group containing a subject and his two closest friends. In support of Sutherland's theory of differential association, Reiss and Rhodes report that the boys in their sample had selected friends who were as delinquent or law-abiding as they were. However, these findings varied according to social class, since working-class male youth demonstrated a clear differential association effect for both serious and less serious offenses, while middle-class boys displayed a differential association effect for less serious crimes but not for more serious ones. In support of our earlier discussion on the limitations of differential association theory relative to the issue of crime specialization, Reiss and Rhodes were unable to verify Sutherland's theorem that delinquents learn specific criminal techniques within the context of peer relationships.

More recent research on differential association theory has been just about as corroborative as were many of the earlier studies. Robins, West, and Herjanic (1975) found delinquency to be strongly associated with sibling delinquency, and Johnson (1979) reports that boys who claim delinquent friends are more likely to engage in criminality than boys who claim no delinquent companions. Using a prospective design, West and Farrington (1977) demonstrated that the antisocial activities of friends and associates predicted delinquent behavior on the part of a group of young Londoners. In a cross-national investigation of crime in developing countries, Clinard and Abbott (1973) uncovered results that were largely congruent with Sutherland's ideas on differential association. Moreover, while Gary Jensen (1972) found differential association theory to be less effective than Hirschi's social control theory in classifying outcomes from the Richmond Youth Project, Ross

Matsueda (1982) determined that differential association theory was actually superior to social control theory in a re-analysis of these data using a better operationalized measure of learned behavioral patterns favorable and unfavorable to law violations.

D. A. Andrews (1980) of Carlton University in Ottawa, Canada, discussed the results of a series of studies he and his colleagues carried out using a community group model of intervention. These community groups accommodated four to seven community volunteers (normally college students) and four to seven prison inmates, and met once a week for a period of eight weeks. Participating inmate members demonstrated decreased tolerance for rule violations and decreased identification with the criminal element, while the community volunteers displayed a converse shift in attitude in the direction of increased identification with criminal values. Subsequent analyses revealed that the observed outcomes were unlikely to have been the result of a more generalized attention/demand effect.

Unfortunately, Sutherland was less than crystal clear in explicating the mechanism underlying differential association; therefore, an assortment of different models has been proposed in an effort to explain exactly how the process of differential association operates. Charles R. Tittle, Mary Jean Burke, and Ellen F. Jackson (1986) not only uncovered support for the theoretical notion of differential association, but they also discovered that the process exerts its effect on behavior indirectly by way of a learned symbolic context (i.e., the motivation to engage in criminality), rather than directly through imitation or modeling.

In a second study carried out by this same group of researchers (Jackson, Tittle, & Burke, 1986), it was determined that while Sutherland was largely justified in calling attention to the importance of peer associations, these associations were criminogenic only to the extent that they elevated criminal motivation and not because they taught attitudes and rationalizations consistent with deviance. These authors continue by encouraging future investigators to explore these issues in greater detail as a way of determining whether definitions favorable to various forms of lawbreaking behavior cluster into several independent loci or assemble around a single domain of crime/deviance.

Borrowing from Sutherland's differential association theory and Becker's (1953) early work on marijuana use, James D. Orcutt (1987) was able to appraise the probability of marijuana utilization in college students given certain motivational and associational conditions. Students with positive, neutral, and negative definitions of marijuana usage were asked to estimate how many of their four closest friends smoked marijuana at least once a month. Results indicated that students with negative definitions of marijuana usage tended to avoid marijuana regardless of how many friends were semi-regular users, while those with positive definitions of marijuana usage were liable to smoke marijuana themselves if at least one of their four closest friends were also a semi-regular user. Of the group with neutral attitudes toward marijuana usage, personal usage was virtually zero if none of the four closest friends were users of this substance, but rose to one in four in cases in which one friend was a semi-regular user and one in two if two or more friends were semi-regular users. These findings are largely supportive of Sutherland's contention that a person will engage in an illegal act if he or she is exposed to an excess of definitions favorable to violating that particular law or social rule.

Though Sutherland's theory of differential association has received a fairly impressive amount of empirical support, it is not without its problems. For one, this theory fails to explain why delinquents and criminals take advice from delinquent peers and associates rather than from noncriminal family members and classmates (Wilson & Herrnstein, 1985). Second, it overlooks the fact that many serious, recidivistic offenders have never integrated well into groups, delinquent or otherwise, and so have had less of an opportunity for differential association than better adjusted adolescents (Hirschi, 1969). Third, researchers have often overlooked the possibility that delinquent associations may be a result, rather than cause, of an early delinquent life orientation. Fourth, critical aspects of the theory have been thought to be untestable (Cressey, 1960), although the results of several recent studies appear to hint that the theory is much more amenable to examination than was once thought (compare Orcutt, 1987; Tittle et al., 1986). Lastly, Sutherland has been criticized for failing to take into account the larger social structural context in which differential rewards and punishments are arranged and made available (Colvin & Pauly, 1983).

In spite of these criticisms, Sutherland's (1939) theory of differential association seems to fare reasonably well when compared against Maddi's six criteria (see Table 2.1). Differential association theory not only appears to concentrate on important relationships, but it also seems strong in terms of its parsimony and precision. In fact, Glaser (1960) comments that differential association theory is superior to most alternative theories in the degree to which observations can be codified and hypotheses established. The copious literature on this theory is testimony to its ability to stimulate investigation, and in most instances the research has tended to support Sutherland's ideas, although several more specific postulates have been found wanting (e.g., uniformity of specific delinquent trends: See Reiss & Rhodes, 1964). If there is a criterion on which differential association falls

TABLE 2.1: Appraising Eight Theories of Criminal Behavior

Theory	Reference	Criteria 1	2	3	4	5	6
Differential Association	Sutherland and Cressey (1978)	H	L	M	H	H	M
Strain Theory	Merton (1957)	M	M	L	M	H	L
Social Control	Hirschi (1969)	H	M	L	M	H	H
Labeling	Schur (1971)	L	L	L	H	H	M
Self Theories	Wells (1978)	M	L	L	M	L	L
Psychoanalytic Theory	Glover (1960)	M	L	L	L	L	L
Pathological Stimulation Seeking	Quay (1977)	M	M	L	M	H	M
Rational Choice Theory	Becker (1968)	L	M	H	M	M	L

Note: Criteria are as follows: 1 = importance, 2 = operationality, 3 = precision, 4 = parsimony, 5 = stimulation, 6 = empirical validity.
Ratings are as follows: H = high (above average), M = moderate (average), and L = low (below average).

short, it is in the area of operationality. Several investigators have, however, developed their own measures of differential association (e.g., Short, 1957), though Sutherland (1939; Sutherland & Cressey, 1978) failed to adequately operationalize his terms, a deficiency that needs to be rectified if research on differential association is to continue to contribute to the criminal science research effort.

Strain Theory

Noted French sociologist Emile Durkheim (1938) theorized that under certain social conditions, traditional societal norms and rules lose their authority over behavior. Durkheim referred to this state of normlessness as anomie, a term that serves as the foundation for Robert Merton's (1957) strain theory of criminal behavior. According to Merton, a society instills in its members a desire for certain goals and then outlines legitimate means through which these goals might be attained. It is reasoned that if a person is thwarted in his or her efforts to realize these goals legitimately, he or she may attempt to achieve them via a variety of illegal maneuvers. Lower-social-class individuals, frustrated by their inability to participate in the economic rewards of the wider society, are said to redirect their energies into criminal activity as a way of obtaining these rewards (Merton, 1957).

Strain theory assumes that man is basically a conforming being who only violates society's law, norms, and rules after the disjunction between goals and means becomes so great that he finds the only way he can achieve these goals is through illegal channels. Consequently, strain theory views man in an optimistic light. In other words, man is basically good since it is the social condition that creates stress, strain, and eventually crime. Due to the fact that legitimate opportunities are unevenly distributed throughout a society, strain theory proposes the presence of a strong link between crime and social class (Merton, 1957). In discussing the foundations of strain theory, Merton maintains that a greater emphasis on goals than the means used in attaining them and a restriction of legitimate opportunities available to portions of the population are necessary conditions in the development of a sense of anomie and strain, which in turn contributes to society's crime problems.

Although strain theory has generated a relatively large number of empirical investigations, many of these studies have yielded results that are largely inconsistent with Merton's original hypothesis. Research on social class, inequality, and the effect of dropping out of school, for instance, calls into question many of the tenets espoused by strain theorists. The results of many of the earlier research studies on social class and crime were consistent with the supposition that more persons from lower than higher socioeconomic backgrounds engaged in various forms of illegal activity (see Reiss & Rhodes, 1961). More recently conducted investigations, however, particularly ones in which self-report data have been utilized, show the relationship between social class and crime to be slight, if not insignificant (see Tittle, Villemez, & Smith, 1978), although controversy continues to surround the proposed association between social class and crime (see Braithwaite, 1981). Research on income inequality, while inconclusive, also tends to be inconsistent with Merton's formulations (see Messner, 1981; Stack, 1982). Finally, several recent studies on school and crime suggest that dropping out of school normally leads to increased rather than decreased (as strain theory would predict) levels of antisocial conduct (see Shavit & Rattner, 1988; Thornberry, Moore, & Christenson, 1985).

In partial support of Merton's theory of criminality, Brennan and Huizinga (1975) found that youth perceptions of limited opportunity, anomie, peer pressure, and negative labeling accounted for 31% of the variance in the frequency of self-reported acts of delinquency in 730 adolescents. Cernkovich and Giordano (1979) discerned that while male and female delinquents expressed a greater sense of blocked opportunity than male and female nondelinquents, this variable explained only 10% of the variance in delinquent behavior. In an effort to examine the primary tenets of strain theory directly, Steven Stack (1983) compared the reported rates of homicide and property crime with the Paglin-Gini index of income inequality for all 50 states. A multiple regression analysis of these data revealed that income inequality was associated with homicide, but not property crime. Stack reports further that a preliminary analysis of data collected on 29 nations yielded similar results. This finding presents problems for strain theory since Merton argues that income inequality should lead to increased levels of economically oriented crime.

Theorists and researchers critical of strain theory argue that this model suffers from redundancy to the extent that goal commitment, in the absence of differential means to goal attainment, may account for a person's involvement in criminal activity (Johnson, 1979; Kornhauser, 1978). Hirschi (1969) was able to demonstrate that commitment to conventional aims was sufficient to explain criminal involvement and that additional factors, such as those adhered to by strain theorists, were largely superfluous to the crime-goal relationship. In an analysis of multiple data sets, Liska (1971) arrived at a similar conclusion.

Finding fault with the Hirschi and Liska investigations, Margaret Farnworth and Michael Leiber (1989) argued that disjunction between economic goals and educational means is a more adequate test of strain theory than the more commonly employed discontinuity between educational aspirations and expectations. Applying this logic to a sample of over 1,600 older adolescents in the Seattle, Washington, metropolitan area, Farnworth and Leiber discerned a moderate relationship between disjunction and utilitarian or property-oriented crime and a slight, but nonetheless significant, connection between disjunction and nonutilitarian delinquency. Though these findings appear to lend support to theorems advanced by strain theorists (i.e., that a sense of blocked opportunity leads to criminal involvements), the correlational nature of this study presents problems of interpretation since it could just as easily be argued that high economic goals and low educational expectations are the result, rather than the cause, of criminal involvement.

In addition to problems with its empirical validity, strain theory has also been criticized for being too general and imprecise (Bahr, 1979), failing to account for the criminality of persons growing up in middle-class homes (Elliott & Voss, 1974), and overlooking important individual differences in behavior (Wilson & Herrnstein, 1985). Moreover, it has been largely unsuccessful in explaining why most working-class youth never resort to crime or why many delinquents abandon the criminal way of life by the time they enter adulthood (Hirschi, 1969). Another shortcoming is that contrary to the predictions of strain theory, high aspirations in working-class youth tend to correlate inversely with later delinquency (Elliott & Voss, 1974; Hirschi, 1969). Operationality and parsimony are other areas requiring additional attention if strain theory is to have much utility in advancing our understanding of crime and criminals (see Table 2.1). Lastly, while there is some support for Merton's contention that most Americans share middle-class goals (see Erlanger, 1980), there is other research that disputes this basic premise of strain theory (Kitsuse & Dietrick, 1959; Lemert, 1972).

In response to many of the criticisms leveled against strain theory, investigators have endeavored to integrate it with other models of criminal behavior. Cloward and Ohlin (1960), for instance, worked to integrate strain theory with Sutherland's differential association approach by arguing that the effects of strain will not operate unless one also has the opportunity to learn from delinquent peers. However, in an empirical test of this theory, Elliott and Voss (1974) found confirmation for the differential association component of the model but virtually no support for the strain/anomie component. More recently, Elliott, Ageton, and Canter (1979) made an effort to enhance the relevance of strain theory by synthesizing it with Hirschi's (1969) social control theory. While the Elliott et al. integration appears to address a number of issues overlooked by strain theory, it has yet to be properly evaluated from an empirical standpoint. Consequently, it remains an interesting possibility awaiting further analysis.

From the research reviewed here, it would appear that strain theory holds very little for those of us interested in unraveling the mysteries of crime. In terms of its ability to explain the development of a criminal lifestyle, this is probably true. However, strain theory may prove more valuable in explaining the aggregate/community aspects of crime. The riots in the Overtown section of Miami, Florida, a predominately black lower-class neighborhood, in January of 1989 are a case in point. Although it is likely that some of the individuals participating in this disturbance were lifestyle criminals, most were citizens frustrated and angry from years of economic inequality and a growing perception that they were being denied legitimate opportunities for advancement. Once the disturbance was over, however, most of these individuals went back to their families, friends, and jobs (if they had them) rather than continuing with their illegalities. This highlights the fact that while strain theory may be useful in describing aggregate level criminality, it does a relatively poor job with individual level data, although in all fairness to Merton, strain theory was never intended for individual level prediction (see Bernard, 1987b).

Social Control

There have been a number of social control theories formulated over the years, but none has had as much impact on contemporary criminological thinking as has the one derived by Travis Hirschi (1969), currently a professor of sociology at the University of Arizona. It is Hirschi's contention that criminal behavior results from a failure of conventional social groups (family, school, pro-social peers) to bind or bond with the individual. Unlike strain theory, the social control argument does not see the individual as intrinsically law-abiding but adopts the antithetical view that man must learn not to offend. Since we are all born with a natural proclivity to violate the rules of society, delinquency is viewed by social control theorists as a logical consequence of one's failure to develop internalized prohibitions against lawbreaking behavior. As such, Hirschi's theory focuses on conformity rather than delinquency. While Hirschi does not dispute the importance of direct or external sources of social control, he adds that internal controls are even more powerful in directing human behavior.

There are four key elements in Hirschi's (1969) social control theory of criminal behavior: attachment, commitment, involvement, and belief. Attachment involves the strength of any ties that may exist between the individual and primary agents of socialization, such as parents, teachers, and community leaders. Consequently, it is a measure of the degree to which law-abiding persons serve as a source of positive reinforcement for the individual. With regard to commitment, we see an investment in conformity or conventional behavior and a consideration of future goals that are incompatible with a delinquent lifestyle. Involvement, which is a measure of one's propensity to participate in conventional activities, directs the individual toward socially valued success. Hirschi states that the more time one spends in conventional activities, the less opportunity one will have to engage in illegal behavior. Finally, belief entails acceptance of the moral validity of societal norms and reflects the strength of one's conventional attitude. Though Hirschi failed to empirically evaluate how these four elements might interact, he hypothesizes the presence of a relationship between attachment and commitment, attachment and belief, and commitment and involvement.

Hirschi (1969) gauged the validity of his social control theory of criminality by administering a questionnaire to a group of 4,000 high school students. Not only was there a meaningful connection between self-reported delinquency and poor attachment to one's parents, as social control theory would predict, but there was also support for the validity of each of the four key elements (i.e., attachment, commitment, involvement, belief). In cross-validating Hirschi's original investigation, Michael Hindelang (1973) observed a negative correlation between delinquency and each of Hirschi's key elements. The only noteworthy difference in the results of the two studies was that where Hirschi observed a negative relationship between peer attachment and delinquency, Hindelang recorded a positive association. Hindelang argued that Hirschi's theory requires greater elaboration in terms of peer attachment since divergent outcomes will likely result from attachment to conventional versus unconventional peers.

Subsequent research has tended to confirm the validity of many aspects and features of Hirschi's social control theory of criminal involvement (see Austin, 1977; Bahr, 1979; Jensen & Eve, 1976; Johnson, 1979; Poole & Regoli, 1979; Rankin, 1977). A possible limitation of this theory, however, is that nearly all of the research has been conducted using samples of juvenile offenders. One might legitimately ask if Hirschi's theory has much applicability to adult forms of criminality. Investigating the behavior of a group of adult misdemeanant probationers, Linquist, Smusz, and Doerner (1985) examined three of Hirschi's key elements (attachment, commitment, involvement), with the intent of appraising their usefulness in predicting success on probation. The results of this investigation revealed that commitment was strongly correlated, involvement moderately correlated, and attachment largely uncorrelated with the dependent variable of success on probation. Linquist et al. concluded that while these results are less than fully supportive of social control theory, they do imply that Hirschi's model holds a certain degree of utility for use with adult offenders. These authors acknowledge that their inability to uncover a relationship between attachment and success on parole may reflect problems with the measures they employed rather than with the theory itself.

Wiatrowski, Griswold, and Roberts (1981) performed a multivariate path analysis of longitudinal data collected on 2,213 Michigan high school students. After controlling for ability, social class, and school performance,

Wiatrowski et al. found general support for the founding tenets of social control theory, although the key elements of social control varied some from what Hirschi originally proposed. Whereas attachment to parents, involvement in conventional activities, and belief in the moral validity of the existing social structure were all part of the multivariate solution, commitment tended to drop out of the analysis (possibly because of redundancy or low reliability), and several factors overlooked by Hirschi (e.g., dating, school attachment) worked their way into the equation. Such findings suggest that while the social control model receives general empirical support, the theory behind the data may be in need of refinement (see also Bernard, 1987a).

Utilizing self-report data from the Seattle Youth Study (Hindelang, Hirschi, & Weis, 1981)[1], Jill Leslie Rosenbaum (1987) conducted a study in which subjects were grouped by offense category (violent behavior, property crimes, drug offenses). In analyzing these data, Rosenbaum noticed that social control theory successfully accounted for drug offenses, but did only a fair job in accounting for property crimes and a poor job in accounting for violent behavior. The absence of a relationship between violent behavior and indices of social control is not necessarily a mark against Hirschi's theory, however, since violent behavior may not be the best indicator of delinquent/criminal trends in juveniles. It is interesting that Rosenbaum found hypotheses generated by social control theory to be more predictive of female, as opposed to male, delinquency. The applicability of social control theory to female forms of delinquency had been documented in several earlier studies as well (i.e., Hindelang, 1973; Jensen & Eve, 1976; Warren, 1983) and augments the generalizability of this particular theory of criminal involvement.

While the applicability of social control theory principles to adults, females, and persons of varying social stature (Brennan & Huizinga, 1975; Wiatrowski et al., 1981) is certainly impressive, the true empirical strength of a theory can often best be demonstrated in comparisons involving several different models. The reader should know that social control theory fares extremely well in this regard. Hence, several recent research studies show that dropping out of school is normally accompanied by increased, rather than decreased, levels of subsequent criminality (Bachman & O'Malley, 1978; Polk, Adler, Bazemore, Blake, Cordray, Coventry, Galvin, & Temple, 1981; Shavit & Rattner, 1988; Thornberry et al., 1985), a relationship that falls more in line with social control theory than the strain model. A cross-national comparison of crime rates in the United States and Sweden by Stack (1982) also revealed support for social control theory relative to the formulations of strain theory. Stephen Cernkovich (1978), on the other hand, found support for both the strain and social control models in a self-report study of 412 male high school students and noted that the combined effect of these two theories accounted for more variance than did either model separately.

In an analysis of data from the Richmond Youth Project, Gary F. Jensen (1972) concluded that control theory was supported over differential association as an explanation of delinquent patterns of behavior, although a re-analysis of these data by Matsueda (1982) uncovered a converse outcome. Although Thompson, Mitchell, and Dodder (1984) report that their findings on family attachment, peer associations, and delinquency are more congruent with differential association than social control conceptualizations, Amdur (1989) finds fault with how the variables in this study were measured. In a somewhat better designed investigation, John R. Hepburn (1976) discerned greater support for social control theory than Sutherland's differential association perspective in a sample of 139 mid-Western males ages 14 to 17. Using a series of partial correlations to test these two theories, Hepburn determined that delinquent definitions (e.g., level of personal restraint and willingness to engage in lawbreaking behavior) preceded delinquent associations. Poole and Regoli (1979) also ascertained support for the social control formulation on peer influence and crime: Adolescents with weak parental support were more susceptible to negative peer influence, while strong parental support served to insulate adolescents from the effects of antisocial peers.

Though strong in most empirical tests, social control theory is not without its detractors. It has been argued that weak bonds alone could not possibly account for all categories of delinquent and criminal behavior since a substantial proportion of poorly bonded persons do not develop delinquent patterns of adjustment (Elliott et al., 1979). Hirschi has also been criticized for not specifying how bonds are severed, broken, or fail to form in the first place (Colvin & Pauly, 1983). Additionally, Colvin and Pauly take Hirschi to task for adopting a largely dichotomous approach (strong-weak) to an issue (bonding) that seems to vary along several dimensions, quantitative as well as qualitative, and for minimizing the significance of the socializing agent in the actual bonding process. Finally, unlike many sociologists, Hirschi appears to consider the impact of individual differences (e.g., intelligence, temperament), although he proposes an indirect effect (via bonding) where Wilson and Herrnstein (1985) argue that some of these individual differences exert a direct influence on crime and delinquency.

Social control theory presents a paradox of sorts. Though widely generalizable, highly fruitful, and reasonably well substantiated from an empirical standpoint, it is lacking in precision and operationality (see Table 2.1). As

Bernard (1987a) points out, Hirschi has failed to adequately define many of his terms, which simply adds to the confusion surrounding certain aspects of his theory. Hirschi's version of social control also lacks an explicit definition of deviance while failing to adequately distinguish between delinquency and deviance or legality and conformity (Bernard, 1987a). Because of this lack of clarity, the theory also tends to be less parsimonious than it might be otherwise. In sum, until the theoretical structure and precision of Hirschi's social control theory of delinquency catches up with the model's impressive record of empirical support, this theory will continue to fall short of its full potential.

Labeling

Labeling theory, sometimes referred to as the labeling perspective, adopts the position that the root cause of crime can be found in the labels society uses to identify certain of its members (Gibbs & Erickson, 1975; Plummer, 1979; Schur, 1971). According to this perspective, lawbreakers are indistinguishable from nonlawbreakers except for the presence of a deviant label. Hence, the criminal is viewed by labeling theorists as a victim of his environment and the labeling practices of conventional society. Labeling theorists argue further that unless a change is made in the way deviance is handled by nations like the United States, the deleterious effects of this negative process will continue to cause the crime rate to rise precipitously.

An outgrowth of attribution theory and symbolic interactionalism, labeling theory hypothesizes that relationships are defined by the meanings people share in common and the characteristics individuals attribute to one another. Once a person is labeled, as typically occurs when one is processed through the criminal justice system, a negative chain of events is set into motion. Not only do changes take place in the individual's self-concept, but there is also a concomitant shrinkage in the person's access to legitimate opportunities. Rather than forming bonds with conventional society, then, this individual is drawn to other labeled deviants and goes about establishing a new set of behavioral norms for him- or herself (Rutter & Giller, 1984).

There are a number of ways in which labeling might interface with criminal behavior. It has been theorized, for instance, that labeling exerts its effect through the development of a negative self-image. Lemert (1951) retorts that assigning a criminal label to a juvenile may eventually lead that individual to begin treating himself as such. A second possibility is that labeling might restrict one's access to legitimate opportunities and make illegal avenues appear more attractive (Tannenbaum, 1938). Third, labeling may create a personal aura that makes the individual less attractive to conventional cohorts but more attractive to antisocial peers (Wilkins, 1965).

As might be anticipated, labeling theory has generated debate, reaction, and investigation. Martin Gold and Jay Williams (1969) compared 35 juveniles apprehended for illegal activities and 35 nonapprehended juveniles matched on age, race, sex, and prior criminality. The outcome of this study tended to support the basic tenets of labeling theory in that apprehended subjects committed more subsequent offenses than nonapprehended subjects, although the authors failed to control for the seriousness of reported offenses. Terence Thornberry (1971) determined that a more severe disposition by the juvenile courts was associated with an increase in the volume, but not the severity, of subsequent criminality in a large sample of Philadelphian youth. Finally, although most juveniles do not perceive a court appearance to be highly stigmatizing (Foster, Dinitz, & Reckless, 1972), there is evidence that teachers (Balch, 1972), employers (Buikhuisen & Dijksterhuss, 1971), and some family members (Snyder, 1971) may, in fact, react less favorably to an adolescent who has appeared before a juvenile court.

After reviewing the literature on legal processing and later delinquency, Rutter and Giller (1984) concluded that a court appearance was reasonably prognostic of later delinquent behavior. Bahr (1979) also found that official processing through the criminal justice system can enhance the probability of future deviance. He is quick to annotate, however, that the labeling effect is not as pervasive as was once thought, is more prominent in first-time offenders, and may exert its influence in ways other than through deprecating the self-concept of the labeled individual. Others have also found differential effects for labeling based on the characteristics of the individual in question. Therefore, the impact of negative labeling is greatest for middle-class youth (Ageton & Elliott, 1974; Short & Strodtbeck, 1965; Thornberry, 1971) and weakest for individuals most likely to be officially processed through the criminal justice system (Ageton & Elliott, 1974; Bernstein, Kelly, & Doyle, 1977; Thomas, 1977). Elliott, Ageton, and Canter (1979), in turn, conceptualize negative labeling as an attenuating process that impacts most heavily upon adolescents with prior commitment to the conventional social order. There is also the possibility that labeling may operate as a deterrent in certain situations (see Thorsell & Klemke, 1972).

Probably the most damning criticism of labeling theory is that it fails to explain deviant patterns of behavior established prior to application of the label (Bahr, 1979; Gibbons, 1971; Rutter & Giller, 1984). Several labeling theorists (see Douglas, 1970; Lemert, 1972) argue that the theory's inability to explain "primary deviance" is compensated for by its ability to elaborate upon the formation of "secondary deviance" (i.e., the stigmatization, diminished self-esteem, and adoption of deviant roles associated with being labeled). However, the notion of secondary deviance itself has been questioned by some scholars. In a review of labeling research through the early 1970s, Anne Mahoney (1974) discerned only a modicum of support for the secondary deviance-labeling hypothesis. Thus, while labeling theory is not without its strengths, to include pointing out the fallacy of assuming that the individual is the seat of all pathology and encouraging the use of symbolic interactionalism to link behavior with its situational context (Colvin & Pauly, 1983), its ahistorical, astructural bent limits its applicability to many forms of criminal conduct (Davis, 1972).

In examining the formal characteristics of labeling theory (see Table 2.1), we notice that this theory is strong on parsimony in the sense that it relies on just a few postulates and assumptions. However, as was mentioned previously, this theory is very limited in scope and suffers from imprecision and diminished operationality. Terms such as primary and secondary deviance need to be more clearly defined and the assumptions surrounding their development elaborated. Nevertheless, labeling theory has stimulated a great deal of scholarly debate and research investigation over the past several decades. It has received a measured degree of empirical support, although the scope of the hypotheses tested within the context of this theory have been rather circumscribed in nature. The argument that self-image is influential in the development of later criminality is a position also advocated by the self theories of criminal behavior, the next theoretical position to be examined in this chapter.

Self Theories

Taking their cue from Carl Rogers's (1951) organismic theory of personality, self theories of crime place a premium on the personal experiences and interpretations of the individual. Exploring the issue of self-image and deviance, L. Edward Wells (1978) speculates that behavior is an attempt by the individual to construct, test, validate, and express one's self. Wells views many forms of emotional distress and behavioral deviance as stemming from the incongruence hypothesized to exist between the self-image and various self-demands (aspirations, expectations). Under such circumstances, self-judgments (subjective feelings about oneself) tend to be negative and the individual is more likely to gravitate toward deviant forms of behavior as a means of establishing a self-image. Self-labeling, of course, is also seen by many theorists as an important link in the development of a deviant lifestyle (Warren, 1974).

Behavior and self-image are linked in at least two ways. First, behavior may be an expression of one's self-concept (Cohen, 1983). Hence, if a person has a low opinion of him- or herself, this would likely be reflected in a wide array of negative behaviors that would include depression, alcohol abuse, and criminality. Behavior may also serve to support or buttress one's self-concept by directing one toward activities that are largely consistent with the self-concept (Cohen, 1983). Therefore, a person harboring concerns about his or her intellectual acumen might tend to restrict activities to more physically oriented tasks, which in turn reinforces the image such a person has of him- or herself as being "all brawn and no brains." The expressive and supportive features of the self-behavior relationship also appear to be operating when one selects crime from available alternatives. Stated somewhat differently, the choice of crime depends upon how it fits with the self-image. Wells identifies three historical trends in self theories of criminal behavior: structural interactionalism, labeling, and socialization-control.

Walter C. Reckless and his colleagues (Reckless, Dinitz, & Murray, 1956; Reckless, Dinitz, & Kay, 1957) developed a theory of criminality, the containment model, which relies quite extensively on the socialization-control view of human behavior. Focusing on push and pull factors and internal and external containment, these authors reasoned that a boy growing up in a high delinquency area could learn to refrain from involving himself in criminal activity if internal constraints against such behavior (ego strength, self-control, self-image) were strong. This theory posits that high self-esteem and personal pride serve to protect one from future episodes of deviant behavior. Follow-up studies of the original sample of subjects used in developing containment theory offer qualified support for the notion that self-esteem provides a form of insulation against later deviance (Dinitz, Scarpitti, & Reckless, 1962; Scarpitti, Murray, Dinitz, & Reckless, 1960).

Other than the research conducted by Reckless and his associates, there is a paucity of empirical investigation on the relationship between self and crime. One exception to this general rule has been the pioneering work of Gresham Sykes and David Matza (1970). After analyzing the thinking patterns of groups of juvenile offenders, Sykes and Matza concluded that "much delinquency is based on what is essentially an unrecognized extension of defenses to crime, in the form of justifications for deviance that are seen as valid by the delinquent but not by the legal system or society at large" (p. 295). These authors go on to describe what they refer to as the process of neutralization, whereby the offender justifies his illegal actions in an effort to maintain a positive view of himself and his actions. By minimizing the significance of rule-breaking behavior, blaming the victims, questioning the motives of condemning authorities, and pointing out how the criminal was forced into a life of crime by various external factors, the criminal attempts to diffuse responsibility for his criminal conduct and protect his already fragile self-image. Although Sykes and Matza's ideas are intriguing and apparently amenable to investigation, there is a conspicuous absence of research on this topic.

In order to become a truly viable model of human behavior, self theories will need to pay greater attention to a number of theoretical and methodological issues. Vague, amorphous references to "the self" will need to be replaced by definitions that are precise, explicit, and operational. Kaplan's (1976) self-attitudes measure is a good example of a more precise measure of self-concept. Researchers also need to clarify the theoretical linkages thought to exist between self-concept, deviance, and social structure before this area of research can live up to its promising beginnings (see Hewitt, 1970). Finally, rather than hold to a unidirectional explanation of the putative connection between self-concept and deviance (i.e., self-concept causing deviance or deviance causing self-concept), Wells (1978) calls for increased attention to structural interactionalism and the reciprocal relationship between self-concept and deviance.

Perusing Table 2.1, we find that self theories of criminal behavior are open to a number of serious criticisms. Like Rogers's organismic theory of personality, self theories of criminality tend to be imprecise and less than fully operational. Taking the Reckless studies as a case in point, we find that a score on a single California Personality Inventory scale served as the criterion measure of self-esteem. Not only are such definitional practices unsound in and of themselves, they also tend to dampen the stimulatory and empirical value of a theory. It is therefore understandable why many criminologists often fail to take these types of theories seriously, although we should not overlook the vast potential embodied in self theories of crime. The fact that researchers have been able to achieve a certain degree of methodological rigor in examining Rogers's theory of personality should serve as encouragement for self theorists investigating the development of criminal behavior. At present, however, self theories of criminal involvement are a good idea awaiting specification, clarification, and empirical verification.

Psychoanalytic Theory

Sigmund Freud, the founder of psychoanalysis, had very little to say about criminals. This is because Freud's attention was drawn to the neuroses and the unconscious factors subsumed within the more general structure of these types of disorders. In the only paper he ever published with specific reference to crime and criminality, Freud (1957) reflected on how our attitude toward criminals in general seems to mirror the attitude we have toward the criminal in ourselves. As Alexander and Staub (1931) state, criminality is part of man's nature. Thus, from a psychoanalytic point of view, the primary difference between the criminal and noncriminal is that the noncriminal has learned to control and sublimate his antisocial drives and feelings.

August Aichhorn (1935) was one of the first analysts to propose a psycho-analytic theory of delinquency development. He hypothesized that a child is born asocial in that he or she demands immediate gratification of primitive needs, drives, and instincts. At this point in his young life, the child's primary concern is for the satisfaction of his basic visceral needs. If the libidinal organization of the child is disturbed by negative experiences, early oedipal conflicts in particular, then he or she will likely remain egocentric and asocial and have a difficult time adjusting to the demands, laws, and rules of society. Aichhorn argues further that this incipient state of "latent delinquency" can lead to actual delinquent behavior if provoked by certain environmental events and situations. It was Aichhorn's belief that the principal goal of treatment was to bring into awareness the unconscious factors responsible for the individual's antisocial behavior.

In several of his writings, Freud intimates that many types of crimes are motivated by the unconscious desire for punishment, although he never elaborated on this theme. In articulating the psychoanalytic approach to crime, Edward Glover (1960) remarked that crime is an unconscious projec-tion of guilt that finds itself transformed into a desire for punishment. Taking this argument a step further, the psychoanalytically oriented theorist would contend that because crime is essentially a symptom of an underlying intrapsychic conflict, techniques designed to modify the behavior, but not the underlying personality structure, are doomed to fail from the very start. In fact, it is thought that such superficial treatment strategies will only result in the reappearance of the symptom in some other, and possibly even more serious, form. Contrary to what psychoanalysts would argue, however, there is no solid empirical support for the occurrence of symptom substitution in behaviorally oriented treatment outcomes (see Baker, 1969; Paul, 1969;

Wollersheim, 1970). This, though, has not prevented psychoanalytic scholars like Karl Menninger (1968) from asserting that socially sanctioned punishment actually aggravates the criminal tendencies of offenders by providing them with the punishment they subconsciously crave.

In a recompilation of some of Freud's ideas on crime and criminals, David J. Dixon (1986) finds two general etiological trends in the development of serious criminal behavior. The most common pathway involves unresolved guilt following inadequate resolution of the oedipal situation relative to the individual's mother and father. An unduly lenient or overly harsh father is thought to be of paramount importance in the development of the type of ego impairments associated with the unconscious desire for punishment. The second major etiological pathway to later criminality reflects a general state of narcissism accompanied by minimal levels of guilt and remorse for one's antisocial actions. Such persons are said to possess weak superegos or superegos that are dysfunctional in specific areas. As a result, these individuals are typically not bothered by the pangs of conscience when they violate society's rules. This particular route to a life of crime is said to evolve out of an isolated and lonely childhood, a supposition that finds some support in John Bowlby's (1946, 1969) work on attachment and delinquency.

Franz Alexander and Edward Glover are two of the more prolific writers on the psychoanalysis of criminal behavior. In separate publications, these two authors have attempted to outline the key postulates of a psychoanalytic theory of criminal conduct (Alexander & Staub, 1931; Glover, 1960). Paraphrasing to some extent, the key postulates of the psychoanalytic theory of criminal involvement are summarized below. First, early family relationships are viewed by psychoanalytic theorists as salient in the development of subsequent acts of antisociality. Second, psychodynamic theory views unconscious intrapsychic factors as predominant in the genesis of criminal and delinquent conduct. Third, because unconscious factors are viewed as predominant in the evolution of a criminal lifestyle, many neo-Freudians believe that there is a great deal of symbolic meaning in the criminal violations of the average offender. Finally, psychoanalysts believe that most lawbreakers desire punishment as a means to assuage the unconscious guilt they experience.

Psychoanalytic theory has stimulated very little empirical investigation on issues of interest to most criminal scientists; of the studies that have been carried out, most have employed a clinical case study approach. Paul Hofer (1988), for instance, observed a number of psychodynamic themes in his therapeutic interactions with selected groups of penitentiary inmates. In discussing various features of the psychoanalytic relationship he entered into with these offenders, he noted that idealization of the relationship with the mother, intense anger toward the father, and heavy reliance on the defense mechanism of splitting were all characteristic of the intrapsychic worlds of these inmates. As was indicated earlier in our discussion of Aichhorn's (1935) work with delinquents, the primary goal of psychoanalytically oriented psychotherapy with delinquents, as well as adults, is to bring the unconscious determinants of criminal behavior into conscious awareness.

Though Freud's writings are colorful, descriptive, and eloquent, they suffer from a lack of precision and paucity of operationality. It is difficult to imagine one conducting a research investigation without benefit of clearly specified criterion measures, although this is exactly what we ask of empirical studies on psychoanalytic theory. This may help explain why so few research investigations have been carried out on the psychoanalytic theory of criminal behavior. Furthermore, the psychoanalytic perspective seems to ignore the prospect of individual choice and personal responsibility despite the presence of research findings that indicate that children have as much impact on their environments as their environments have on them (Bell, 1979; Shaffer & Emerson, 1964). In the absence of precision, parsimony, and explicit, testable hypotheses, it is concluded that the psychoanalytic approach has little to offer a science of criminal behavior at this point in its development (see Table 2.1).

Pathological Stimulation Seeking

Herbert C. Quay (1965) has proposed a theory of criminality based on the observation that many crimes seem to provide one with a sense of excitement and thrills. According to Quay, criminality is a manifestation of the offender's "inordinate need for increases or changes in the pattern of stimulation" (p. 181). The primary abnormality is thought, therefore, to be seated in the person's physiological response to sensory input. More specifically, it is hypothesized that criminals possess nervous systems that are hyporeactive or underresponsive to stimulation. Following this general line of reasoning, Quay proposed that the criminal views higher than normal rates of sensory stimulation as optimal and so pursues an augmented level of such activity as a means of compensating for an intrinsically low rate of cortical arousal. This tendency eventually finds itself converted into behavior designed to create excitement and alleviate boredom. It is significant that unlike many of the sociologically based theories of criminal behavior, Quay's model considers individual differences to be important.

In 1977, Quay modified his theory somewhat to include environmental factors. As with the original theory, it was proposed that the future criminal is born with a hyporeactive nervous system. However, it was further reasoned that this cortical underresponsiveness does not exist in a vacuum but interacts with the individual's particular home environment. In many cases, the stimulus-seeking behavior of the young child helps create a sense of frustration and anger in the parents, who might then reject the child or fall victim to inconsistent patterns of disciplinary practice. These types of parental responses, in turn, contribute to increased deviancy on the part of the child. Since the pre-delinquent child tends to habituate quite rapidly to punishment and aversive stimulation, this simply adds to the growing sense of frustration on the part of the parents. This pattern then evolves into a vicious cycle of negative parent-child interactions; in the end, it produces a child who as an adolescent and adult is hostile, resentful, poorly socialized, and has a high need for various forms of sensory stimulation.

There are a number of research studies that support Quay's (1965, 1977) notion that stimulation-seeking tendencies are part of the criminal picture. Kipnis and Wagner (1967) found a positive correlation between scores on the Sensation Seeking Scale (SSS) and measures of impulsivity and psychopathy, while Shostak and McIntyre (1978) report the presence of a nexus between psychopathy/criminality and sensation-seeking tendencies on the Kinesthetic Aftereffect Test but not on the SSS. Although there have also been negative findings (see Stewart & Hemsley, 1984), the majority of evidence has been supportive of the pathological stimulation-seeking hypothesis (see Rutter & Giller, 1984). In addition to the generally positive results obtained with adult males, a relationship has been found to exist between stimulation seeking and delinquency/criminality in children (DeMyer-Gapin & Scott, 1977), females (Farley & Farley, 1972), and white (Farley & Cox, 1971), as well as nonwhite (Farley & Sewell, 1976), adolescents. Summarizing the research literature on stimulation-seeking and crime/psychopathy, psychologist Dennis Doren (1987) found a modest connection between criminality and sensation-seeking in studies employing the SSS scale, but a much stronger link when various behavioral measures and indices of sensation-seeking were considered.

David Lykken's (1957) classic study on avoidance conditioning in psychopaths revealed that as a group, these individuals displayed lowered sensitivity to noxious stimuli and more rapid recovery to basal galvanic skin response (GSR) following the onset of stimulation. This finding suggests that a diminished level of basal reactivity, as well as an elevated rate of habituation, may both be involved in the derivation of psychopathic and criminal behavior. Fairweather (1953), utilizing a syllable-learning paradigm, uncovered results that were supportive of the lowered sensitivity/rapid adaptation explanation as to why criminals tend to seek out higher than normal levels of environmental stimulation. In examining this issue, Quay (1965) directs our attention to the outcome of a study by Fox and Lippert (1963) in which a group of psychopathic offenders exhibited significantly lower spontaneous GSR activity relative to a group of nonpsychopathic offenders. Quay used these results to argue that it was probably more rapid adaptation to stimuli, rather than lowered basal reactivity, that is behind the stimulation-seeking tendencies of psychopaths and criminals.

After reviewing research conducted since Quay published his original thesis on pathological stimulation-seeking and psychopathy in 1965, Robert Blackburn (1978) concluded that there was little evidence in favor of Quay's habituation hypothesis. Supporting his argument with his own data (Blackburn, 1978), as well as the data of others (Fenz, 1971; Hare & Craigen, 1974; Hare & Quinn, 1971), Blackburn observed greater levels of spontaneous fluctuation on such physiological measures as skin conductance in primary psychopaths and criminals compared to groups of secondary psychopaths and noncriminal controls. Such a finding is obviously inconsistent with Quay's habituation hypothesis. The reader should not assume, however, that just because the habituation hypothesis failed to find support in these studies that this necessarily reflects positively on the hyporeactive hypothesis since the latter is also lacking in empirical corroboration (see Hare, 1978; Zuckerman, 1975).

In the 1977 edition of his theory, Quay evinced greater interest in environmental factors than had been the case in earlier versions of the theory. The environmental factor emphasized most fervently in Quay's (1977) revision of pathological stimulation-seeking theory was the nuclear family. In considering the evolution of delinquency, crime, and antisocial behavior, Quay proposed two primary models of person×situation interaction. First, it was hypothesized that negative and inconsistent parental response to the stimulation-seeking behaviors of the child was an essential etiological force in the development of subsequent criminalistic tendencies. The second general hypothesis was that the child's physiological abnormality makes it difficult for him or her to anticipate the painful consequences of his or her actions. Both factors are viewed as contributing to the vicious cycle of negative parent-child transactions that eventually culminate in a pattern of serious criminality. While these two postulates have yet to enjoy empirical confirmation, they have received ample indirect support in several reviews of the literature (e.g., McCord & McCord, 1959; Wilson & Herrnstein, 1985).

Quay's critics have charged him with concocting a theory that is incomplete and difficult to verify. Thus, while his theory has stimulated a great deal of scholarly investigation and received a fair amount of empirical support, we still do not know why criminals and psychopaths generally view abnormally high levels of sensory stimulation as optimal. Is it more rapid habituation, a lowered rate of basal reactivity, or some third variable that is responsible for the criminal's apparent desire for increased levels of excitement and stimulation? Moreover, as Smith (1978) carefully points out, this theory is lacking in clarity since a wide variety of divergent stimuli, presented to a number of different sensory sites, has been used to test the theory. While this practice enhances the generalizability or importance of the theory, it does so at the cost of precision (see Table 2.1). Hence, if Quay's theory is to play a consequential role in future investigations on the criminal lifestyle, it will need to be made more precise and verifiable.

Rational Choice Theory

Evolving out of deterrence theory, the rational choice perspective borrows heavily from contemporary economic theory and applies many of these concepts to criminal behavior. Where deterrence theory highlights the influence of punishment on subsequent behavior, rational choice theory emphasizes the anticipated utility (rewards and punishments) of lawful versus unlawful behavior. An early proponent of rational choice theory, Gary Becker (1968) asserted that criminal outcomes were a function of the immediate choices and decisions offenders make relative to the opportunities available to them. Basing his ideas on the Neumann-Morgenstern expected utility paradigm, Becker proposed that the individual considering a criminal option will act on this thought only if the anticipated outcome or expected utility of committing the crime exceeds the anticipated outcome or expected utility of not engaging in that particular criminal act. In other words, rational choice theory contends that the individual weighs the various possibilities and then selects the optimal solution.

Assessing the supply and demand of human interaction can be a truly demanding task. As Cook (1980) points out, there are a variety of individual and personal factors that contribute to the complexity of the human decision-making process. It follows, then, that this process is much less mechanistic than most rational choice theorists would have us believe. The outcome of a study directed by John Carroll (1978) illustrates the complexity of the human decision-making process and points out that our decisions are often nonrational and noneconomic in nature. It has also been determined that the probabilities considered by the human decision-maker are subjective, rather than objective, and that aspects of the criminal choice scenario (e.g., cost, benefit) are considered individually rather than multiplicatively as expected utility theory predicts (Cimler & Beach, 1981). Findings such as these make it difficult to ignore Carroll's (1978) conclusion that human judgments are accomplished in a manner that makes less than optimal use of various probabilities and opportunities.

Economic theory is concerned with the availability and distribution of resources. Therefore, an increase in income or expanded economic opportunity should reduce, not only the incentive for crime, but also actual criminal behavior, according to the rational choice perspective. Likewise, economic recession or decreased economic opportunity should lead to increased levels of criminality by reducing legitimate opportunities for advancement. However, the research on economic indicators (such as unemployment) and criminality is mixed, with a few studies highlighting the presence of a crime-unemployment association (i.e., Devine, Sheley, & Smith, 1988; Sampson & Castellano, 1982), but with many more studies failing to find a link between these two variables (see Orsagh & Witte, 1981). It should be noted further that even if a connection were to exist between unemployment and criminal behavior, the clinical significance of this relationship is brought into question by the results of an investigation by Freeman (1983), who estimates that a 50% reduction in unemployment would lead to no more than a 5% reduction in the overall rate of criminality.

Most of the research on rational choice theory has been conducted using aggregate data (Brier & Fienberg, 1980; Cook, 1980). However, research on individual subjects seems to be a more appropriate experimental paradigm due to the fact that the primary focus of the rational choice model is on crime and criminal events rather than on criminality and criminal involvement. Therefore, while aggregate level investigations appear to be largely supportive of the rational choice hypothesis, individual level studies are much less so (Paternoster, 1987; Piliavin, Gartner, Thornton, & Matsueda, 1986). An individual level study directed by Ann Witte (1980), on the other hand, provides some measure of support for the economic perspective on crime in the sense that both the expected certainty and severity of punishment displayed a relatively weak, but nevertheless significant, deterrent effect with respect to subsequent criminal behavior. Still in all, rational choice theorems are rarely assessed through individual level data. Unless efforts are made to extend economic and rational choice theories of criminal behavior to the individual, it will remain, as Rutter and Giller (1984) assert, a partial explanation of antisocial conduct at best.

In addition to being narrow, circumscribed, and drawn more to trivial than important relationships, rational choice theory has trouble explaining a number of phenomena that have been observed in variegated investigations on human decision-making. These phenomena include, but are not limited to, "context effects" (Hershey & Schoemaker, 1980), short-cut decision-making (Corbin, 1980), processing heuristics (Kahneman & Tversky, 1979), and perseverative choice selection (Einhorn & Hogarth, 1978). As much of the criticism toward rational choice theory has been aimed at the expected utilities model, modifications have been proposed by various theorists in the field. Some of the more popular modifications of expected utilities theory include Edwards's (1955) subjective expected utility model, the differentially weighted product-averaging approach (Lynch & Cohen, 1978), and prospect theory (Kahneman & Tversky, 1979).

Lattimore and Witte (1985) determined that the expected utility model and prospect theory lead to very different predictions when asked to assess how changes in criminal justice policy would impact the decision-making tendencies of criminal offenders. However, we still need to determine whether prospect theory fares any better than the expected utility model when individual level data are plugged into the equation. As it now stands, rational choice theory is a useful, but incomplete, explanation of criminality. Its strength can be found in its precision, operationality, and ability to clarify specific criminal events, while its weakness is revealed in the circumscribed nature of the relationships observed, its lack of explanation for a variety of empirical phenomena, and its inability to account for criminal behavior over time (see Table 2.1). Future research will need to address these sundry issues if rational choice theory is to have a place in the criminal science research effort.

Conclusion

The eight theories of criminal behavior discussed in this chapter were selected on the basis of their popularity, originality, and distinctiveness. Thus, they range from the traditional sociologic (strain theory), to the classic psychodynamic (psychoanalytic theory), to the neo-biologic (pathological stimulation-seeking). A reasonable conclusion would be that these eight models reflect a wide spectrum of theoretical thought on criminal behavior.

While several fairly popular perspectives, like the deterrence model (Blumstein, Cohen, & Nagin, 1978), Marxist theory (Colvin & Pauly, 1983), and the subcultural approach (Cohen, 1955), have been omitted from this discussion, it is felt that each overlaps substantially with one or more of the theories that were covered. Consequently, while this review may have been limited on the depth at which individual theories were examined, I don't believe it can be faulted for unfounded selectivity.

Fred Kerlinger (1973) reminds us that the null hypothesis can never be proven, just disproven. In much the same manner, a theory of human behavior can never be proven since there is always the exception to the rule. Thus, rather than work to establish the absolute truth or validity of any particular theoretical perspective, a more profitable approach would be to assess the theory's usefulness or utility. This, in fact, was the rationale behind selecting Maddi's (1976) six criteria (importance, operationality, precision, parsimony, stimulation, empirical validity) as the standard against which these eight theories were measured and compared. Hence, the degree to which a theory is precise, stimulating, and empirically valid also reflects the degree to which it is useful. Similarly, a lack of operationality or attenuated generalizability and importance will tend to limit a theoretical model's usefulness. Without belaboring the point, it is a theory's utility, rather than its absolute verity, that should serve as the milestone against which theories of criminal conduct are assessed.

In contrasting the eight theories of criminal behavior discussed in this chapter, we find that the differential association, social control, and pathological stimulation-seeking models produce the most consistently positive outcomes in terms of Maddi's six criteria. Conversely, the self and psychoanalytic perspectives perform rather poorly when gauged against these criteria. It is important to keep in mind, however, that the "stronger" theories are no more a complete explanation of criminality than the "weaker" theories are totally without merit. In fact, there are aspects of the self and psychoanalytic approaches which, if integrated properly, could actually enhance the utility of the differential association, social control, and pathological stimulation-seeking perspectives. Hence, none of the theories of criminal behavior discussed in this chapter are unremittingly useful or completely useless, but rather vary in the degree to which they further our understanding of lifestyle criminality.

If we compare criteria instead of theories, we find that the major theories of criminal conduct, as a group, are important, parsimonious, and stimulating. However, these same theories also tend to be imprecise and poorly operationalized. Further, while these theories have stimulated a fairly impressive amount of research and scholarly debate, they have been less than fully useful from an empirical/predictive standpoint. Much of this would appear to stem from the fact that the postulates are imprecise and the terms poorly operationalized, for it is difficult to verify a theory's predictability without clearly stating the hypotheses and employing variables that are behaviorally referenced. Future efforts in this area would be well advised to strive for increased experimental control over the relevant hypotheses, postulates, and criterion measures without sacrificing the importance, parsimony, and stimulatory value of the underlying theory—a challenging task to say the least.

As I was reviewing the research literature on theories of criminal conduct, I was reminded of the children's story about the six blind men and the elephant. As the reader may recall, these six unsighted gentlemen each focused on the part of the elephant they came across first. Thus, one man held the squirming trunk in his hands and deduced that the elephant was much like a snake, while a second man felt the smooth, pointed tusk and reasoned that the animal was similar to a spear. The other four men approached the ear, leg, side, and tail and concluded that the elephant resembled a fan, tree, wall, and rope, respectively. An analogous case of myopia seems to have afflicted many of the theorists attempting to explain the behavior of criminal offenders. Each of the eight theories reviewed in this chapter is responsible for uncovering potentially useful relationships, but all, like the six blind men, have explored only a portion of the picture. In order to gain a more complete and useful perspective on crime, we therefore need to remove our self-imposed blinders and realize how the different parts are capable of forming a meaningful and integrated whole. Then we will be in a better position to understand the behavior of criminals, convicts, and other lawbreaking members of society.

In concluding this chapter on theories of criminal behavior, I feel obligated to warn the reader that we still have one more theory to review: the theory that criminality exists as a lifestyle. As it will become increasingly apparent as we proceed through the next several chapters, the theory of lifestyle criminality borrows liberally from each of the models thus far reviewed. Although many criminologists would consider the lifestyle theory of criminal conduct a mixed model, it does, in fact, possess a number of the integrating features discussed in the Pearson and Weiner (1985) and Thornberry (1987) papers. Unlike many past attempts at integration, a finite number of key concepts will serve as the theoretical underpinnings of this theory that crime can be conceptualized as a lifestyle. Consequently, it is hoped that the confusion that sometimes accompanies attempts at synthesis and eclectism can be avoided. With the intent being to develop a theory that is important, precise, operational, parsimonious, stimulating, and empirically/predictively useful, we now turn our attention to the underlying foundation of the theory of lifestyle criminality.

NOTE

1. There have been a number of major crime/delinquency data collection projects instituted within the past several decades. Since these projects have given rise to multiple data analyses, it is important that we not treat studies conducted on the same data set as though they were yielding independent outcomes (see Hirschi, 1969; Jensen, 1972; Matsueda, 1982). The Cambridge Study of Delinquent Development (West & Farrington, 1977), National Crime Survey (Bureau of Justice Statistics, 1988), New York Youth Survey (Hindelang, 1973), Philadelphia Birth Cohort (Wolfgang, Figlio, & Sellin, 1972), Richmond Youth Project (Hirschi, 1969), and Seattle Youth Study (Hindelang et al., 1981) are among the more prolific data collection projects with relevance to the question of crime and delinquency.

3. Crime as a Lifestyle

It has been postulated that a large portion of serious criminality is committed each year by a small segment of the criminal population. This observation has been made cross-nationally (Clinard & Abbott, 1973; Cooper, 1971; Kobayashi, Ono, Ooe, & Sakumichi, 1982; Russell, 1964), as well as historically (Gurr, 1989; Kempf, 1987), and is valid for individuals of varying social, ethnic, and economic status. A recent examination of this issue by a group of researchers working under the auspices of the Figgie Corporation of Cleveland, Ohio (1988) revealed a similar outcome. In directing this investigation, these authors interviewed 589 incarcerated property offenders as they were being processed through a prison admissions program. Subsequent analyses revealed that 9% of the interviewees accounted for 55% of the crimes committed by the overall group of 589 inmates. Results such as these have led some criminal scientists to the conclusion that there exists in any criminal population a relatively small cluster of individuals who can claim responsibility for the majority of serious offenses committed.

The theory of lifestyle criminality to be discussed in this and subsequent chapters should not be confused with Hindelang's, Gottfredson's, and Garofalo's (1978) lifestyle model of criminal victimization. Where Hindelang et al.'s model examines the likelihood of one's being victimized through a consideration of lifestyle variables, the current perspective adopts the argument that crime can be conceptualized in lifestyle terms. Hence, while the former theory probes personal victimization relative to aspects of one's daily routine, the latter explores aspects of one's daily routine that seemingly reflect a lifestyle in which the rights of others and the rules of society are violated. The fundamental difference between the lifestyle model of criminal victimization and the lifestyle theory of criminal involvement will become even more apparent once we have explored the early precursors and guiding principles of the latter.

In order that we might achieve a better understanding of the theory that conceptualizes crime in lifestyle terms, I believe it is vital that the ideas that served to stimulate the development of the present model be discussed first. Toward this end, we will be exploring Yochelson and Samenow's (1976) notion of the criminal personality, research on criminal careers, developmental life-span theory, and the rational choice perspective. While probing the early precursors of a particular theoretical position is certainly a vital step in effective theory building, so is examining the theory's conceptual roots. Accordingly, the philosophical underpinnings of the theory of lifestyle criminality (i.e., the nature of man, development, deviance, and change) will also be points of discussion in this chapter. First, however, we turn our attention to the early precursors and Yochelson and Samenow's (1976) work on the criminal personality.

Early Precursors

The Criminal Personality

In 1976, Samuel Yochelson, a psychiatrist, and Stanton Samenow, a clinical psychologist, published the first of their three volumes on *The Criminal Personality.* Basing their conceptualizations on the interviews they conducted with approximately 250 offenders (all but three of whom were male), they focused on subjects who had been adjudicated not guilty by reason of insanity and remanded to the custody of officials at St. Elizabeths Hospital in Washington, DC. In fact, Yochelson and Samenow logged as many as 5,000 interview hours per subject in a dozen or so cases. If nothing else, these two clinicians appear to have uncovered a wealth of information about the thinking and behavior of the subjects in their sample. Thus, while Yochelson and Samenow have been criticized for taking a case study approach to the question of crime, the time they spent interacting with the subjects of their investigation adds significance to their findings and contrasts sharply with the more commonly encountered practice of formulating a theory on the basis of secondhand data.

Several years after initiating their project at St. Elizabeths Hospital, Yochelson and Samenow (1976) found themselves disenchanted with nearly all of the organic, psychological, and sociological theories of crime causation in vogue at the time. Rather than derive another theory of criminality, they chose instead to focus on the content and process of criminal thought. In the end, they had developed a system of 52 thinking errors that supposedly subserve the behavior of most criminal offenders. Several of the more prominent cognitive errors discussed by Yochelson and Samenow were superoptimism, criminal pride and perfectionism, and a very self-serving attitude toward school, work, other people, and society in general. In discussing their treatment model, Yochelson and Samenow offer four points that summarize the philosophical foundation of their approach: Man can will; man can choose; deterrents exist that are capable of correcting a criminal's erroneous thinking; and constructing a "moral inventory" of one's daily thoughts is an essential step in the correction process.

Yochelson and Samenow's treatment model appears to coalesce and blend with the earlier work of William Glasser (1965) and Albert Ellis (1962). Extending beyond the issue of treatment, Carl Gacono and J. Reid Meloy (1988) undertook the task of tying Yochelson and Samenow's ideas on criminal cognition to psychodynamic speculation on the unconscious determinants of human behavior, with defense mechanisms in particular. Therefore, while Yochelson and Samenow's notion of a power thrust is postulated by Gacono and Meloy to reflect projective identification, and fragmentation the unconscious defense mechanism of splitting, there is an underlying philosophical difference between Yochelson and Samenow's thinking and the psychoanalytic model that makes integration difficult, if not impossible. Ergo, where the former features behavior, thought, and choice, the latter is encrusted in a framework of psychosexual development and psychic determinism. Equating Yochelson and Samenow's notion of lying, for instance, with the psychoanalytic view on denial and rationalization, is like assuming a fundamental kinship of Jews and Arabs based solely on their common Semitic ancestry. Moreover, it unwittingly reinforces the misconception that Yochelson and Samenow's criminal personality is nothing more than a potpourri of antiquated and best-forgotten theories (see Hagan, 1986).

It is understandable why Yochelson and Samenow's (1976) work has been so poorly received by the majority of theorists and researchers in the criminal science field. For one, the theory is poorly operationalized and difficult to evaluate empirically (Hagan, 1986). Second, Yochelson and Samenow cavalierly dismiss the role of environmental factors in the etiology of criminal conduct despite evidence to the contrary (see Vold, 1979). Third, Yochelson and Samenow's approach rests almost entirely on the case study approach and so may be lacking in generalizability (Meier, 1983). Finally, Yochelson and Samenow have taken an atheoretical approach to the question of crime; while they provide a wealth of descriptive information, their ideas lose a certain degree of applicability by not being tied to a coherent theoretical framework.

Before relegating Yochelson and Samenow's ideas to the realm of lost and forgotten theories, it is important that we consider a recent investigation by Michael L. Benson (1985). After interviewing a sample of 80 white-collar offenders, Benson arrived at the conclusion that these individuals employed a variety of rationalizations and cognitive distortions in an effort to assuage guilt feelings, minimize the seriousness of their rule-breaking behavior, and retain a view of themselves as "good people." Though these findings were obtained using a sample of predominately Caucasian, middle-class, white-collar criminals, they are remarkably consistent with the patterns Yochelson and Samenow (1976) witnessed in a group of predominately black, lower-class, person-oriented offenders. This would seem to suggest that at least some of Yochelson and Samenow's concepts have a fair degree of general-izability.

Though it may have sparked the imagination of many correctional work-ers, the manner in which Yochelson and Samenow (1976) constructed their theory of criminal behavior was not without its shortcomings. This concep-tualization does, however, serve to open our minds to new possibilities, while questioning notions that have gone unchallenged for too long. It also high-lights issues (e.g., choice, thought, and personal responsibility), which seem to have largely been ignored these past several decades in our efforts to make the study of criminal behavior more "scientific." Yochelson and Samenow argue that the criminal is free to choose his path in life, that thinking is the primary vehicle through which this choice is expressed, and that for change to take place, the offender must assume greater responsibility for his or her actions. These three features would appear to be Yochelson and Samenow's principal contributions to the developing theory of lifestyle criminality.

The Career Criminal

Beginning with the work of Park, Hughes, and Burgess at the University of Chicago in the early 1900s, there has been an expanding interest in the career concept of criminality (Sutherland, 1937). Previously referred to as the repeat or habitual offender, the term for this category of criminality may have changed over the years, but the behavior has remained remarkably consistent since New York state's passage of the first career criminal law in 1797. The notion of career criminality has been advanced by several contem-porary researchers and theorists, including Jan and Marcia Chaiken (1982), Peter Greenwood (1983), and Alfred Blumstein (Blumstein, Cohen, & Hsieh, 1982), and appears to have been a driving force behind the Comprehensive

Crime Control Act of 1984. It does not take much to appreciate how pertinent research on the career criminal is to the development of a theory of lifestyle criminality.

Since a theory is only as good as the procedures and principles upon which it is based, a model's life force is tied directly to its methodology. In the case of the career criminal, there have been at least four methodologies implemented: the cohort approach, the survey method, the target sample technique, and the longitudinal criminal history procedure. The cohort method entails selecting a cohort or population of individuals and then examining the official arrest records of that group over a specified period of time. Wolfgang, Figlio, and Sellin (1972) used this approach to explore the criminal behavior of all males born in Philadelphia in 1945 and still living in that city some 10 to 18 years later. The results of this investigation revealed that approximately 6% of the sample was responsible for 51% of the offenses committed by members of the cohort. Lyle Shannon (1982) conducted a similar study using a birth cohort from Racine, Wisconsin, and had comparable results.

The survey method, though related to the cohort approach, is unique in the sense that subjects are considered individually, rather than as a group or cohort. Hence, while such a procedure provides one with more options in terms of subjects and often allows for the collection of a greater wealth of information than the cohort method, it is vulnerable to the effects of selection bias and differential responsiveness. Kip Viscusi (1983) utilized this method to investigate self-reported criminality in a group of over 2,000 young black males living in three major urban areas. In support of what has been observed in cohort studies, Viscusi determined that the majority of crimes attributable to subjects in his sample were perpetrated by a small group of high-rate offenders. Similar results were obtained by West and Farrington (1977), who also employed the survey method to explore the correlates of crime and delinquency in a group of 411 working-class male adolescents residing in London, England.

A third methodology used to study the career criminal is something I refer to as the target sample procedure. Here one selects a group of high-risk individuals, often incarcerated offenders, and then questions them about various aspects of their criminal careers. A study conducted by the Rand Corporation was one of the first to employ a target sample methodology. In the initial phase of this project, Petersilia, Greenwood, and Lavin (1978) interviewed 49 incarcerated robbers in regard to their past criminal activities. The pattern of results obtained in this study revealed that even in this sample of imprisoned felons, the distribution of crimes was skewed toward a low rate of offending and that the majority of crimes was committed by a relatively small group of high-rate offenders. In an extension of this project to 625 California prisoners, Peterson and Braiker (1980) note that while half the robbers in their sample committed fewer than five robberies a year and half the burglars reported fewer than five burglaries per annum, in excess of 50 robberies and 150 burglaries were perpetrated by 10% of the robbers and burglars, respectively. The Figgie Corporation research group (1988), which also analyzed target sample data, arrived at a similar conclusion, with 51 (9%) of the 589 felons interviewed reporting involvement in 100 or more crimes a year.

A fourth methodology relevant to our discussion of career criminality is something known as the longitudinal criminal history approach. Investigators promoting this method of data collection start out by identifying a group of known offenders and then follow these individuals for a specified period of time with the aid of official arrest records. The primary advantage of this procedure is that it avoids the problem of an unwieldy data base, as often happens in target sample research, and features serious criminality, rather than be sidetracked by a relatively large number of minor offenses, as sometimes occurs with the cohort technique. The principal disadvantage of the longitudinal criminal history approach is that one is normally restricted to crimes known to the police. In one study using the longitudinal criminal history approach, Blumstein and Cohen (1979) of Carnegie-Mellon University in Pittsburgh ascertained that the average robber in their sample committed approximately 5 robberies per year, although a small subgroup of offenders (5% of the sample) was responsible for an annual rate of between 180 and 400 robberies each. In a 22-state study of young parolees, it was determined that 10% of the releases accounted for 40% of all subsequent arrests (Beck & Shipley, 1987).

It would appear that no matter which of these methodologies one utilizes, the results lead us to a similar conclusion: There exists a group of criminals who, while constituting a minority of offenders, account for the majority of serious criminal acts committed in any particular city, state, or country. One might well ask if these career criminals don't tend to specialize in certain specific lawbreaking activities. In research conducted on the Philadelphia cohort (Figlio, 1981), the London survey group (Farrington, 1982), and the Rand target sample (Petersilia et al., 1978), there was no evidence of specialization in the behavior of career or habitual criminals. Consequently, while there may be some crimes an offender may choose to avoid, such individuals are opportunists who will pursue just about any criminal possibility that comes their way. On the other hand, Kempf (1987) reanalyzed the Philadelphia cohort data and found that criminal careers follow along several paths, some of which are more specialized than others, and Bursik (1980) discerned that except for whites committing personal-injury offenses, there was a moderate likelihood of crime repetition for all of the offense categories considered as part of his investigation. Likewise, Holland and McGarvey (1984) failed to observe specialization in violent criminal careers but did note a trend toward moderate specialization for certain types of nonviolent property-oriented offense categories.

Though existing data suggest the possibility of a certain degree of specialization in the careers of some nonviolent offenders, preparation is more the exception than the rule. Hence, while the habitual or recidivistic offender may scheme more than the occasional lawbreaker (Erez, 1980; Figgie Corporation, 1988), the vast majority of all crimes take place with minimal planning and forethought. Edna Erez (1980), for instance, found that 80% of the crimes committed by members of the Philadelphia birth cohort were accomplished without benefit of a specified plan, and only 6% of the first offenses and 14% of the last offenses had been planned at least one day prior to commission of the felony. Another common misconception about criminals is that they become more skilled and their plans more organized as they grow older. As Petersilia et al. (1978) point out, however, those offenders who plan have tended to do so from an early age; rather than refine their criminal skills while incarcerated, immured criminals are motivated primarily by the desire to survive the prison experience and attain status in the prison subculture.

In examining the criminal careers of 24,398 middle-aged inmates, Langan and Greenfeld (1983) observed four types of criminal career, spanning three age periods: adolescence (ages 7 to 17), young adulthood (age 18 to 39), and middle age (age 40 and older). The most common pattern observed was one in which individuals had been crime-free during the first two periods and then found themselves involved in crime during middle age. This group of individuals exhibited the lowest levels of prior violence and the most stable record of past employment. In many cases, this was their first incarceration, and Langan and Greenfeld speculate that many of the men in this group were serving time for offenses emanating from domestic violence. Whether or not this is true, it is clear that the vast majority of individuals in this group do not qualify as career criminals. The career criminal group, constituting just 14% of the total sample, had not only been involved in crime during all three life periods, but also exhibited the highest rates of prior arrest, confinement, family criminality, and drug abuse. Furthermore, they were the group most likely to have fathered an illegitimate child and also exhibited the highest rate of unemployment in the month prior to commission of the instant offense.

The career criminal concept appears to hold for blacks as well as whites (Viscusi, 1983; Wolfgang et al., 1972), juveniles as well as adults (Smith, Smith, & Noma, 1984), and females as well as males (Warren & Rosenbaum, 1986). In fact, the career criminal has probably been with us as long as there have been societal rules to violate. The conception that a relatively small group of individuals account for the majority of serious offenses appears to be both self-evident and empirically valid. Furthermore, it contains features relevant to a theory of lifestyle criminality. However, steps need to be taken to distill and synthesize this information in a manner that not only does justice to the basic premise, but is useful to those of us interested in advancing a theory of criminal behavior that is as meaningful as it is fruitful. For as Robert Tillman (1987) discovered after analyzing data from the California Bureau of Criminal Statistics, though a relatively small subgroup of offenders were responsible for a disproportionate number of the serious crimes committed in California during the time period studied, a sizeable segment of the general state population had been in conflict with the law at one time or another.

Three of the better researched features of career criminality with applicability of the criminal lifestyle are: (1) the observation that past criminality is one of the better predictors of future criminality; (2) the fact that early-onset criminality is a strong predictor of serious lawbreaking behavior later on in life; and (3) the realization that high-rate criminality is often associated with heavy alcohol and drug abuse (Holden, 1986). The career criminal approach is not without its problems, however, the most prominent seemingly being that it fails to take into account life-span development issues and often restricts analyses to offender types rather than including groups of noncriminals for comparative purposes (Hirschi & Gottfredson, 1983). In fact, after interviewing a group of Canadian robbers, Normandeau and Lanciault (1983) conclude that the notion of career criminality should be replaced by the concept of criminal stages.

Life-Span Development Theory

As we saw in the preceding section, such issues as specialization and planning present problems for the concept of career criminality as it is typically understood. However, these issues might be better clarified if we were to examine them over the course of an offender's criminal career rather than at specified points in time. In this regard, Hirschi and Gottfredson (1983) acknowledge the durability of age as a correlate of crime, but they argue that age alone does not effectively predict crime over the life cycle of offenders. Therefore, while it may not be necessary for us to conduct longitudinal research in order to achieve a complete understanding of the career crime concept, it may be useful to scrutinize different career-line or life-span patterns. I offer this commentary in the knowledge that the crime-age relationship has been examined almost exclusively using aggregate or group level data, a practice that may have ensconced important individual crime patterns.

In examining the delinquent career lines of 767 adolescents incarcerated in New Jersey correctional facilities, Randall Smith, William Smith, and Elliot Noma (1984) ascertained that the majority were chronic offenders with an average of 11.7 arrests each. A variance centroid analysis of their data revealed four primary dimensions of crime: crimes against persons-crimes against property, person offenders-status offenders, serious-less serious, narcotic possession-other offenses. After examining individual career lines, Smith et al. concluded that delinquent careers may develop along several different trajectories, one common branch commencing with serious crimes against property (burglary) and evolving into serious crimes against persons. Other career paths observed in this study include one in which status offenses were followed by automobile theft and another in which a variety of different crimes preceded drug abuse. Results such as these suggest that career movement is possible even with juvenile crimes.

A great deal of research has been directed toward examining the advent or onset of criminality (see Hirschi & Gottfredson, 1983; West & Farrington, 1977; Wolfgang et al. 1972). Much less is known, however, about how persons leave or exit crime. In a study of Canadian robbers, Cusson and Pinsonneault (1986) discerned that the shock and stress of a criminal lifestyle, a gradual wearing down of the criminal drive by an accumulation of punishments and incarcerations, and a build-up of fear relative to the negative consequences of one's criminal actions all entered into offenders's decisions to desist from crime. Likewise, Thomas Meisenhelder (1977) found desistance to be associated with the development of a meaningful bond with the conventional social order and symbolic certification by a noncriminal that the offender had changed and was no longer a criminal. John Irwin (1970), an ex-robber and now respected criminologist, encountered a fear of future incarceration, insight into the futility of continued criminality, reduced expectations, development of a satisfying relationship with a woman, and involvement in extravocational and extradomestic activities in the stories of a group of 15 ex-convicts who had remained free of legal entanglements for a substantial period of time following their most recent incarceration.

Neal Shover (1983), a sociologist at the University of Tennessee, interviewed 36 men who had been previously convicted and confined for a variety of property offenses. He observed changes in both temporal contingencies (i.e., redefining their youthful criminal identities as foolish and self-defeating; fear of losing their last remaining opportunities for accomplishing something of value; a shift in aspirations and goals; a growing sense of tiredness with prison life) and interpersonal contingencies (i.e., establishment of a mutually satisfying relationship with another person, often a woman; commitment to a legitimate means of employment). Other than not finding extravocational activities and "verification" to be particularly useful in helping offenders resist crime, these results are in general agreement with Irwin's (1970) and Meisenhelder's (1977) earlier findings. It would appear, then, that the development of noncriminal associations, a reorientation in one's life goals, and a rapidly growing sense of fear are prominent in offender's decisions to abandon crime.

In considering life-span development issues relative to crime, Daniel J. Levinson's theory of adult development (Levinson, Darrow, Klein, Levinson, & McKee, 1978) may be particularly useful. Levinson et al. propose a system of age-linked developmental stages for men that center around three transition periods: the early adult transition, the mid-life transition, and the late adult transition. This model contains both internal (core values, identity, personal perception of events) and external (lifestyle, social roles) dimensions that change as the individual grows older. Even more germane to our discussion of life-span development and crime, however, is the mid-life crisis and the three tasks this crisis brings to light: review and reappraisal of one's life trajectory; changing the negative aspects of one's life; and confrontation and integration of the four polarities (young-old, feminine-masculine, attachment-separateness, creative-destructive). This might help explain certain aspects of desistance from crime since, as Gove (1985) notes, the individual becomes less self-absorbed, rebellious, and pleasure-seeking and more other-oriented, conforming, and introspective as the transition is made from early adulthood to middle age.

Annette Jolin and Don C. Gibbons (1987) interviewed 19 ex-offenders (mean age = 47) and 30 prison inmates (mean age = 45) and found that the majority of ex-offenders and inmates experienced mid-life changes in their attitudes, values, and behavior consonant with Levinson's theory. A handful of individuals, however, seemingly failed to experience the reevaluation that commonly occurs during the mid-life transition and consequently continued to engage in significant criminal behavior. It would therefore seem to follow that desistance from crime reflects life-span development issues as well as the influence of environmental and socially contingent experiences (see Irwin, 1970). In combination, these two factors serve to bring about an increased number of terminated criminal careers as the individual approaches middle age.

The Rational Choice Perspective

The rational choice theory of criminal behavior was a major topic of discussion in Chapter 2. Consequently, we will restrict our present discourse on this theory to an examination of how this model interfaces with the three models of human behavior previously discussed (i.e., criminal personality, career criminal, life-span development). Since choice and erroneous thinking are fundamental in defining Yochelson and Samenow's (1976) criminal personality, rational choice theory would appear to have a great deal of relevance to this particular model of criminal cognition. There is ample research to suggest that criminals do in fact make choices relative to their criminal activities (Cornish & Clarke, 1986), although these decisions are often nonoptimal and flawed (Carroll, 1978). In a study comparing 17 novice and 17 expert shoplifters, Frances Weaver and John Carroll (1985) determined that both groups based their decisions to shoplift on models of the environment that were simplified and oftentimes incomplete.

An interface also appears to exist between rational choice theory and the career concept of criminality. As we saw in the section on career criminality, there is little evidence of either specialization or planning in a majority of criminal careers. Moreover, research on rational choice theory has shown that a lack of utilitarian precision is the rule rather than the exception when it comes to human decision-making, criminal or otherwise (Carroll, 1978; Cimler & Beach, 1981). It would appear that instead of spending the majority of our time entertaining rational thoughts, our thoughts tend to resonate around irrational, self-defeating themes more often than we realize or are willing to admit (Ellis, 1962). This may be particularly true of the lifestyle criminal who, while not psychotic, chooses to think in ways that are clearly self-destructive. A reasonable conclusion might therefore be that while criminal thinking is logical, in that it follows from certain premises, it is also irrational, in that the premises themselves are often faulty and misleading.

The rational choice model would also appear to dovetail with life-span development theorizing. Choice and decision-making both seem inherently relevant to such developmental issues as one's initiation into crime or desistance from same. In exploring the reasons felons give for exiting crime, for example, we find that decision-making principles have a great deal to do with desistance. As Neal Shover (1983) aptly points out, "individuals, based on personal experiences, may alter their expectations of potential outcomes of criminal behavior" (p. 216). Subsequently, he found age-related changes in the anticipated likelihood of success in criminal ventures, which in turn led to a decrease in actual criminal behavior. While some of these changes in thinking were the result of experiences within the criminal justice system, others involved modification of goals and aspirations in an adult development sense. These findings clearly suggest that the rational choice and life-span development theories interface in a meaningful and potentially important way.

Guiding Principles

In defining a theory of human behavior, it is imperative that certain fundamental issues be addressed. Put another way, we need to appreciate the underlying philosophy of any system of theoretical thought. In what manner does the theory conceive of the nature of man, conceptualize development, explain deviance, and define change? These questions are of particular interest to persons aspiring to understand the theoretical underpinnings of various models of human behavior. In Chapter 2, we examined eight of the more popular theories of criminal conduct. We will now use these eight theories as a backdrop (see Table 3.1) against which the guiding principles of the theory of lifestyle criminality are explored.

Nature of Man

In broaching the nature of man issue, I have selected an artificial, but descriptive, trichotomy by which to categorize the eight theories of criminal conduct probed in Chapter 2. In essence, this trichotomy holds that man's basic nature can be conceived of in one of three ways: positively, negatively, or neutrally. The strain, negative labeling, and self viewpoints, for instance, adopt a positive or optimistic approach to the nature of man question. Strain theorists argue that man is a social being whose natural inclination is to conform, and that deviance is a function of the stress and strain generated by an inequitable social system (Merton, 1957). Labeling theory holds to a similar perspective, not only by postulating the basic goodness of man, but also by localizing deviance in the labels society imposes on its young lawbreakers (Schur, 1971). While self theories assume a positive stance on the human nature conundrum, they stop short of ascribing deviance to the inequities and attributions found in society. Rather, deviance is viewed by self theorists as an outgrowth of an individual's efforts to implement a

**TABLE 3.1: Eight Models of Criminal Conduct as Defined by the Four
Fundamental Principles of a Theory**

Theory	Nature of Man	Normal Development	Cause of Deviance	Implementing Change
Differential Association	Neutral	Modeling & social learning	Association with delinquents & criminals	Associating with noncriminals
Strain Theory	Positive	Pursuit of sociallysanctioned goals	Disjuncture between goals & available means	Increased opportunity for everyone
Social Control	Negative	Internalized sense of social control	Weak/broken bond to conventional social order	Attachment to the conventional social order
Labeling	Positive	Attributions & symbolic interactionalism	Negative labeling experiences	Changes in criminal justice system's approach to deviance
Self Theories	Positive	Defining one's self relative to society	Implementation of a self-image consistent with crime	Challenging old beliefs about self & developing a new self-identity
Psychoanalytic Theory	Negative	Gratification of instinctual drives within the limits established by society	Inadequate resolution of early conflicts resulting in either guilt or weak superego development	Developing greater insight into the unconscious determinants of behavior
Pathological Stimulation Seeking	Neutral	Achieving an optimal level of sensory stimulation	Drive for increased levels of stimulation coupled with negative family experiences	Finding socially appropriate outlets for stimulation seeking tendencies
Rational Choice Theory	Neutral	Maximizing gains and minimizing costs	The cost: benefit ratio for crime exceeds the cost: benefit ratio for noncrime	Increase the cost of crime and/or increase the benefit of noncrime

self-image consistent with his experience of himself as a person (Wells, 1978).

A second group of theories hold to a largely negative or pessimistic view of man. The two theories of criminal conduct adopting the perception that man is principally bad are the psychoanalytic and social control perspectives. Psychoanalysis is well known for its assumptions concerning the egocentric, selfish, and pleasure-oriented aspects of man's nature. According to this particular point of view, society forms a necessary link between civilization and order, since without society's intervening and organizing influence, the individual would tend to act on destructive and primitive impulses (Freud, 1963). Hirschi's (1969) social control perspective, on the other hand, attempts to explain noncrime rather than crime based on the premise that criminal behavior is a natural consequence of one's own humanness. Both viewpoints conclude that man is driven by antisocial tendencies that can only be harnessed through the controlling influences of society and various socializing agents.

A third class of theories conceptualize man as neither good nor bad, but neutral in terms of his proclivity for crime or noncrime. These behaviorally oriented perspectives view the individual as a sort of "blank slate" whose behavior is determined by various environmental experiences and contingencies. The differential association approach (Sutherland & Cressey, 1978), with its strong social learning bent, and rational choice perspective (Becker, 1968), with its penchant for describing behavior in cost:benefit terms, both paint a neutral or uncommitted picture of human nature. Quay's (1977) revision of pathological stimulation seeking theory also sets forth a neutral view of human nature, although unlike the differential association and rational choice models, Quay's perspective eschews the "blank slate" notion. On the contrary, the individual is said to be born with a nascent neurobiological predilection that interacts with various environmental contingencies to either bolster or weaken one's resistance to criminal temptation.

The lifestyle model of criminality approaches the nature of man issue in much the same manner as does Quay (1977), with one notable exception. Hence, man is viewed as largely neutral in terms of his propensity for engaging in prosocial or antisocial activity, although genetic and prenatal factors cannot be discounted as important in subsequent behavioral development. The fundamental difference between this and Quay's position is that the criminal lifestyle perspective finds man to be unmistakably oriented toward self-interest, hedonism, and the immediate gratification of certain biological drives. Accordingly, this theory holds to the viewpoint that man is born with certain needs and impulses that take precedence over a consideration of the welfare of others. It is only through the process of socialization that the individual even becomes aware of the fact that others may take a somewhat different perspective on certain issues. Consequently, the lifestyle approach to criminality involves a blending of the neutral and negative positions concerning the nature of man.

Normal Development

There are a number of ways in which behavioral development can be conceptualized. The three most popular positions considered by theorists assessing the question of crime are stage theories, task theories, and continuity theories. Stage theories approach human development as a series of discrete and definable stages, steps, or levels, culminating in a particular outcome or result. Of our eight theories of criminal conduct, only the psychoanalytic viewpoint posits a clear stage theory of human development. According to this particular theory, the individual progresses through the oral, anal, phallic, latency, and genital stages of psychosexual development, each with its own set of conflicts and pertinent issues. Problems occurring during the phallic and latency stages are assumed to be particularly influential in the evolution of criminal patterns of behavior (Glover, 1960). Stage theories of human behavior therefore equate maturity with successful movement through a series of universally applicable steps or stages.

Task theories are akin to stage theories but presuppose certain early developmental tasks that the individual must resolve rather than a series of stages through which the individual progresses. Strain theory hypothesizes that man is confronted with the task of finding a means to socially defined success (Merton, 1957), while social control theory postulates the presence of a link between the task of bonding to the conventional social order and a low level of subsequent criminality (Hirschi, 1969). The self theories of criminal conduct define human development in terms of a specific early life task, namely achieving a sense of personal identity (Wells, 1978), while Quay's (1965, 1977) pathological stimulation seeking explanation also finds itself in line with task theories of criminal development in the sense that attaining a satisfying or optimal level of sensory stimulation is assumed to be a primary organizing motive for human behavior.

Instead of conceptualizing human development as a series of discrete stages or life tasks, our third category of theory, the continuity model, presumes an uninterrupted flow of internal and external events that do not differ significantly from one period to the next. Differential association theory, for instance, posits that the associations the individual forms with other people will have wide-ranging effects in shaping, defining, and rein-forcing particular behavioral patterns, regardless of the age at which these associations are made (Sutherland & Cressey, 1978). Labeling theory also shows evidence of holding to a continuity view of human development since the attributions ascribed to persons follow an adjoining or contiguous, rather than discrete or step-defined, path (Schur, 1971). Rational choice theory subscribes to a modified continuity perspective since the individual must attain a certain level of cognitive awareness/maturity before he or she is capable of weighing the advantages and disadvantages of a particular course of action; once this occurs, however, there are no universal psychological transformations, stages of human development, or life tasks that the individ-ual must undergo or confront in order to move forward.

The lifestyle theory of criminality finds itself most closely allied with task theories of human development. In fact, the specific tasks assigned a preem-inent role in this developmental theory of criminal behavior—attachment/bonding, stimulus modulation, and self-image—correlate closely with tasks examined individually by Hirschi (1969), Quay (1977), and Wells (1978), respectively. Going a step or two further, the lifestyle theory of criminality contends that it is not the resolution of these three early life tasks that determines subsequent criminality, but rather the choices the individual makes relative to these tasks. The theory further argues that the person who goes about establishing a pattern of delinquent or criminal choices also constructs a system of thought that serves to support and buttress the criminal choices he or she has made and continues to make. Eventually, the three Cs of human development (conditions, choice, cognition) emerge into a self-reinforcing system of interacting influences and behavioral tendencies that reflect deviant patterns of development as well as normal ones.

Cause of Deviance

There are a number of ways in which our eight theories of criminal conduct can be classified in terms of their position on deviance. One possible classification scheme might involve a dimensional analysis of theories that view deviance as a continuum versus those that conceptualize deviance as categorically distinct from nondeviance. Thus, the former group of theories view criminals as quantitatively, but not qualitatively, distinct from noncrim-inals (labeling theory, rational choice theory), while the latter adopts the perspective that criminals and noncriminals are qualitatively, as well as quantitatively, different (social control theory, pathological stimulation seeking). We might also classify these theories into those that conceive of deviance as being seated in the individual (social control theory, psychoanalysis); attribute deviance to external conditions (strain theory, labeling theory); or take a more interactive approach (self theories, pathological stimulation seeking). A third classificatory strategy might entail comparing theories that hold to a multi-causal explanation of deviance (psychoanalysis, pathological stimulation seeking) with theories advocating a more unidimensional approach to crime causation (labeling theory, differential association).

Regardless of what these conceptual schemes tell us about crime and criminals, it would appear that the most striking aspect of these various models is that a theory's views on deviance follow directly from its position on normal development. Stated somewhat differently, deviance or pathology constitutes a disturbance in normal developmental patterns. Hence, where attributions are applied indiscriminately, deviance is the logical outcome (labeling theory), just as lawbreaking behavior is the natural consequence of poor or weak bonding (social control). In a similar vein, crime is viewed by self-theorists as the implementation of a self-concept that is deviant, while Quay (1977) argues that delinquency is innervated by an aberration of normal development (i.e., stimulus seeking behavior). It would appear, then, that a theory's position on deviance is simply an extension, albeit a pathological extension, of its views on normal development.

Like the eight theories of criminal conduct presented in Table 3.1, the lifestyle theory of criminal behavior conceptualizes deviance as an anomalous extension of normal developmental patterns. As such, the three Cs play a predominant role in the evolution of deviant behavior. According to lifestyle theory, the pre-criminal deals inadequately with the three early life tasks (attachment, stimulus modulation, self-image) and makes certain delinquent choices relative to these early experiences. These choices lead to various positive or negative consequences for the individual which, in turn, may enter into future decisions he makes relative to the laws, rules, and dictates of society. Over time, the evolving lifestyle criminal formulates a pattern of thinking designed to reinforce his decisions, rationalize his actions, and promote a view of himself as a good person despite his lawbreaking behavior. In classifying the lifestyle theory of criminality according to the three dimensions discussed at the beginning of this section, I would maintain that this theory holds to a view of deviance that is categorical, multidimensional, and interactive in nature.

Implementing Change

In developing a program of change, our eight theories propose a number of alternatives, although the most noteworthy aspect of these recommendations is that they follow from a given theory's ideas on normal development and deviance. Accordingly, the differential association perspective emphasizes the formation of associations with noncriminals (Sutherland & Cressey, 1978); social control theory, the development of attachments to the conventional social order (Hirschi, 1969); self theories, the derivation of a more positive self-identity (Wells, 1978); and pathological stimulation seeking theory, the exposition of more socially acceptable outlets for one's high sensation seeking tendencies (Quay, 1977). In each of these theories, change is viewed as something the individual must implement rather than being the responsibility of society or its various representatives.

Environmental solutions, on the other hand, have been advocated in the writings of several theorists in the criminal science field. Strain theorists, for instance, contend that an escalation in the number of opportunities for legitimate advancement will result in a parallel reduction in criminality (Merton, 1957), and labeling theorists argue that crime can only be meaningfully attenuated through a concerted effort by society to suspend the practice of labeling youthful offenders (Schur, 1971). The philosophy behind change from a rational choice or deterrence standpoint is raising the costs of crime while increasing the benefits of noncrime (Becker, 1968). These and other ideas would appear to place some, if not all, of the responsibility for change squarely on the shoulders of society, a position I find untenable from a lifestyle point of view.

The theory of lifestyle criminality adopts a person-oriented approach to change. In other words, change is the sole responsibility of the individual and encompasses a variety of techniques designed to encourage the individual to examine his thinking and current criminal choices. Thus, while the change agent plays an important role in teaching the criminal about his cogitation and encouraging him to challenge his thinking, whether or not the individual changes is determined by the time, effort, and energy he himself invests in the change process. This is not to say that society is blameless when it comes to crime development or that society cannot serve as a catalyst for change; it is just that in order for change to take place, the individual must be willing to acknowledge the need for personal transformation and be committed to taking the steps that will make such change a reality. As we can see from this brief discussion, personal responsibility is afforded a central position in the lifestyle model's approach to change, although this does not negate society's obligation to find more efficient means by which to facilitate the change process.

Conclusion

This chapter has served to introduce the reader to the philosophical underpinnings of the theory that crime can be conceptualized in lifestyle terms. As previous research unquestionably demonstrates, lifestyle criminals exert a substantial drain on society's legal, emotional, and financial resources. Consequently, while lifestyle criminals constitute a relatively small percentage of all persons processed through the criminal justice system, they account for the majority of serious offenses committed, a relationship that has been witnessed historically as well as cross-nationally. The lifestyle criminal engages in behaviors that have long-term negative consequences for all of society but exact the greatest toll from the personal victims of his crimes. It is therefore incumbent upon us as a society to learn how to identify and deal more effectively with this often misunderstood group of offenders.

It would appear that the progress of the U.S. systems of criminology, jurisprudence, and penological thought has been slow and disappointing. Though we are able to put a man on the moon and are capable of manufacturing computer chips small enough to fit inside a shirt pocket, yet powerful enough to generate 128 kilobytes of computer memory, we remain largely ignorant of what motivates the behavior of those persons responsible for the lion's share of serious criminality in this country (i.e., the lifestyle criminal). Part of the explanation would seem to rest with the previously noted observation that the major theories of criminal behavior have focused their attention on only a small portion of the relevant data. Though it may be defensible for a field to supply unidimensional answers to multidimensional questions when it is at an immature level of development, the criminal science field, much like the lifestyle criminal himself, appears stuck in a state of protracted adolescence.

It may seem unduly harsh of me to attribute blame for our lack of success in explaining criminal behavior to the seeming superficiality of a large portion of criminal science research. After all, criminal scientists are not alone when it comes to dealing ineffectively with lifestyle criminals. Politicians, the courts, and society itself must assume a certain degree of responsibility for the general state of nescience that seems to dominate our way of thinking about criminals. Society, in fact, has become an unwitting accomplice to the lifestyle criminal's efforts to avoid responsibility by providing him with a plethora of seemingly legitimate excuses for his illegal acts (see Walters & White, 1988). As a society, we have thrown money at problems without fully appreciating the extent or nature of these problems, and implemented programs without articulating the program's mission, goals, or general purpose. Until society is willing to take a more candid look at the problem of lifestyle criminality and entertain reasonable solutions instead of campaign slogans, any efforts undertaken at this point in time, no matter how well intended, are bound to fail.

In the next four chapters, we will be examining the theory of lifestyle criminality in much greater detail than was possible in this preliminary chapter. Though this model is continually being revised as new information is brought to light, it appears to offer a perspective on crime that is generally consistent with existing clinical and research data. As we progress through these next several chapters, I believe the reader will begin to realize how this theory's relevance has been enhanced by the practice of restricting the scope of my investigation to a circumscribed group of offenders—lifestyle criminals. Additional study should also reveal the subtle interplay of conditions, choice, and cognition as they affect criminal behavior. In the next chapter, we will be examining the postulates that serve as a foundation for this theory that holds to the view that serious criminality can be understood as a lifestyle.

4. Postulates and Key Terms

If the early precursors and guiding principles supply a theory with its roots, the defining postulates constitute its heart and soul. Postulates are unquestionably a vital rung in the stepladder of behavioral theory building. As such, they should be provided a prominent position in any theory of human behavior. I have therefore set aside an entire chapter for the express purpose of defining the founding postulates of the theory that crime can be conceptualized as a lifestyle. As we witnessed in Chapter 2, a theory should not only be important and useful, but it should also be precise and sufficiently operationalized. Imprecision and inadequate operationality give birth to drifting hypotheses and flaccid conceptualizations that divert our attention from the meaningful analysis of human behavior. Organizing one's theoretical ideas around specific postulates can help avoid the problem of ambiguity since it allows for increased accuracy and clarity of expression.

Though unambiguously defined propositions may encourage greater precision and specificity in our thinking about a particular issue, a postulate-based theory of criminal conduct is no panacea. Sutherland, in presenting his differential association model of criminality (Sutherland & Cressey, 1978), offered a series of postulates, yet failed to define behaviorally many of his terms. In fact, operationality is one of the areas in which most theories of criminal behavior fall well short of the mark. Consequently, for a theory to be both precise and properly operationalized, the postulates need to be rich in terms that are clearly defined and behaviorally referenced. Without benefit of both explicit postulates and concisely-defined terms, we will find ourselves adrift in a sea of confusion with no oars, motor, or steering mechanism.

In this chapter, we will be examining ten postulates that subserve the theory of lifestyle criminality. These suppositions provide the substance and foundation of this theory that conceptualizes crime as a lifestyle of personal irresponsibility and social victimization. Attempts have been made in this chapter to clarify pertinent hypotheses, operationalize key terms, and formalize the sequence of events responsible for the criminal lifestyle, while at the same time retaining a high degree of personal and clinical relevance. Unfortunately, as I believe the subsequent discussion will bear out, these efforts have met with less than total success. Accordingly, it is imperative that the reader understand that these postulates are currently at a preliminary, rather than final, stage in their development and will require additional refinement as new information is brought to light. This, then, is the working hypothesis approach to theory building referenced in the opening chapter of this book.

Postulate #1: Crime can be understood as a lifestyle characterized by a global sense of irresponsibility, self-indulgent interests, an intrusive approach to interpersonal relationships, and chronic violation of societal rules, laws, and mores.

The focal point of this first postulate is that criminality is defined in lifestyle terms. This does not mean that there are no other categories of crime, just that the particular genus that is of prime importance here exists as a lifestyle. The reader may recall from our discussion on career criminality that this is a group of offenders who can lay claim to the vast majority of serious criminality perpetrated worldwide. Thus, rather than conceive of crime as a momentary lapse in morality or an atypical response from an individual experiencing high levels of psychological distress, the lifestyle theory features criminal acts that reflect a relatively enduring life pattern of violation. This should not be taken as evidence against the possibility of a momentary lapse in morality or increased levels of environmental stress that explain certain types of crimes; but rather that the present theory is primarily concerned with crime committed within the context of a wider lifestyle, a lifestyle characterized by irresponsible, self-indulgent, interpersonal intrusive, social rule breaking behavior.

As our definition of lifestyle criminality suggests, this particular category of deviance is characterized by four primary behavioral characteristics. These are the behaviors that demarcate the criminal lifestyle and accord precision and specificity to the idea that crime exists as a lifestyle. I would hypothesize further than an unequivocal pattern of lifestyle criminality will reflect all four characteristics. Consequently, a person might be irresponsible, self-indulgent, and a regular violator of society's laws and mores, but in the absence of intrusive behavior cannot legitimately be classified within the lifestyle rubric. There are, in fact, many individuals who restrict their antisocial activity to nonpredatory forms of criminality and cannot justifiably be categorized as lifestyle criminals using the criteria delineated herein. With these considerations in mind, we direct our attention to the four primary behavioral characteristics of lifestyle criminality.

Irresponsibility

We have all been irresponsible at times. The lifestyle criminal, however, has forged this characteristic into a life pattern. He is irresponsible in his attitude toward school, work, finances, family, and friends, Moreover, this irresponsibility in attitude culminates in an habitual epitome of conduct in which the criminal fails to account for his actions and regularly neglects his social and moral obligations to others. This irresponsibility is global and persistent rather than circumscribed and periodic, and it is a constant source of irritation to those most affected by the criminal's undependability, namely parents, spouses, teachers, and employers. It is his reckless, impulsive, unreliable approach to situations that serves to make the criminal's life so chaotic, unpredictable, and tumultuous.

As the reader may have gathered from our discussion of the nature of man issue in Chapter 3, a major assumption made by the lifestyle theory of criminal behavior is that responsibility is a learned, rather than innate, characteristic. A child who is not reinforced for responsible behavior will see no value in acting responsibly and will fail to develop accountability for his or her actions. School often is the first environment in which the evolving criminal's global sense of irresponsibility is displayed publicly. Such is the case because the school setting demands a certain degree of accommodation, a task a young child who has not been taught a rudimentary sense of accountability will have difficulty managing. Hence, an important interaction takes place between the person and his or her school environment, although the role of individual choice should also not be overlooked.

The evolving criminal appears to enter into a conflictual relationship with the school environment from the very outset. Most lifestyle criminals have experienced academic problems since grade school, though this appears to be more a function of languishing interest, initiative, and responsibility than of limited academic/intellectual ability. Consequently, most lifestyle criminals drop out of school long before they reach the twelfth grade (Glueck & Glueck, 1968; Polk & Schafer, 1972; Walters & White, 1987). Take the example of one subject from Walters and White's (1987) Leavenworth 500 sample:

Despite average intellectual ability (IQ = 99) and good academic performance prior to the fifth grade, S received low ratings from his high school teachers for leadership ability, as well as cooperativeness. Enrolled in the tenth grade at the time, he was failing all of his classes, in large part because of excessive absenteeism and repeated truancy. Several months later S dropped out of school with no job or apparent means of support.

Employment is another area in which this global sense of irresponsibility is expressed. Research has consistently demonstrated that the work records of most career and lifestyle offenders are sparse, meager, and grossly deficient (Chaiken & Chaiken, 1982; Langan & Greenfeld, 1983; Petersilia, Greenwood, & Lavin, 1977; Walters & White, 1987). When working, most lifestyle criminals will take advantage of their employer's generosity or good nature. However, the majority of such individuals have never worked the same job longer than one to two years at best, often quitting or being fired within several months of being hired (Walters & White, 1987). The lifestyle criminal's irresponsible attitude toward work is illustrated in another case vignette from the Leavenworth 500 study:

Of the eight jobs C ever held, the longest lasted 17 months and the shortest 2 days, with an average length of six months. C quit one job so that he could move to another state and then quit this job 15 months later because he was homesick. After working three months as a barber's apprentice, he quit, taking $300 worth of barber tools with him. He evidently sold the barber tools in order to get money to purchase drugs. C was eventually picked up by the police but the owner of the barber shop refused to press charges because, as he puts it, "C was always a good worker on the days he showed up."

A second case illustration from this same sample of offenders shows how the lifestyle criminal's irresponsible attitude toward work affects other areas of his life as well:

A bright, verbal young man, M was hired to work in a restaurant as a cook and part-time waiter. Reports from the restaurant's owner indicate that from the first several weeks of his employment, M made a habit of lying to enhance his standing among other employees. Moreover, he would inform patrons of the restaurant that he was a law student receiving guidance from a local judge, though in actuality he hadn't even graduated from high school. M had been observed taking tips meant for other waiters and had written a half dozen "bad checks" at local establishments which the employer ended up having to cover. To top things off, M acted like a jealous suitor of the owner's daughter despite being a married man with a pregnant wife at home. After four months the owner, fed up with M's antics, fired him, but not before M raided the restaurant cash register and made off with some $1,700, most of which was never recovered.

The lifestyle criminal is also irresponsible in terms of managing money, paying bills and utilities, meeting his social obligations to others, and taking care of his family. The lifestyle criminal may father a number of children but rarely does he meet his financial and personal responsibilities in raising and caring for these offspring:

> Never before married, D fathered two children by two different women. One child was raised by its mother and the other by a maternal aunt. D provided no financial support despite holding several construction jobs in the community and actually never even met either of his two children.

It would seem, then, that irresponsibility is a cardinal behavioral characteristic of lifestyle criminals. It is further hypothesized that this particular attribute of the recalcitrant lawbreaker has its foundation in the cognitive interpretations of the individual. In fact, all four of the primary behavioral features of lifestyle criminality mirror a characteristic attitude and style of thought. Though irresponsibility is a part of growing up, in the case of the lifestyle criminal, it persists well beyond early adolescence. In line with the work of Yochelson and Samenow (1976), the lifestyle theory of criminality proposes that the habitual offender must not only become more responsible, but he must also find the responsible way of life intrinsically reinforcing if meaningful change is to take place.

Self-Indulgence

According to the present formulation, we are not only born irresponsible, but self-indulgent as well. Though I find a great deal about psychoanalysis with which I do not agree, this skepticism does not extend to the psychoanalytic position regarding the role of pleasure in motivating the behavior of young children. Like Freud, I believe that we are all born with a tendency to maximize pleasure and minimize pain. By means of socialization, however, we learn that we must delay satisfaction of certain desires in order to achieve various long-term goals. The lifestyle criminal has never learned the value of postponing gratification and consequently tends to be impulsive, pleasure-oriented, and self-indulgent. The abuse of alcohol or drugs is a particularly obvious expression of the self-indulgent attitude of the lifestyle criminal. In this regard, research on career criminality shows that high-rate lawlessness is often accompanied by a history of alcohol and/or drug abuse (Holden,

1986). Such was certainly the case with at least one member of the Leavenworth 500 sample:

> L began drinking alcohol and smoking marijuana when he was approximately 13. His first documented arrest occurred one year later, although he had been shoplifting from stores and strong-arming school-mates since age 11. By the time he was 16 years of age, L had graduated to "harder" drugs like PCP, cocaine, and heroin and before his 18th birthday had a full-blown drug habit. Two years later he was serving a 5- to 10-year sentence in a medium security state prison for burglary. While his drug usage may have accentuated his descent into crime, it did not appear to have caused it.

Yochelson and Samenow (1976) found a great deal of sexual promiscuity in the backgrounds of offenders in their sample of criminal personalities. Sexual promiscuity, an unstable marital history, and tenuous emotional ties to others would all appear to reflect the lack of self-restraint so characteristic of the self-indulgent attitude. Taking as an example the behavior of one subject from the Leavenworth 500 sample, we see just this:

> By age 35 G had been married and divorced five times. Each one of these marital relationships had been marked by extramarital affairs and a lack of commitment and loyalty to each marital partner. Not only did this individual indulge in regular drug binges, but he would achieve a sense of excitement and exhilaration while successfully posing as a mental health professional, though he was neither properly trained nor appropriately credentialed for such work.

The nature of self-indulgence is that the individual seeks to achieve satisfaction and pleasure irrespective of the consequences of his or her behavior. One way of achieving such gratification is by bringing attention to one's physical appearance. Hence, wearing garish jewelry, flaunting expensive clothing, or adorning oneself with tattoos may all reflect self-indulgence, although other factors also need to be considered since these behaviors, in and of themselves, are not criminogenic. Tattooing, for instance, not only correlates with delinquency (DeRen, Diligent, & Petiet, 1973) and adult criminality (Yamamoto, Seeman, & Lester, 1963), but it also tends to discriminate between personally assaultive and nonassaultive felons (Newman, 1982). The advisability of considering body graffiti as an expression of self-indulgence is supported by the results of a study by Bennahum (1971), in which a high rate of tattooing was observed in a group of heroin addicts.

There is a distinctly self-destructive flavor to the self-indulgent adventures of the typical lifestyle criminal. Drugs, sex, and tattooing all have negative long-term consequences for the lifestyle criminal, particularly in light of present-day concerns about hepatitis, genital herpes, and AIDS:

> R was a chronic complainer. Whether the complaints were physical, psycholog-
> ical, or administrative, he demanded an immediate response from staff. While
> confined in Disciplinary Detention he had sexual relations with a known homo-
> sexual. As he waited for the medical test results to come back from the lab, he
> continually demanded that staff do something to relieve the anxiety he was
> experiencing relative to the possibility of him having contracted a sexually-trans-
> mittable disease.

As the above example illustrates, the lifestyle criminal's self-indulgent activities will often bring about long-term negative consequences for himself and others. However, rather than accept responsibility for these outcomes, the criminal looks to blame other people and outside circumstances for the misery and discomfort he has brought upon himself.

Interpersonal Intrusiveness

The lifestyle criminal repeatedly violates the rights, dignity, and personal space of others. This third cardinal characteristic of lifestyle criminality, interpersonal intrusiveness, is different from irresponsibility and self-indulgence in the sense that one is not born intrusive, but rather learns to act in this manner. I say this because interpersonal intrusiveness involves a deliberate attempt on the part of the individual to encroach upon the rights and personal feelings of others. There is no such intent on the part of the young child, regardless of how disturbing his or her behavior may be to the parents. Interpersonal intrusiveness is therefore an essential link in the chain of behaviors defining lifestyle criminality since, in some cases, it is the only behavioral feature that distinguishes lifestyle from nonlifestyle patterns of offending.

Interpersonal intrusiveness is often expressed in aggressive, violent acts, especially those encompassing specific criminal events. The true test of an action's intrusiveness is whether it violates the personal space or dignity of one or more specific persons. Consequently, crimes like rape, murder, and robbery are usually considered to be more intrusive than offenses like larceny, shoplifting, and drug trafficking. However, we need to examine the criminal act in detail if we are to obtain an accurate estimate as to the degree of intrusiveness of that particular act:

> T was only 9 years old when he had his first brush with the law. He and his 12 year old brother stole their father's .22 caliber pistol, some ammunition, and the family car. Confronted by two policemen several miles out of town, they held these officers at bay for six hours with the firearm, surrendering only after they had run out of ammunition. From this point onward, T regularly engaged in intrusive actions, commencing with extorting other juveniles for their lunch money and progressing to robbing passersby of their possessions by the time he was 16. It wasn't long before he was running into banks with a shotgun demanding that everyone "drop to the floor" as he and his cohorts went through the teller drawers.

Expressions of interpersonal hostility and physical abuse directed toward significant others can also reflect a tendency toward intrusive action. Physical and/or emotional abuse of a spouse or child, for instance, shows designs of an interpersonally intrusive nature. This was clearly evident in the behavior of one Leavenworth 500 subject:

> N had always been a rather aggressive individual. Since second grade he had been a nuisance in the classroom and a bully on the playground. He spent more time in the principal's office than he did in the classroom and was suspended some 15 times for fighting. N was finally expelled from school in the 11th grade when he attacked and beat up the high school vice principal. This behavior continued well into adulthood, for in addition to winding up in a large number of fights at local bars and nightclubs, the police were being called to his home on a weekly basis on complaints from neighbors that he was beating up on his wife and various girlfriends. N's wife finally left him after his abuse of their 5-year-old son landed the youngster in the hospital with a broken arm.

Social Rule Breaking

The human infant tends to march to the tune of his own drummer. In fact, it has been the observation of many a parent raising their first child that the newborn infant seems preoccupied with inner tensions and pleasures and is largely inattentive to the world around him or her. It is not until the child begins differentiating itself from the wider social and physical environment that we see the gradual waning of this primitive state of egocentricity (Piaget, 1954). Hence, the lifestyle theory of criminality finds itself in agreement with

Hirschi's (1969) position on man and society—namely, that man is born to violate the rules and conventions of society and that only through the process of socialization do we learn to abide by the laws and dictates set down by an outside authority. Consequently, irresponsibility, self-indulgence, and social rule breaking, but not interpersonal intrusiveness, are viewed as inherent parts of man's nature.

In general, social rule breaking reflects a blatant disregard for societal norms, laws, and mores. Such behavior normally commences relatively early in life and often is observed in situations where the individual is being asked to conform to certain rules and standards. As such, the school environment is a regular target of the developing criminal's rule-breaking activities:

> A belligerent student who frequently got himself involved in fights at school, D was suspended from school in excess of 20 times between grades 4 and 10. He was finally expelled from school midway through the tenth grade.

The lifestyle criminal also does poorly in responding to the demands of military life:

> B spent six months in the Army until he was thrown in the stockade for stealing from the other soldiers in his unit. He was also considered by the company commander to be a serious behavioral problem who did not like taking orders. After spending five months in the stockade on the aforementioned larceny charges, he received a bad conduct discharge from the military.

Though school and military adjustment problems reflect a proclivity for norm-violating conduct, social rule breaking is probably most plainly expressed in various criminal acts. In this regard, it is important to know the frequency, intensity, and duration of lawbreaking behavior, as well as the age at which the individual was first arrested, in order to obtain an accurate reading of an individual's social rule breaking tendencies. Moreover, research conducted over the past several years demonstrates that the onset of lawbreaking behavior at an early age is strongly prognostic of high-rate criminality later in life (Holden, 1986):

> E was first arrested around age 12. His general delinquent demeanor consisted of petty larceny, breaking into houses, violating the local curfew, and being chronically truant from school. Over the next twenty years he accrued a record of 22 arrests for offenses ranging anywhere from DWI to rape and spent 14 years confined in various jails, prisons, and correctional facilities.

Irresponsibility, self-indulgence, interpersonal intrusiveness, and social rule breaking constitute four distinct, but interrelated, behavioral functions. Consequently, while each is important in its own right, there is a clear bond of commonality tying these four behavioral characteristics to each other, statistically as well as theoretically (see Walters & White, 1987). In fact, this was the rationale that guided the development of the Lifestyle Criminality Screening Form (LCSF), a rationale that found support in the form of a relatively high degree of inter-scale correlation (.44 to .74) between the Irresponsibility, Self-Indulgence, Interpersonal Intrusiveness, and Social Rule Breaking scales that comprise this instrument (Walters, White, & Denney, in press). We shall see later that the LCSF provides us with a fairly reliable and robust measure of the lifestyle criminality concept.

Postulate #2: Conditions impact on the development of the criminal lifestyle principally through three domains (physical, social, psychological).

As was discussed in Chapter 1, the conditions prominent in the later development of criminality can be conceptualized as interacting within three domains: the physical, the social, and the psychological. The factors interacting in the physical domain determine how the early life task of stimulus modulation will be played out. In other words, what level or magnitude of sensory stimulation does the individual view as optimal? In the social domain, the person and situations variables merge to bring about the individual's response to the early life task of attachment or bonding relative to one or more parental figures. The resolution of this early life task will have far-reaching consequences for subsequent interpersonal behavior. Finally, the person×situation interaction taking place in the psychological domain influences how one will handle the life task of defining oneself as an individual. As we shall see in the next chapter, these early life tasks are normally resolved within the first four to five years of life.

The person×situation interaction continues despite the fact that the individual has moved beyond the early life tasks. Actually, the resolutions achieved within the bulwark of these early life events enter into the variegated interactions taking place within the physical, social, and psychological domains later on in life as well. In the physical arena, we find the later life task of deciding whether to organize behavior internally or externally. The later life task of empathy and social bonding is situated along the social dimension, while the later life task of role identity falls within the purview of the psychological domain. These later life tasks are thought to arise in response to demands placed on the individual by extrafamilial sources of social influence, though resolution is never fully achieved since the later life tasks guide behavior and development over the entire life span.

> Postulate #3: Conditions may limit one's options, but they do not determine one's choices.

We have seen how conditions appear to cluster into three primary domains of influence. However, it is the attitude one adopts toward these life tasks, rather than the tasks themselves, that determines subsequent criminality. In other words, crime is a function of the choices we make specific to the early and later life tasks occurring in the physical, social, and psychological domains. For most of us, these choices are congruent with socially acceptable goals. The aspiring lifestyle criminal, on the other hand, makes choices that bring him into continual conflict with societal rules, laws, and mores. It is a primary tenet of the lifestyle approach to criminality that conditions do not cause crime directly but exert their influence through an expansion or narrowing of one's options relative to some future course of action.

The decision-making component of the lifestyle model of criminal conduct serves as the framework within which the criminal choice can be understood. Of particular importance are risk/protective and exacerbating/mitigating factors. It is theorized that risk factors serve to increase the probability of one's involvement in criminal activity, while protective factors function to decrease the prospect of such an outcome. Likewise, exacerbating factors augment one's chances of committing a particular criminal act, while miti-gating factors serve to reduce one's likelihood of engaging in a specific criminal act. Hence, conditions characteristically exert their effect through one of these four actions, increasing or decreasing one's options in a given situation, but never determining the final outcome. Consequently, in spite of the influence of various personal, situational, and interactive conditions, the individual still makes choices, though these choices are limited by the alternatives available to the person at any particular point in time.

A potential limitation of both the second and third postulates revolves around finding a methodology by which to evaluate hypotheses educed from these postulates. Though there has been an abundance of research on such issues as attachment and stimulus modulation, there is a lack of consensus as to how these various elements should be assessed. Therefore, while a great deal of research has been conducted on attachment in infants and young children, there is a paucity of information on attachment in adults. Moreover, though copious attention has been paid to examining sensation seeking behavior, there is disagreement as to how sensation seeking should be measured. As such, it is essential that a unified and congruent research methodology be found that will permit us to probe meaningfully the impact of conditions and choice on the criminal lifestyle.

> Postulate #4: The behavior of the lifestyle criminal is directed toward losing in dramatic and destructive ways.

One obvious manifestation of lifestyle criminality involves a clear poverty of self-awareness and personal insight. Thus, while the lifestyle criminal appears to set himself up to lose in ways that are obvious to everyone but himself, he expends a great deal of time and effort trying to blame his problems on external factors. In truth, the lifestyle criminal sets himself up to lose in a manner that frequently is dramatic and consonant with his desire for increased sensory stimulation. However, the criminal lifestyle is a destructive lifestyle, pernicious to the individual as well as society. As such, the drama in the criminal lifestyle unfolds into self- and other-destructive behavior. The self-destructive side of the criminal lifestyle is a reflection of the particular self-image the individual has adopted, while the other-destructive component relates to the fact that the criminal is poorly bonded to others. In the end, this lifestyle takes the individual down a deleterious path of irresponsible, self-indulgent, interpersonally intrusive, and social rule breaking actions.

The following case illustration from the Leavenworth 500 sample reveals the loser's mentality that is so apparent to the outside observer, yet so difficult for the lifestyle criminal himself to see:

> P had been a management problem since early adolescence. His first several arrests were for general delinquency, petty larceny, and public drunkenness. On one occasion he was observed wandering around a parking lot peering into car windows. When approached by a police officer about this behavior, he resisted arrest by punching the officer in the abdomen. On another occasion he broke into a nightclub, intent on burglarizing the establishment, but then drank himself into a stupor when he happened across several bottles of liquor. The next morning the owner of the night spot walked into his business only to find it in a shambles, the perpetrator passed out at the bar. However, in discussing his various predicaments in life, P seemed completely oblivious to the fact that in most cases he was the primary agent of his own destruction.

Like the vast majority of lifestyle criminals I have met, P did not approach crime as a profession geared toward long-term success, but rather as a vehicle through which he might lose in dramatic and destructive ways.

The notion that habitual criminals assume a loser's stance in life is similar to what Eric Berne (1961), the founder of Transactional Analysis, referred to as a life script. Claude Steiner (1974), who has probably written as much about script analysis as anyone, states that scripts are like a blueprint of one's life. He goes on to argue that the life script has features that parallel the three parts of a Greek tragedy: prologue, climax, and catastrophe. The prologue is the individual's life during childhood; the climax, the adult period in which the protagonist struggles against his or her destiny (as defined by the script); and the catastrophe, the tragic ending wherein the life script is fulfilled.

The primary difference between the life script and the loser's lifestyle is that the life script is said to be written by the time the individual is still very young. This, in fact, is what makes the life script so tragic—it is based on decisions construed when the individual had a very limited understanding of the world. While the loser's mentality also begins at a very early age, it continues to develop over time and actually does not reach its full potential until the individual is well into his adult years. Consequently, it is an evolving life decision to lose in dramatic and destructive ways, rather than a life script, which is said to direct the criminal lifestyle.

If we were to terminate our discussion on the losing life decision at this juncture, I believe our explanation of criminal motivation would be incomplete, if not tautological. To contend that one is a criminal because of the choices one makes without then exploring why these particular choices are made does not appear to be a particularly insightful or useful approach to the complicated question of crime causation. At least part of the answer as to why the pre-criminal selects certain behaviors over others lies with decision-making models of human cognition (see Carroll, 1978; Cornish & Clarke, 1986). However, there is another important factor that is often overlooked by these decision-making models of cognition: the element of fear. Fear is seen by the lifestyle theory of criminal conduct as a primary motivator of repetitive antisocial behavior.

As we know from the psychology of learning and motivation, a motivator energizes as well as directs behavior (Mowrer, 1960). Conditions and reinforcement patterns would appear to supply the direction, but the actual impetus would seem to derive from a strong sense of fear. The lifestyle criminal fears many things, but he fears responsibility, commitment, intimacy, and failing in conventional pursuits most of all. He therefore finds refuge in the criminal world, where there are as many excuses for failure as there are targets for predation. Since the lifestyle criminal avoids learning about conventional society, this fear of failure grows with each criminal act. Hence, this fear is what fuels the evolving life decision to lose (from the standpoint of society) in a manner that is both dramatic and destructive.

It is one thing to hypothesize that a loser's mentality subserves lifestyle criminality, and it is quite another to support such a hypothesis with data. The loser's life decision, while intriguing, is probably the most difficult element in the theory of lifestyle criminality to verify. How do we measure this loser's mentality? Even more important, how exactly is losing being defined here? Are we arguing that the lifestyle criminal is a failure from a conventional point of view, or are we saying that he is a loser even from the standpoint of being a criminal? These and other questions will be addressed in the next chapter, which is devoted exclusively to exploring the developmental features of lifestyle criminality. It should be noted, however, that the lifestyle theory of intervention is founded on the premise that the lifestyle criminal is driven to lose in dramatic and destructive ways. Consequently, this fourth postulate needs to be as operationally explicit as possible.

> Postulate #5: There is a distinctive thinking style that derives from the lifestyle criminal's decision to engage in delinquent and criminal acts.

As we have discussed several times previously, the theory of lifestyle criminality rests on the 3 Cs: conditions, choice, and cognition. The first two, conditions and choice, interact to form the third, cognition. The criminal thinking style develops in an effort to support, buttress, and reinforce one's criminal decisions. In many respects (particularly when it comes to supporting irresponsible and self-indulgent aims), the process of criminal thought is an extension of the cognitive patterns present in normal adolescents, although in many respects (particularly in reference to interpersonally intrusive actions) the content of thought is very different between these two groups. The problem appears to be that the evolving lifestyle criminal has found the irresponsibility of adolescence so reinforcing that he makes the decision to continue this pattern indefinitely, even though he may not be fully aware of his own sentiments in this regard.

The urge to extend adolescence is clearly evident in the unusual story of one Leavenworth 500 subject:

> In high school F was a star athlete whose grades also were better than average. The other students looked to him with awe and respect and he was always dating one of the more popular girls in school. He went to college on a football

scholarship but was injured and cut from the team. He subsequently dropped out of college since he was failing all of his classes. One year later, posing as a 16-year-old orphan, he enrolled in high school and again became a football star and one of the more popular students in school.

The desire to be a star and to receive the adoration and attention of others is an important motivator of behavior for the lifestyle criminal. It is well to keep in mind, however, that there are many persons who have acted on the desire to forestall the responsibilities of adulthood but have never engaged in serious criminality. Thus, it would appear that while the lifestyle criminal is prepared and willing to infringe upon the rights of others in order to perpetuate this adolescent-like lifestyle, the noncriminal is not.

The extended or persistent adolescence interpretation of the behavior of society's most incorrigible outlaws finds support in research that shows offenders to be impulsive, self-justifying, and externally oriented, and having hair-trigger tempers and short-time horizons (see Wilson & Herrnstein, 1985). One might well wonder why all adolescents don't engage in habitual lawbreaking behavior if their thinking is analogous to that displayed by the average lifestyle criminal. The reader needs to realize that what I am referring to here is a similarity in process rather than content. The lifestyle criminal evidences a style of thought that in many ways mirrors patterns found naturally in children and early adolescents. The content of thought, particularly as it relates to violating the laws of society and the rights of others, however, is as different in the criminal and normal adolescent as day and night. It may therefore be useful to construct a model highlighting these criminogenic thinking patterns. Such a model will be the subject of our next postulate.

Postulate #6: The content and process of criminologic thought are reflected in eight primary cognitive patterns.

The lifestyle criminal thinks in ways designed to perpetuate the irresponsible, self-indulgent, interpersonally intrusive, and social rule breaking decisions he has made in life. This thinking style manifests itself in eight primary cognitive patterns, which were originally published as an article in the *Criminal Justice Research Bulletin* (Walters & White, 1989c). Predicated upon Yochelson and Samenow's (1976) 52 thinking errors and Walters's own clinical work with groups of incarcerated offenders, these thinking patterns were derived, modified, and evaluated over a period of five years. What started out as a fragmentary model encompassing five specific thinking errors evolved into an integrated system of eight separate, but interrelated, primary cognitive features of lifestyle criminality. These features were subsequently labeled mollification, cutoff, entitlement, power orientation, sentimentality, superoptimism, cognitive indolence, and discontinuity.

Mollification

Mollification involves an attempt by the individual to lay blame for his irresponsible, intrusive acts on various external sources. With its roots in the rationalizations and self-justifications of adolescence, mollification helps the lifestyle criminal avoid responsibility for his own actions. Mollification will often assume the form of pointing to the inequity and unfairness of life. What the lifestyle criminal fails to appreciate is that acknowledging the presence of injustice elsewhere does nothing to excuse, justify, or attenuate his irresponsible, social rule breaking actions.

> In therapy sessions W would point out how his life had always been rough; how he grew up poor and never really knew the difference between right and wrong. In discussing his case he blamed the FBI, government attorneys, and prison officials but never once considered the possibility that it was his behavior, rather than a government conspiracy, which put him behind bars.

Cutoff

A common misconception about criminals is that they are unresponsive to deterrents (see Cleckley, 1976; Hare, 1970). The truth of the matter is that the lifestyle criminal is just as sensitive to deterrents as the next guy (see Phillips & Votey, 1981); he just happens to be more adept at eliminating these deterrents from his decisions. One way the lifestyle criminal eradicates deterrents is through the use of what Yochelson and Samenow (1976) call the cutoff. This cutoff may consist of a simple phrase ("fuck it"), visual image, or even a musical theme. What's important is that the cutoff eliminates the anxieties, fears, and deterrents that prevent most of us from engaging in serious criminal action.

> Subsequent to his release from a state prison K spent several weeks in the community before entertaining the prospect of committing another crime. K relates that his problems first began when he lost his construction job. Rather

than seeking other employment, however, he decided to start robbing again. Though he considered the possibilities, to include getting caught and going back to prison, he purged these thoughts from his mind with the aid of a two-word phrase, "fuck it." It wasn't long before he found himself sitting in a jail cell, feeling hopeless, despondent, and persecuted.

Entitlement

Most criminals believe that the law, including the police, serve a necessary function in any society. However, they also believe that they are somehow personally exempt from the rules that govern the rest of us. This sense of entitlement is what provides the lifestyle criminal with permission to violate societal laws and the personal rights of others. Through the vehicle of entitlement, the lifestyle criminal believes that he is privileged to take whatever he wants from whomever has what he desires, be it property, money, or sex. An essential component of this entitlement process, then, is the mislabeling of wants as needs. Accordingly, the lifestyle criminal elevates his desire for money, fancy clothes, or expensive jewelry to the level of a need. He reasons that since he is only taking care of his needs, he is justified in taking whatever steps he deems necessary to procure that to which he feels entitled.

H had been referred to a private psychologist for a forensic evaluation. In discussing the events leading up to his arrest for assault and battery, he advised that he didn't conceive of himself as guilty of assaulting his wife since he was entitled to "put her in her place." After all, she was his wife. A review of previous convictions, to include a number of intrusive offenses, revealed a similar sense of entitlement and privilege.

Power Orientation

The lifestyle criminal adopts a rather simplistic view of the world. He cerebrates that people fall into two categories: those who are strong and those who are weak. He reasons further that if a person is conceptualized as weak, then he or she can be intimidated, used, or manipulated for one's own benefit. The power orientation involves an attempt on the part of the criminal to control his surroundings. This orientation to power embodies two cognitive elements discussed by Yochelson and Samenow (1976): the zero state and power thrust. Where the zero state reflects a feeling of impotence and powerlessness at not being able to control people or events, the power thrust describes a style of thought designed to achieve a sense of power and control over others. In fact, the power thrust is viewed by the lifestyle criminal as a remedy for zero state feelings.

> J often monopolized the group discussions and at such times would resist other group member's efforts to speak or intervene. Rarely did a group session go by that this individual did not attempt to gain control by trying to outshout other group members or by refusing to listen to another's point of view. As the power thrusts began to subside in group, so did J's problems on the prison compound. This change in behavior was one of the first indications that J was beginning to challenge his criminal thinking.

Sentimentality

Sentimentality is what Yochelson and Samenow (1976) refer to as the criminal's tendency to express tender feelings and aesthetic interests in a fickle and self-serving manner. According to the theory of lifestyle criminality, sentimentality involves an attempt by the criminal to present himself in as favorable a light as possible despite his interpersonally intrusive actions. Where mollification embraces a justification of rule-breaking behavior by way of pointing out the problems and injustices in one's environment, sentimentality is justification based on a consideration of one's positive qualities or "soft" side. However, just as it is illogical to rationalize one's behavior on the basis of world inequalities or injustice in the legal system, it is also irrational to try to palliate one's negative behavior by pointing to the "good things" one has accomplished.

> Despite a life sentence for murder, T enjoyed telling stories about his life to anyone who would listen. He would proudly point out how he had bought turkeys for the poor people in his neighborhood each Thanksgiving and how he had helped open a juvenile center for the neighborhood kids to use during the evenings and weekends. A drug dealer, he always had extra money readily available and could be observed handing out dollar bills to the youngsters who would gather around his Cadillac on Saturday mornings. In his own mind he reasoned that what he did to get the money was less important than the fact others in the community "looked up" to him. What he failed to inform his listeners, however, was that he had been involved in several shoot-outs in the neighbor-

hood where innocent bystanders had been injured and was profiting personally from the misery of those in the community who were addicted to the drugs he sold.

Superoptimism

Yochelson and Samenow (1976) see the criminal's tendency to be extremely optimistic and self-confident as reflective of superoptimism. In much the same way as a young child contemplates his invulnerability while donning a superman costume, the lifestyle criminal is unrealistic in how he appraises himself, his attributes, and his chances of avoiding the consequences of his antisocial actions. Experience has taught many high-rate offenders that the crimes they get away with greatly outnumber the crimes for which they have been caught. This simply reinforces the superoptimistic attitude they have about themselves, and their ability to elude detection helps promote a vicious cycle of criminal thinking followed closely by lawbreaking behavior.

> E realized from an early age that crime was easy. He started stealing candy bars from convenience stores when he was 7 years old but soon graduated to shoplifting music tapes, clothing, and small radios from various department stores in town. After engaging in over 50 separate shoplifting episodes he was finally apprehended. Although the police were called, the charges were eventually dropped and it wasn't long before he was back on the streets pilfering goods from local stores. As he entered adulthood, E moved on to more serious crimes and by age 25 had robbed his first bank. However the thinking behind the bank robberies was the same as the thinking which motivated him to shoplift as a youth. He reasoned that all he needed was a solid plan, a big gun, and a fast car and he could go on robbing banks indefinitely. It was a genuine shock for him when after his third robbery he was identified by a teller, arrested, convicted, and sentenced to 20 years in a federal penitentiary.

Cognitive Indolence

Anyone who has had regular contact with criminal offenders can attest to the fact that most are exceptionally lazy. In actuality, the lifestyle criminal is as lazy in thought as he is in behavior. Like water running downhill, the lifestyle criminal's thinking takes the path of least resistance. Hence, this is an individual who is exceedingly lazy, easily bored, and overly accepting of his own ideas. Walters and White (1989c) hypothesize that the lifestyle criminal pursues excitement in the outside world as a means of compensating for a shallow and understimulating inner world. As the following case vignette illustrates, cognitive indolence is not only a source of frustration for others, but is also a major impediment to meaningful long-term change for the offender.

> Nearly every behavior R engaged in reflected the presence of cognitive indolence. His speech was slow, his gait slothful, his thinking unimaginative, and his appearance messy. He was late to work, late for medical appointments, and late to group therapy sessions. In fact, it took him 22 months to complete a 10-month drug treatment program due to the fact that he keep getting himself locked up in Segregation for various petty infractions.

Discontinuity

The lifestyle criminal fails to follow through on commitments, carry out intentions, or remain focused on goals over time. This inconsistency, which affects both the behavior and thinking of the recalcitrant offender, is what I refer to as discontinuity. Not only is the lifestyle criminal distracted by environmental events, but he demonstrates such a high degree of impersistence that he often does not complete that which he starts. Therefore, while he may genuinely desire change, the lifestyle criminal has difficulty maintaining this commitment to change from one context or situation to the next.

> C transacted with others in a disjointed and fragmentary manner, switching topics and ideas in mid-paragraph. He had been previously diagnosed as suffering from schizophrenia and manic-depressive disorder by various psychiatrists but his speech was more suggestive of discontinuity than of loose associations or a psychotic-like flight of ideas. While C would resolve to make changes in his behavior while discussing his situation with the institution psychologist, he was constantly getting himself into trouble with prison officials for using drugs and involving himself in a prison-based gambling operation. Though he continued meeting with the institution psychologist for weekly sessions of individual psychotherapy, he had a great deal of difficulty seeing the inconsistency between what he said in therapy and what he did outside the psychologist's office.

Postulate #7: For a criminal event to transpire, a criminal opportunity must be present.

Opportunity is an important precondition for any criminal event. This would appear to go without saying, but it seems a point worth reiterating. According to the lifestyle theory of criminal conduct, the high-rate offender is the eternal opportunist. His mind may be closed to conventional activities, but it is indefatigably open to a wide assortment of criminal opportunities. Where most of us will walk past a parked car without a second thought, the average lifestyle criminal vigilantly scans the automobile for unlocked doors, unattended purses, or misplaced keys. In a world full of naive, trusting people, the criminal is like a wolf amid a flock of sheep. Consequently, while opportunity is a necessary step in the sequence leading up to the commission of various criminal acts, it is crucial that we remain mindful of the fact that there is, in any free society, a plethora of criminal opportunities and that the lifestyle criminal has become quite sensitive to these opportunities.

Opportunity not only determines the timing of a particular criminal offense, but also the form or substance of the offense. The crime of embezzlement, for example, presumes a certain degree of knowledge about financial transactions as well as the fiscal status of the person or company being embezzled. Likewise, someone incapable of charming or beguiling others would be incapable of pulling off a sophisticated fraud. To involve oneself in the drug trade implies certain criminal and underworld connections that are unavailable to most noncriminals. Robbery, burglary, and assault, on the other hand, require very little in the way of specified skills or prerequisites. I am inclined to refer to these as equal opportunity crimes. The point being made here is that opportunity is an essential link in the sequence of events culminating in a specific criminal act, both in terms of timing as well as offense category.

Postulate #8: The motivation for specific criminal events is derived through the process of validation which is comprised of four secondary organizing motives: anger/rebellion, power/control, excitement/pleasure, and greed/laziness.

As part of Postulate #4, we discussed the primary organizing motive of fear and how it energizes and directs the evolving life decision. Thus, while fear may be a cardinal force behind the criminal lifestyle, it does not explain why individuals give different reasons for their involvement in selected criminal acts. Money may be an important reinforcer for most bank robbers, but what motivates the rapist or child molester? The robber would argue that such individuals are "sick" or "perverted." I, on the other hand, view their primary organizing motive as being no different than that of the robber; what differs is the secondary organizing motive. Where many robbers are driven by greed, sex offenders tend to be motivated more by the desire for power and control over another person.

In addition to the presence of a criminal opportunity, the offender must be able to justify or explain to himself his motives for engaging in a particular antisocial act. Though the motives we observe as crucial to the commission of a particular criminal event and the ones assigned importance by the offender may not always coincide, a psychological process known as validation seems to bridge the gap between internal and external explanations for criminal behavior. Floyd Feeney (1986), for instance, writes that 60% of the robbers he interviewed reported using their stick-up money to purchase drugs, fancy clothes, and expensive automobiles, while the other 40% engaged in robbery as a means of controlling others, venting their anger, or experiencing a sense of excitement and exhilaration. Findings such as this one have led me to conclude that the validation process organizes itself around four primary motives—anger/rebellion, power/control, excitement/ pleasure, greed/laziness. What follows is a brief discussion of each of these four secondary organizing motives of lifestyle criminality.

Anger/Rebellion

Motivation can come in many forms, shapes, and sizes. Basic human needs, such as the requirements for air, food, and water, accentuate the physiological drive of the individual and motivate him or her to engage in behavior designed to reduce those drives. While drive reduction may explain the behavior of certain species of animal, it accounts for only a small portion of human behavior. Human conduct, including criminality, is much more a function of social needs than physiological ones. Toward this end, psychologists like Henry A. Murray have developed theories of human behavior around a theme of learned motivation.

One of the social needs identified by Murray (1966) was something he referred to as autonomy. The autonomy motive involves not only an assertion of one's independence, but it also inspires a resistant attitude toward authority figures and the influence of others. In many lifestyle criminals, autonomy expresses itself in a motive of anger and rebellion. An offender operating on the basis of this motive is angry and validates his criminality by pointing out all of the injustices he believes have been inflicted upon him by persons in positions of power. For him, crime is a venting of his anger, a reflection of his frustration, and an expression of his rebellious attitude toward the authority of society.

Power/Control

An early student of Murray's, David C. McClelland (1971), has examined three social needs in some detail: achievement, affiliation, and power. The power motive seems to be particularly relevant to our discussion of power and control as a secondary organizing motive for crime. As conceptualized by McClelland, the power motive reflects a desire to exert control or influence over others. This control can be either physical or psychological, direct or indirect. Consequently, subtly attracting attention to oneself by means of one's attire may be as indicative of the power motive as ordering a subordinate about. The defining characteristic of the power motive would therefore appear to be the desire to exercise power and control over one's external environment.

The power motive takes on added significance when we consider it within the context of the criminal lifestyle. The lifestyle criminal seems to treat acquiring power and control over others as a sort of reaffirmation of his personal virility. In validating his criminality through a secondary organizing motive of power and control, the lifestyle criminal achieves a sense of authority over his environment. Some robbers even report experiencing an orgasmic-like "rush" when in the process of robbing a bank or store. In fact, many sex crimes appear to be motivated more by power goals than sexual ones (see Burt, 1983; Groth & Hobson, 1983; Rada, 1978). Power/control therefore exists as a powerful motive for criminality, particularly in reference to certain categories of crime.

Excitement/Pleasure

Research suggests that when deprived of sensory stimulation, subjects tend to become bored and irritable (Hebb, 1972). If these subjects are exposed to such privation over a period of several days, they typically report experiencing "visions," "images," and other apparitions (Heron, 1957). Thus, while there appears to be a great deal of controversy surrounding research on sensory deprivation, there is evidence that we all require a certain level of sensory stimulation to function effectively. This would appear to be particularly germane to the case of the lifestyle criminal, who, as mentioned earlier, has a high need for excitement, thrills, and stimulation. Excitement and pleasure therefore compose the third secondary organizing motive for criminal behavior as established by the lifestyle theory of criminal conduct.

The excitement/pleasure motive has its foundation in the immediate gratification that a crime frequently provides the criminal. This motive would appear to be well suited to the type of crimes committed by youthful offenders (e.g., automotive theft, petty larceny). Hence, excitement/pleasure looms in significance during the early criminal years, but then tapers off as the individual grows older. I suspect that this effect is due, in large part, to the fact that the excitement/pleasure motive has its origin in visceral expressions of physical pleasure and sensation, both of which tend to decline with age. Just as the excitement/pleasure motive lessens with age, a fourth secondary organizing motive, greed/laziness, takes on added importance as one grows older.

Greed/Laziness

One of the strongest social drives found in man is the need for achievement or mastery. According to Murray (1966), the achievement motive provokes the individual to action wherein he strives for excellence and success in as rapid a time frame as possible. The impact of this drive for mastery on later success was clearly demonstrated in a study directed by Teevan and McGhee (1972). What these researchers observed was an increase in financial and occupational success in persons displaying a high need for achievement during childhood. However, this motive assumes a distorted silhouette in the mind of the lifestyle criminal. Though he desires the rewards offered by society, he is often too lazy to pursue them via legitimate channels; hence, ambition turns to avarice and industry gives way to indolence. Consequently, greed/laziness is the fourth and final secondary organizing motive to be discussed within the framework of this theory of lifestyle criminality.

Previous research has clearly supported the hypothesis that greed is a powerful motivator of such crimes as robbery, burglary, and grand larceny (Feeney, 1986; Walters & White, 1988). Involvement in drug sales is also often a reflection of the greed/laziness motive, particularly if the individual is not a user of drugs himself. The person who engages in crime as a shortcut to extrinsically defined "success" yearns to achieve this outcome as quickly as possible while exerting the least amount of effort. Just as power and control can be used to bolster a sagging self-image, the criminal operating on the basis of greed and laziness sees a direct correlation between the amount of material goods he can accrue and his own value as a person.

It is hypothesized that the motivation for any specific criminal event can be found in one or more of the four motives discussed here. Hence, a particular act may reflect greed and laziness, or it may mirror a combination of power/control and anger/rebellion. This, however, is a fairly superficial explanation of motivation relative to the behavior of the lifestyle criminal. Consequently, in order to obtain a satisfactory level of understanding into what motivates the criminal lifestyle, one must consider these four secondary organizing motives as they interact with the primary organizing motive of fear.

Postulate #9: Criminal events can be understood as incorporating a complex inter-linking of thoughts, motives, and behaviors.

A primary tenet of the lifestyle theory of criminality is that cognition, motive, and action are meaningfully connected. It is reasoned further that the convergence between certain thoughts, motives, and behaviors is stronger in some instances than in others. Stated somewhat differently, there appear to be several clusters of behaviors that correspond more closely with certain thoughts and motives than others. This possibility was initially explored by Walters and White (1989c) in their paper on criminal thinking. As these authors pointed out, however, differential cognitive-motive-behavioral relationships are far from absolute. In truth, nearly all of the thoughts, motives, and actions associated with the criminal lifestyle are correlated to one degree or another, though certain groupings are more strongly correlated than others.

In that social rule breaking involves a general disregard for societal norms, values, and mores, the cognitive features most closely aligned with rule-breaking behavior would appear to be mollification and the cutoff. Mollification is included in this cluster because it involves justifying one's rule-breaking tendencies by considering circumstances that are largely irrelevant to one's own situation. The cutoff plays a major role in social rule breaking since it provides an avenue through which the lifestyle criminal eliminates common deterrents to rule-breaking activity. The anger/rebellion motive seems to fall within this initial cluster as well since it reveals the sense of injustice that seems to fuel chronic rule-breaking behavior and such cognitive operations as mollification and the cutoff.

Interpersonal intrusiveness captures the manner in which the lifestyle criminal infringes upon the rights of others. As such, both entitlement and the power orientation would appear to reflect interpersonal intrusiveness; entitlement because it provides one with privileged status and the prerogative to satisfy one's own desires at the expense of others and the power orientation because this entails downgrading others as a means to feeling good about oneself. The motive of power/control would appear to fit snugly within this framework of criminogenic thoughts and actions since the individual's intrusive behavior, as well as his entitled and power-oriented thinking, is geared toward achieving a sense of control and power over others.

Self-indulgence reflects the lifestyle criminal's single-minded pursuit of personal pleasure and lack of concern for the negative long-term consequences of his actions. The hedonism and selfishness that are so much a part of the criminal lifestyle are similar in form to the secondary organizing motive of excitement/pleasure since both are coordinated around a common theme: the desire for immediate gratification and increased sensory stimulation. Sentimentality also falls within the purview of this particular cluster since it, too, is an expression of self-centered concerns (i.e., to appear as an innocent victim or "good guy" in the eyes of others). Superoptimism is a second cognitive feature with ties to self-indulgence and the excitement/pleasure motive since this aspect of lifestyle criminality portends a high degree of self-stimulation in the form of a thoroughly unrealistic appraisal of one's chances of escaping the negative consequences of a specific criminal act.

Irresponsibility is a measure of the lifestyle criminal's eschewal of responsibility and disinclination to account for his conduct and obligations. Cognitive indolence would appear to represent the psychological manifestation of this particular behavioral pattern; discontinuity also seems to fit well within the irresponsibility constellation since it lends itself to inconsistency and a lack of commitment to a reliable course of action. The secondary organizing motive most closely affiliated with this particular cognitive-behavioral cluster is greed/laziness. The cognitive indolence and discontinuity found in the thinking of all lifestyle criminals not only feed the criminal's irresponsible attitude, but they also supply fertile soil for crimes committed out of a sense of avarice and laziness.

The theoretical significance of linking behavior, thought, and motive together is fairly self-evident. The clinical applicability of this procedure may be less clear. Exploring the pertinent issues for a moment, we can see that if we were able to match specific aspects of criminal thought with particular motives and behaviors, further examination of these interconnections might generate useful clinical information on specific offenders. Consequently, if we knew an individual had a history of serious self-indulgent behavior, we might expect high levels of sentimentality and superoptimism and crimes motivated more by excitement than greed or anger. We might even be able to predict future problems using these interlinkages since we would anticipate that an individual possessing a strong power orientation and sense of

entitlement might tend to display an increased rate of intrusive activity and
crimes motivated by the desire to control others than an individual whose
thinking is dominated by superoptimism or discontinuity.

> Postulate #10: Since behavior is a function of the attitude and thoughts one adopts
> toward a particular situation, criminal behavior will not change unless the
> offender first changes his thinking.

Though cognition develops in response to the actions of certain conditions
and the choices one makes relative to these conditions, cognitive factors
should be provided a preeminent position in any program of behavioral
change. I would go so far as to argue that a change in criminal behavior is
not possible without there first being a change in cognition. This does not
mean, however, that an offender must enter a formal program of therapy or
rehabilitation to succeed in the community. To the contrary, there are many
ex-felons who never attended a single therapy group or completed one
vocational course but who have managed to live as law-abiding citizens
despite a long history of prior criminality. Likewise, there are even more
offenders who, having spent several years in therapy and having completed
their college education in prison, continue to return to jail in ever-increasing
numbers.

In research on desistance, researchers have asked ex-felons who had
adopted a noncriminal lifestyle after many years of antisociality to describe
their reasons for exiting crime. This research suggests that this change in
lifestyle is mediated by a change in attitudes and values that are the result of
both developmental and various stressful/shocking experiences (Cusson &
Pinsonneault, 1986; Irwin, 1970; Meisenhelder, 1977; Shover, 1983). In the
conclusion of his report, Shover, for instance, calls attention to the fact that
"even offenders who committed serious crimes while young are capable of,
and do, change as they get older" (p. 216). The present theory embraces the
philosophy that desistance from crime is a natural cognitive process that can
be escalated in persons genuinely desiring change. Hence, as we shall see in
Chapter 7, therapeutic interventions with the lifestyle criminal simply take
advantage of a natural change process found in all individuals, criminal as
well as noncriminal.

Conclusion

In presenting this theory of lifestyle criminality through a series of postulates, I had several goals in mind. First and foremost, I wanted to present the

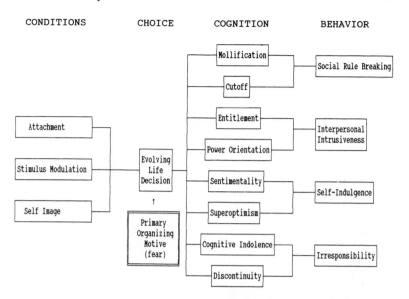

CONDITIONS   CHOICE   COGNITION   BEHAVIOR

Figure 4.1. Schematic Diagram of the Lifestyle Theory of Criminal Involvement

theorems that comprise this particular system of thought. Second, I set out to organize the theory around a framework that was clear, concise, and meaningful. Finally, I wanted to clarify the key concepts and consummate my discussion on the philosophy behind the theory that commenced in Chapter 3. With regard to this last goal, I believe there are three additional points that should be made. The cardinal postulate of this theory is that crime can be conceptualized as a lifestyle marked by four behavioral characteristics: global irresponsibility, blatant self-indulgence, interpersonally intrusive actions, and habitual violation of society's laws and rules. Equally important, however, is the recollection that while conditions play a role in crime, it is the choices one makes relative to these conditions that actually determine subsequent criminal behavior. It also is essential that the reader understand that choice is expressed through a conduit of cognition and that intervention with the lifestyle criminal is founded on the premise that cognitive change precedes behavioral change.

When we examine the lifestyle theory of criminality, we notice that it actually incorporates two models in one: the lifestyle theory of criminal involvement and the lifestyle theory of criminal events. The lifestyle theory of criminal involvement is outlined in Figure 4.1. Commencing with the important interactive conditions of attachment, stimulus modulation, and self-image, we proceed to the evolving life decision and eight primary

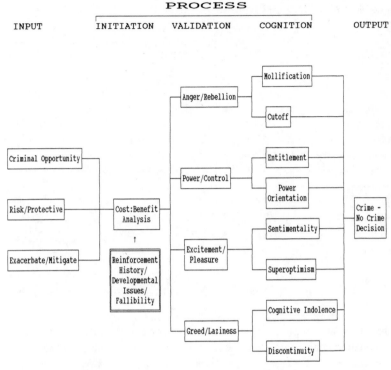

Figure 4.2. Schematic Diagram of the Lifestyle Theory of Criminal Events

cognitive features of lifestyle criminality, again highlighting the condition-choice-cognition sequence. I think it is important that one grasps the role of the primary organizing motive of fear in the development of the evolving life decision as well as the interconnections hypothesized to exist between the eight cognitive features and four behavioral characteristics of lifestyle criminality. As was pointed out in our discussion of the ninth postulate, however, we need to be cognizant of the fact that while the lines connecting specific thoughts to specific actions reflect certain cognitive-behavioral linkages, other thought-action relationships also exist.

The lifestyle theory of criminal events profiled in Figure 4.2 demonstrates the significance of criminal opportunities, risk/protective factors, and exacerbating/mitigating variables in the criminal decision-making process. In addition to impacting on the decision-making procession directly, they also influence the validation procedure by steering the individual toward one or more of the four secondary organizing motives that comprise this process. Cost:benefit analysis also assumes a prominent position in the lifestyle theory of criminal events, although it is important to keep in mind that this analysis is influenced by historical (Skinner, 1953), developmental (Piaget, 1954), and psychological/emotional (Carroll, 1978) factors. As Figure 4.2 illustrates, the secondary organizing motives tie into specific cognitive features of lifestyle criminality. However, as discussed earlier in reference to the connections thought to exist between different patterns of cognition and behavior, the proposed linkages of various motives and beliefs, though theoretically meaningful, are less indubitable from an empirical standpoint.

It is of particular consequence that the lifestyle models of criminal involvement and criminal events, instead of being independent, actually complement one another and overlap through their common association with the eight primary cognitive features of lifestyle criminality. These theories, however, are limited, in part, by a lack of specificity and operationality in certain key terms and concepts, particularly those centering around the evolving life decision and primary organizing motive of fear. Pains need to be taken to bolster the definitional clarity of such terms and breathe life into concepts that seem to be largely theoretical at this point in time. In several instances, tighter parameters need to be drawn and more specific hypotheses formulated. This, in fact, will be a primary goal of our next two chapters, the first one dealing with developmental issues and the second one probing the principal cognitive features of lifestyle criminality.

5. Developmental Issues

One drives by a group of about 100 third-graders taking part in recess on the playground of an inner-city school located somewhere in the northeastern United States. Some of the children are playing tag, others are jumping rope, and a few are preparing themselves for a life of crime. Collins (1976) reports that 47% of the male subjects in the 1945 Philadelphia cohort had experienced at least one officially recorded police contact for something other than a traffic violation by the time they had reached age 30. In the 1947 and 1949 Racine (Wisconsin) cohorts, this figure ranged anywhere from 48% to 56% for officially recorded nontraffic police contacts by age 33 (Shannon, 1982), while in a sample of working-class male Londoners, it was determined that 31% had been convicted of at least one offense by age 21 to 24 (West & Farrington, 1977). We would therefore anticipate that about one-half of the male third-graders in our school sample will eventually come into contact with police authorities. However, as we know from our discussion of career criminality, 5% to 10% of this group of future offenders will account for the majority of all crimes committed. Consequently, this sample of 100 inner-city schoolchildren will likely yield only one or two lifestyle criminals.

Examining our school yard vignette further, we might ask ourselves what separates the one or two future lifestyle offenders from the rest of the class. Don't we all start out the same way? Innocent toddlers scampering about in a communal sandbox, so to speak. The fact of the matter is that we do not all start out the same, for even at birth there are characteristics and traits that leave some individuals more vulnerable than others to various "criminogenic" conditions. If we were to examine the one or two children in our third-grade sample likely to grow up to become lifestyle criminals, we would inevitably find a number of telltale signs even though our subjects are but 8 or 9 years of age. The teacher probably perceives these budding lifestyle criminals as less cooperative and more aggressive than many of the other pupils in class, while the other children are liable to view them as bullies and intimidators. The lesson to be learned here is that lifestyle criminality is just that—a lifestyle characterized by habitual violation of society's rules, a pattern that begins at a relatively early age.

In this chapter, we find ourselves exploring the developmental features of lifestyle criminality. As part of this investigation, we will be asking ourselves why certain individuals engage in habitual lawbreaking behavior when many of those convicted of juvenile offenses abandon the criminal way of life long before entering adulthood (see Greenwood & Zimring, 1985). This chapter will provide us with an avenue through which we might probe the kinds of developmental changes that antedate serious adult criminality. This voyage will be directed by a familiar guide, the three Cs of lifestyle criminality (conditions, choice, and cognition). Where conditions and choice will be the focus of attention in the present chapter, cognition will be addressed in Chapter 6. We turn our attention now to the conditions facilitating the development of a criminal lifestyle.

Conditions

The correlates of criminality, as mentioned previously, cluster around three primary functions or domains: the physical, the social, and the psychological. This, then, is how the theory of lifestyle criminality conceives of the role played by various conditions in the later development of criminal behavior. The various conditions prominent in the evolution of a criminal lifestyle exert their primary influence through the person×situation interaction occurring in each domain. This does not mean, however, that some variables do not also exert a more direct effect on criminality. A case could most certainly be made for the direct influence of intelligence (Moffitt, Gabrielli, Mednick, & Schulsinger, 1981), family atmosphere (Loeber & Dishion, 1983), and peer associations (Hanson, Henggeler, Haefele, & Rodick, 1984) on later criminal behavior. Nonetheless, the principal means through which conditions affect criminality, according to lifestyle theory, is via the early and later life tasks taking place in each of the three primary domains of human experience: physical, social, and psychological.

Early Life Tasks

The early life tasks take place during the first four or five years of life. It is important to note, however, that since we are all confronted with these early life tasks, it is the manner in which we respond to the challenges of each task, rather than the task itself, that defines lifestyle criminality. We now examine how each of these early life tasks affect the individual in ways that facilitate the development of recidivistic patterns of criminal behavior.

Stimulus Modulation: Within the physical domain, there exists the desire for increased sensory stimulation. Prior research has clearly established that humans require a certain amount of stimulation in order to function effectively (Hebb, 1972). There are, nevertheless, important individual differences in the level of sensory stimulation that is sought (Wachs, 1977). Because of genetic and early environmental factors, the criminal negotiates this particular early life task by seeking higher levels of sensory stimulation and excitement. However, this does not mean that stimulus-seeking tendencies are a direct cause of criminality, since there are many people who realize their desire for increased stimulation in ways that are more congruent with socially ascribed goals.

That criminal offenders view higher-than-average levels of sensory stimulation as optimal is reflected in a variety of different behaviors. Extreme stimulus amplification tendencies have been found to correspond with drug usage (Zuckerman, Tushup, & Finner, 1976), sexual promiscuity (Zuckerman, Neary, & Brustman, 1970), and gambling or risk behavior (Waters & Kirk, 1968), all of which are quite commonly found in the behavior of most lifestyle criminals. It is the rule, rather than the exception, for habitual offenders to enjoy "living on the edge" in the sense that doing so seems to provide them with the sensory stimulation and excitement so many of them crave. Even when confined, many offenders find it difficult to avoid "high-risk" activities like gambling, homosexuality, and drug usage. However, there is more to lifestyle criminality than high sensation seeking.

Attachment: The early life task arising from an interaction of person and situation variables in the social domain is known as attachment. The human infant is dependent upon his or her caregiver for life itself. It has been suggested by some that evolution has given rise to a natural proclivity for attachment and bonding between the infant and primary caregiver and that problems occur when this attachment process breaks down (see Ainsworth, 1979). Books directed at the general reader, like the one written by Ken Magid and Carole McKelvey (1987) or Frank Bolton's (1983) work on bonding and family violence, outline how problems with attachment create interpersonal difficulties for the individual in later life. Magid and McKelvey describe in some detail the interaction that takes place between the newborn and his or her parents to bring about a vicious cycle of "non-responsiveness," which they state ties into later criminal behavior.

While the relationship between attachment difficulties during infancy and serious adult criminality may not be as direct as Magid and McKelvey (1987) would have us believe, it does appear to play a significant role, particularly in terms of one's attitude toward others. It is hypothesized that future criminals resolve the early life task of attachment by taking an avoidant approach to others. In examining 40 mother-father-child triads, Mary Main, Nancy Kaplan, and Jude Cassidy (1985) observed that individual differences in attachment actually reflected individual differences in the internal working models (mental representations) children derived of themselves relative to the issue of attachment. The results of this study also demonstrate the interrelatedness of the three primary domains in which the life tasks take place since the final early life task involves the formation of a self-image.

Self-Image: Framed within the psychological domain are the interactions comprising the self-image life task. Rather than existing as a global, unitary impression, however, this image is composed of a collection of separate, yet interrelated, self-conceptualizations that focus not only on self-esteem, but body image, self-definition, and personal expectations as well. Though there has been ample support for the presence of a link between low self-esteem and criminality in both adults (Fitts & Hammer, 1969; Wrightsman, 1974) and adolescents (Conger & Miller, 1966; Patterson, 1986), self-esteem is but one facet of self-image. Moreover, considered in isolation, self-esteem can be rather misleading. Jensen (1972), for instance, discerned that self-definition as a delinquent was associated with a high rate of officially recorded criminality in lower-class white youth, but that the relationship between self-esteem and delinquency was moderated by both race and social class (i.e., minimal levels of concordance between self-esteem and official delinquency in white juveniles; while a positive relationship existed in lower socioeconomic status blacks, and a negative relationship in higher status blacks).

Ageton and Elliott (1974) witnessed racial variations in the relationship between police contact and self-concept, as measured by scores on the Socialization Scale of the CPI, in a four-year longitudinal study on labeling and criminality. Ergo, while police contact was associated with a decline in the self-concept scores of white juveniles, it had little effect on the self-conceptualizations of Mexican and black youth. While a single score on a measure like the CPI fails to capture the complexity of the self-image concept as it relates to lifestyle criminality, these and the results of Jensen's (1972) investigation clearly denote that ethnic status should be considered in evaluating the connection hypothesized to exist between criminality and self-concept. Even though I am steadfast in my belief that the early life decisions involved in formulating a self-image play a compelling role in the development of lifestyle criminality, this life task does not operate independently of such personal characteristics as social class and race.

Jensen's (1972) observations, as well as the results of a study directed by Harris and Lewis (1974), indicate that lower socioeconomic status blacks may tend to view crime as enhancing their self-worth and thus may have managed the self-image task somewhat differently than white or higher status black criminals. Nevertheless, there are aspects of a negative self-image that can be observed in the behavior of nearly all lifestyle criminals. Walters and White (1989b) discuss four such trends. First, based on various messages the offender may have received as a youngster, he sees himself as isolated and not lovable. Second, he comes to the conclusion that he can never be successful in conventional pursuits and that any effort on his part will invariably lead to failure. Third, he adopts an "I'm it" attitude whereby he believes that he can expect little help or support from others. Within the context of the "I'm it" attitude, the lifestyle offender experiences himself as special, different, or separate from others. Finally, there is a fatalistic bent to his thinking in that he reasons he can do nothing to change his lot in life. These are the early thoughts of an individual who has had problems negotiating the self-image life task.

Later Life Tasks

The later life tasks come into play after the early life tasks have been resolved, normally commencing at the age of 5 or 6. However, resolution is never fully realized in the case of the later life tasks since they continue to guide behavior and development over the course of one's life. These later life tasks exist in the form of a subtle interplay of personal and situational influences resonating around a common vortex established by the product of the early life tasks, as well as individual person and situation variables. Like their forerunners, the later life task cluster into three primary domains: the physical, the social, and the psychological.

Internal-External Orientation: Rising out of interactions taking place in the physical domain is the later life task of deciding whether to take an internal or external approach to one's environment. Similar to Rotter's (1966) locus of control concept, the orientation task confronts one with the necessity of problem resolution. The capacity for problem-solving is common to all persons; where individual differences come into play is with the specific approach utilized and the overall efficacy of one's problem-solving efforts.

Hence, the internally oriented individual seeks to resolve problems by thinking them through, while the externally oriented person tends to act on his or her environment. Either tendency in the extreme can be self-defeating, and the lifestyle criminal gravitates toward a near exclusive external orientation. Consequently, the lifestyle criminal values immediate pleasure over long-term success (Ross & Fabiano, 1985). Rather than seek an efficacious balance between thought and action, he endeavors to find an external solution, even to problems that are clearly internal in nature.

From our discussion of stimulus modulation, we know that the evolving lifestyle criminal seeks higher-than-normal levels of sensory stimulation. In effect, he seeks out situations in the external world that will provide him with the stimulation he craves. This tendency interacts with later life issues taking place in the physical domain which the criminal resolves by adopting a strong external position. Consequently, the lifestyle criminal engages in a variety of activities designed to achieve a sense of stimulation, excitement, and thrills, the end result being a powerful external orientation. This, incidentally, is the reason why some offenders tend to decompensate psychologically when placed in environments where the level of sensory input has been significantly reduced (e.g., solitary confinement). Such persons, therefore, may lack the internal skills necessary to keep themselves occupied under such circumstances.

Social Bonding/Empathy: Once the early life task of attachment has been resolved, the individual begins to develop his or her interpersonal attitude in a manner that encompasses the wider social environment. This process is referred to as the later life task of social bonding/empathy, which is similar in form to the bonding process referenced in Hirschi's (1969) theory of criminal behavior. Within the context of these social bonding/empathy issues, the individual derives a strategy upon which future interpersonal relationships are based, a strategy that is influenced by the outcome obtained with the early life task of attachment.

Magid and McKelvey (1987) state that the poorly bonded individual treats people as objects and demonstrates a miniscule amount of empathy for the feelings of others. It is reasoned that the lifestyle criminal has negotiated the later life task of social bonding/empathy by shutting himself off from others. Though he may be charming, outgoing, and persuasive, these attributes are but superficial accessories in an individual who has very little investment in other people. Consequently, most lifestyle criminals proceed through life encroaching upon the rights and personal feelings of others, often with very little insight into how negatively their behavior is viewed by those around them.

Role Identity: The later life task of role identity evolves out of interactions taking place in the arena of psychological concerns. During the first several years of life, the individual derives a general image of him- or herself, an image that supplies him or her with a sense of personal identity and individuality. However, this image is galvanized around various individual characteristics, thoughts, and perceptions. Role identity, on the other hand, involves an expansion of the self-image task in a manner that incorporates the larger social environment. Also implicit in the later life task of role identity is consideration of one's role or place in society.

A person confronting the later life task of role identity asks how he or she fits into the wider scheme of things. This person is making a decision about him- or herself relative to society. The evolving lifestyle criminal reaches the conclusion that he really doesn't fit into "straight" society and goes about carving a niche for himself in an area that is antagonistic to the conventional social order. This is also one of the reasons why many habitual offenders have difficulty exiting the criminal lifestyle—they have committed themselves to this lifestyle and thus experience problems when they try to integrate into the fabric of conventional society. Moreover, there is the associated problem of effecting the transition from prison, where the individual may be well known and "respected," to the community, where he is just another face in the crowd.

Learning and Lifestyle Criminality

The conditions that have an impact on the early and later life tasks, as well as the person and situation variables that exert a more direct effect on the criminal lifestyle, find themselves translated into behavior through learning. A muscularly built youngster learns that he can get his way by bullying peers and intimidating adults. If he is successful in this sort of activity over time, the bond between stimulus and response strengthens and becomes increasingly resistant to extinction. Likewise, an adolescent who acquires status with peers for having been the first one on the block to spend time in juvenile hall is being reinforced for the rule-breaking behaviors that earned him a trip to the detention center in the first place. Eliminate this negative reinforcement and we would not see the level of continuity observed in the behavior of some of society's worst lawbreakers (Kazdin, 1987).

A primary tenet of the lifestyle theory of criminal conduct is that we tend to engage in those behaviors for which we are reinforced. Most high-rate offenders view a conventional lifestyle as unnecessarily confining and largely unrewarding. On the other hand, the criminal lifestyle, with its accompanying irresponsibility and self-indulgence, is quite inviting to this group of individuals. In fact, there are aspects of the criminal lifestyle that are intrinsically appealing to many of us since they are consistent with our irresponsible, self-centered beginnings. However, where most of us ultimately find responsibility and self-discipline to be reinforcing because of the long-term benefits to be accrued, most lifestyle criminals establish short-term gratification as their life goal and very rarely consider the long-term consequences of their actions.

While reinforcement augments the probability of a particular response being emitted, punishment reduces the likelihood of such an occurrence. Psychologists define punishment as anything applied to behavior that decreases the probability of that behavior being displayed in the future. Consequently, for a specific condition or situation to be considered truly punishing, we would need to witness a decreased incidence or suppression of the behavior presumably being punished. Research suggests that many persons refrain from serious legal infractions for fear of getting caught and going to jail or prison (Snyder, 1971; Stuck, Ksander, Berg, Laughlin, & Johnson, 1982). This external or objective fear of confinement may therefore be responsible for the avoidance of criminal activity on the part of an appreciable portion of the population. Unfortunately, a dawning realization for persons who have been exposed to the criminal justice system early on is that the sanctions society imposes on its lawbreakers are nowhere near as aversive as most people initially anticipate (Walters & White, 1989b).

Whether placed on probation, conscripted into the military, forced into a mental-health treatment program, or sent to jail, the youthful offender learns to survive and sometimes even prosper (Petersilia, Greenwood, & Lavin, 1978) under such circumstances. In the process, most such individuals lose the fear that serves to impede criminal action on the part of many persons who have never been exposed to such sanctions early in life. This certainly would appear to have been the case with convicted mass murderer Charles Manson: "Jails, courtrooms and prisons have been my life since I was twelve years old. By the time I was sixteen, I had lost all fear of anything the administration of the prison system could dish out" (Manson, 1986, p. 21).

Choice

A point made throughout this book is that it is the attitude or perspective one adopts relative to various life conditions, rather than the conditions themselves, that serves to fuel criminal behavior. As such, conditions exert their effect on behavior by limiting or restricting one's options instead of determining one's choices. These variables consequently impact on criminal behavior in a risk/protective or exacerbating/mitigating capacity, increasing or decreasing one's chances of engaging in criminal behavior but not forcing one into such a lifestyle. Making sense of the risk/protective and exacerbating/mitigating scheme, however, requires that we correlate it with the choice process. We therefore turn our attention to the feature that links choice to criminal behavior, the evolving life decision to lose in destructive and dramatic ways.

Evolving Life Decision

Society often adopts one of two seemingly antithetical views of the individual criminal. One group sees the criminal as a victim, while the other views him as a monster. As most people who have spent any time working with criminal offenders will attest, neither of these two perspectives is terribly accurate. The lifestyle theory of criminal behavior offers a third possibility: The lifestyle criminal is an individual who sets himself up to lose in ways that are both dramatic and destructive. The drama generated by the criminal lifestyle can be traced back to the offender's desire for increased levels of stimulation and excitement. The other-destructive aspect of his behavior reflects a lack of attachment, bonding, and empathy, while the self-destructive component corresponds with the nefarious self-image and antagonistic role identity the individual has developed for himself during childhood and adolescence.

The U.S. system of jurisprudence is founded on the premise that the pain and discomfort of punishment should outweigh the anticipated pleasure of any criminal act and therefore deter one from engaging in serious criminality. However, the system is predicated on the assumption that all persons desire socially defined success and weigh the costs and benefits of crime in much the same manner. Charles P. McDowell and Norman Thygusen (1975), however, argue that this is a false assumption when applied to a group they refer to as "society's losers." Even psychoanalysts like Karl Menninger (1968) recognize that criminality is more often characterized by "stupidity, clumsiness, and inefficiency" (p. 153) than a deliberate desire to harm others. An article in *Newsweek* magazine (Tanner, 1987) outlines the madcap adventures of a gang that robbed banks in rural Kansas over a period of several months. One time, the gang tunneled its way through a bank wall only to miss the vault entirely, while on another occasion, the acetylene torch that was used to cut into the bank caught a stack of papers on fire, filling the bank with smoke and aborting the heist. Though at the time the article was written the gang had burglarized 12 different banks, the average take was only $5,000, an amount that would hardly seem worth the risk.

The lifestyle criminal finds the immediate gratification provided by crime more reinforcing than the long-term stability of conventional life. In fact, many of the high-rate offenders I have interviewed view the "straight" or "square" life as exceedingly boring and something to avoid at all costs. The lifestyle criminal therefore isolates himself from conventional peers and surrounds himself with losers like himself (McDowell & Thygusen, 1975). The criminal justice system unwittingly feeds into this process by labeling the youthful offender with a figurative seal of disapproval that is similar in spirit to the puritan practice of burning a letter into the foreheads of seventeenth-century criminals. Unlike puritan times, however, there is no dominating system of informal social control in the United States today to prevent most juveniles from experimenting with crime. In addition, many lifestyle criminals view modern-day society's sanctions against lawbreaking behavior as nothing more than an occupational hazard. Consequently, prison not only fails to deter the lifestyle criminal from future criminal involvement, but it actually validates his life position as a loser and perpetuates a life pattern of losing in dramatic and destructive ways.

As was mentioned in Chapter 4, the evolving life decision to lose in a manner that is dramatic, as well as self- and other-destructive, is similar in form to the life script notion advanced by theorists operating out of a Transactional Analysis framework (Steiner, 1974). What differentiates the two is that the life script is normally established by the time the individual is 5 or 6 years of age, while the life decision continues to evolve throughout the adult years. This decision becomes more ingrained and patterned as the evolving criminal restricts his social contacts to individuals sharing his basic attitudes toward life. These early patterns become reinforcing for the individual and before long have formed their own network of behavioral contingencies. A common theme expressed by the majority of recidivistic offenders I have interviewed is that while they initially entered crime for the excitement and easy money, this pattern was eventually replaced by one in which their behavior seemed driven and out of control. Many lifestyle criminals, particularly those heavily involved in drugs, acknowledge that being sent to jail probably saved their lives, while Cusson and Pinsonneault (1986) determined that criminals who successfully exited crime did so with the knowledge that to continue in a criminal lifestyle meant certain failure, if not death.

The next logical step in our discussion would be to explore how the lifestyle theory of criminality defines losing. I believe there are at least three ways in which losing and failure can be conceptualized relative to the early life decision. First, the lifestyle criminal is a loser in terms of the crimes he chooses to engage in, a point supported by the self-reports of older offenders (see Jolin & Gibbons, 1987). Nearly all "street" and violent offenses are viewed as "loser crimes" in the sense that the risk associated with these crimes is nearly always high and the anticipated gain relatively low. Bank robbery is a perfect example of a "loser's crime" as witnessed by the fact that the FBI identifies and arrests over 80% of all bank robbers, that the conviction rate for bank robbery is 90%, that the average sentence for bank robbery is upwards of 15 years, and that the average bank robber nets only $3,000 per heist (Haran & Martin, 1984).

As part of their research on the business of commercial theft, John Gibbs and Peggy Shelly (1982) observed that thieves get caught because other thieves get caught (and oftentimes turn state's evidence for a lighter sentence) and because the thieves themselves make certain fundamental mistakes. Therefore, it would appear that the risk associated with such crimes as robbery and theft outweigh the gains one could realistically anticipate, in clear support of the old adage that crime doesn't pay. However, this maxim may not ring true for all criminal offenses. Take, for instance, the illegal stock manipulations of Michael R. Miken, whose earnings topped the $1 billion mark over a 4-year span, yet who, if convicted, will likely spend no more than 5 years in a minimum security federal prison camp. Regardless of whether Miken is eventually convicted, I would scarcely consider the activities he chose to engage in as "loser" types of crimes.

Second, the general lifestyle of the recalcitrant offender can be conceptualized as a "loser's" lifestyle. Be it within the context of school, work, finances, or one's personal life, the habitual lawbreaker has recorded very few meaningful successes in life. It is not uncommon for a lifestyle criminal to have held numerous jobs, yet never to the point of occupying the same position for more than six months to a year (Walters & White, 1987). Although at various times in their lives they may have had in their possession large sums of money, these individuals normally squander their ill-gotten gains on a variety of luxury items, including expensive jewelry and cars; to purchase illicit drugs; and to engage in prosmiscuity. Gibbs and Shelly (1982) report that several of the offenders in their study spent in excess of $50,000 annually on entertainment alone. Moreover, the interpersonal lives of many criminals are characterized by instability, nonsupport, and a lack of commitment, even to persons who have supported them in the past. In general, there is a conspicuous lack of continuity in the behavior of the lifestyle criminal over time. Except for brief periods of momentary self-gratification, his life is marked by long periods of incarceration, failure, and social alienation.

A third aspect of losing for the lifestyle criminal is that he appears to set himself up for failure despite opportunities for success. In the words of one lifestyle criminal taking part in group therapy: "Everything I touched seemed to turn to shit." The lifestyle criminal appears to have a "minus touch" for many things in his life despite the fact that there are nearly always one or two persons in each criminal's background who believed in him and encouraged him to strive for socially defined success. The case of the only inmate to escape from the federal penitentiary at Leavenworth during the 1980s illustrates the loser's mentality nicely. Despite an admittedly ingenious escape from this maximum-security facility, the inmate apparently set himself up in various ways so that he was back in custody within one month of his escape (Rizzo, April 12, 1989). Several of the lifestyle criminals I have worked with in therapy have possessed a variety of talents and abilities but lacked the initiative, persistence, and discipline to direct these skills toward socially useful goals.

Whether we conceptualize losing in terms of the criminal's selection of crimes, overall lifestyle, or general problem-solving approach, it is difficult to escape the conclusion that he is a loser. Many lifestyle offenders will go to lengths to "prove" to themselves and others that they were, in truth, successful in their criminal pursuits on the streets, and that several months of self-indulgence more than compensate for the many years they will spend in a state or federal penitentiary. There are even examples of convicts who document their "success" with picture albums. These albums might include a picture of the Rolls Royce they purchased with the proceeds of their illegal activities, newspaper clippings of their exploits, or a snapshot of themselves standing behind several large stacks of dollar bills. Many will share these albums with friends and associates in the penitentiary as a means of demonstrating their success in the community. However, the victories they enjoy on the outside typically are as short-lived as the pictures in their photo albums are superficial.

Many lifestyle criminals take exception to the term *loser* and interpret it to mean that they are being viewed as innately inferior to other people. However, as our previous discussion clarifies, this is not how the lifestyle theory of criminality construes losing. Rather, the loser is someone who, by his or her own actions, sets him- or herself up for failure. The lifestyle criminal is but one type of loser, a type who chooses to fail in ways that are dramatic and destructive to himself and others. Moreover, although the formal definition of lifestyle criminality relies on a history of criminality, the phenomenological definition centers on losing. In other words, crime is just a convenient way for the lifestyle criminal to fulfill his early life decision to lose in dramatic and destructive ways.

Primary Organizing Motive

Existential philosophers have been arguing for decades that human behavior is motivated by various fears, anxieties, and doubts relative to our very existence (May, 1958; Sartre, 1956). The lifestyle theory of criminality also considers fear to be a primary motive for behavior. Unlike the objective fear of incarceration referenced earlier, the fear that serves as a fundamental motivator of the evolving life decision to lose in dramatic and destructive ways is more subjective and existential. The primary organizing motive exists as a fear of responsibility, commitment, intimacy, and failure in the conventional world. This fear is sometimes expressed in the form of a desire to gain control over a situation the individual perceives as uncontrollable. One inmate I interviewed used the analogy of a soldier whose foxhole was about to be overrun by the enemy. Instead of waiting to be shot in his foxhole, the soldier charges the enemy, thereby gaining a greater sense of control over his admittedly dire situation.

While many aspects of this fear have their foundation in the human condition, the primary organizing motive, like the evolving life decision, tends to strengthen over time. The sense of inadequacy the criminal feels relative to attaining conventional success and the fear he has of being "found out" (Yochelson and Samenow, 1976) tend to build the longer the criminal continues functioning within the criminal lifestyle. Some high-rate offenders surround themselves with expensive material goods as a means of defending against this fear because they believe they are incapable of attracting the attention of others on the merit of various personal attributes. The external orientation, so much a part of the criminal lifestyle, can also be explained, in part, by the primary organizing motive of fear. In fact, it is the fear that drives the criminal lifestyle to the point where the individual is continually searching for external verification of his own worthwhileness.

The early antecedents of the primary organizing motive can be observed in all humans. Alfred Adler (1927) was one of the first theorists to address the universal sense of inferiority that afflicts us all. Adler postulated that we all enter the world as inferior beings, surrounded by persons who are both larger and more knowledgeable than ourselves. Most of us learn through compensation (Adler, 1927) to deal with these concerns and go on to lead lives as productive, contributing members of society. The lifestyle criminal, on the other hand, never really confronts this primary existential fear, hiding from his anxieties with exaggerated displays of bravado and ultramasculinity. Perhaps Charles Manson (1986) sums it up best: "I do come on pretty strong, but boldness and aggressiveness is sometimes just an effort to hide fear, weakness, and doubt" (p. 130). In the end, the lifestyle criminal has set himself up to become the victim of his own childish fears.

The manner in which many of us handle the fear associated with our existence is by developing a sense of social obligation. In other words, we can achieve a sense of purpose and focus by directing our energies toward helping others, or, as Adler notes, by learning to live on the socially useful side of life. This, of course, is not the only way inferiority feelings can be managed since Scrooge, in *A Christmas Carol* by Charles Dickens, expressed very little social obligation prior to his "conversion," though he could hardly have been considered a lifestyle criminal. This point also highlights the invaluable role of personal choice in the development of the criminal lifestyle in the sense that inadequate handling of the inferiority feelings we all must face does not, in and of itself, cause criminality. However, the decisions the lifestyle criminal makes relative to the early life tasks and innate sense of personal inadequacy tend to metastasize beyond their humble beginnings, leaving no area or function unscathed.

Yochelson and Samenow (1976) observed chronic anger in the behavior of many of the criminal offenders they interviewed at St. Elizabeths Hospital in Washington, DC. However, as Aaron Beck (1976) has shown, anger is not a primary emotion but actually emanates from a variety of more fundamental feelings. Therefore, while we may experience anger toward a spouse who has left us after twenty years of marriage or at the driver of an automobile who abruptly cuts in front of us on the expressway, these angry reactions stem from more basic human emotions: hurt in the first case and fear in the second. As Yochelson and Samenow note, criminals are angry about a great many things. They are angry when the teller does not hand over the money as quickly as they would like, they are angry when they are sent to jail for their transgressions, and they are angry when they don't feel they are being treated with respect by prison officials or fellow inmates. However, what lies beneath this anger is the primary organizing motive of fear, a fear that is intrinsic to the individual's antisocial attitude and behavior.

Over time, the primary organizing motive branches out into four secondary organizing motives: anger/rebellion, excitement/pleasure, power/control, and greed/laziness. Where the primary organizing motive supports the evolving life decision directly and the general behavior of the lifestyle criminal indirectly, the secondary organizing motives are more highly correlated with specific criminal events. Through a process known as validation, these

TABLE 5.1: Age Breakdown for Arrests (1983 Index Crimes)

Age	U.S. Population (1980) (percentages)	Index Crime Arrestees (1983)	
		Violent Crimes (percentages)	Property Crimes (percentages)
Under 15	23	5	14
15-19	9	23	32
20-29	18	43	32
30-39	14	19	13
40-49	10	7	5
50-59	10	3	2
60 & Older	10	1	2

Source: Bureau of the Census, Statistical Abstract of the United States, 1981; FBI, Crime in the United States, 1983

secondary organizing motives provide the criminal with an explanation as to why he or she participates in a particular criminal act. Even though these secondary organizing motives help clarify the motivation behind specific criminal events, they do not operate independently of the primary organizing motive. In truth, these secondary organizing motives are enmeshed with the existential fear that guides the evolving life decision to lose in dramatic and destructive ways. It is hoped that this discussion, albeit brief, clarifies the interrelatedness of the early and later life tasks, the evolving life decision to lose in ways that are dramatic destructive, and the primary/secondary organizing motives.

Stages of Criminal Development

A four-stage model of criminal development was outlined in a recent paper (Walters & White, 1989b). This model is based, in part, on the observation that crime is a young man's occupation. Data extracted from the 1983 version of the FBI's Uniform Crime Reports indicate that persons between the ages of 15 and 39 account for two thirds of all index crime arrests (see Table 5.1). Although the four stages that comprise the lifestyle theory of criminal development follow certain age guidelines, there are individual differences that may place one 25-year-old offender at one of the earlier stages and a second 25-year-old offender at a more advanced stage. Hence, while age provides a general estimate of where an offender might fall within the scope of this particular developmental scheme, the stages of criminal development are actually defined by the pattern of primary and secondary organizing motivation that is observed in each.

The arrangement of primary and secondary organizing motive strength varies over the criminal life span. Consequently, while the excitement/pleasure motive may peak during adolescence, the anger/resentment and greed/laziness motives tend to peak at a later point in life. As we discussed previously, the primary organizing motive tends to build slowly over time and then drops off as the individual enters the final stage of criminal development, a stage that embodies the mid-life transition (Jolin & Gibbons, 1987). Figure 5.1 illustrates motivational trends for the primary organizing motive and four secondary organizing motives over the four stages of criminal development: the pre-criminal stage, the early criminal stage, the advanced criminal stage, and the stage of criminal burnout/maturity.

Pre-criminal Stage

The pre-criminal is normally a juvenile somewhere between the ages of 10 and 18. While the pre-criminal may engage in a relatively large number of criminal violations, the majority of arrests occurring during this stage are for nuisance, misdemeanor, and status-type offenses (Petersilia et al., 1978). Though the criminal behavior of individuals during this stage is rarely specialized (Hindelang, 1971; Wolfgang, Figlio, & Sellin, 1972), larceny, burglary, and auto theft are among the more popular felonies committed by members of this particular group (Jamieson & Flanagan, 1987). It should also be pointed out that peers are often instrumental in the criminal conduct of pre-criminals, and many pre-criminal stage offenses are committed in the company of adolescent cohorts (Petersilia et al., 1978).

As demonstrated in Figure 5.1, thrill-seeking is a salient motive for the criminal activities of persons at a pre-criminal stage of development. This theoretical conceptualization of pre-criminal motivation finds support in everyday experience that tells us that auto theft for the purposes of joyriding is quite prevalent in juveniles but practically nonexistent in adults (Wilson & Herrnstein, 1985). This stage would appear to hold the greatest prospect for change, and there are a significant number of juvenile offenders who decide not to carry their criminality into adulthood (Greenwood & Zimring,

Stages of Criminal Development

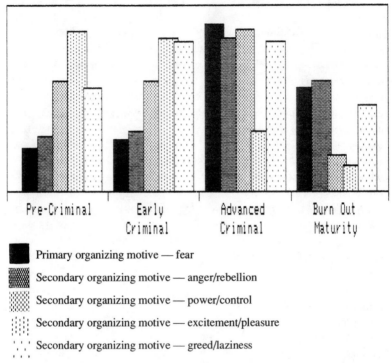

Pre-Criminal   Early   Advanced   Burn Out
                      Criminal   Criminal   Maturity

■ Primary organizing motive — fear

▨ Secondary organizing motive — anger/rebellion

▨ Secondary organizing motive — power/control

⫶⫶ Secondary organizing motive — excitement/pleasure

˙ˌ˙ Secondary organizing motive — greed/laziness

Figure 5.1. Bar Graph of Changes in Motive Strength Hypothesized to Occur over the Course of Criminal Development

1985). However, crime is still very reinforcing for many persons functioning at a pre-criminal level of adjustment; consequently, a healthy proportion move on to later, and more serious, stages in the criminal development sequence.

The pre-criminal stage is probably more densely populated than any of the four stages of criminal development. This is because attrition tends to lower the numbers as we proceed through the criminal development sequence. Some of the persons in this initial stage of criminal development will decide that a life of crime is not for them and exit the lifestyle before entering adulthood. Many others, however, will use this stage as a springboard for future, and more serious, forms of criminal involvement. Case History 5.1 outlines the early criminal life of a boy whom we will call Eric. This juvenile

Case History 5.1: "Eric"

A 15-year-old single white male, Eric was interviewed during his participation in an inpatient chemical-abuse treatment program for adolescents. He had been discharged from the program several months earlier after he had run off on two separate occasions. Between admissions, he had been in jail, on the psychiatric wing of a general hospital, and in the juvenile ward of a state mental hospital. His behavior was disruptive and his adjustment poor in all three placements, and he was discharged from the general hospital after it was learned that he was giving the other adolescents explicit instructions on how to shoplift, beat up their parents, and live on the streets. The day before he was scheduled for discharge from the state hospital, he and several associates ran off for "something exciting to do." With long stringy hair, a large earring dangling from the left ear, and several small tattoos blazoned on the left arm, Eric had "thug" written all over him.

Eric's parents were divorced when he was a young child, and his mother had remarried at least three times and divorced twice. The most recent stepfather was serving a 1- to 5-year sentence for larceny, and the family had moved to this particular community for the express purpose of being near the state prison in which he was incarcerated. Eric's early years were punctuated by instability and constant change as the family moved from state to state and from low-rent quarters, to trailer parks, to community shelters. Reasonably bright but largely unmotivated for academic success, the subject did poorly in school. He reported having been suspended from school on at least eight separate occasions for fighting with other students. Eric acknowledged regular use of alcohol and drugs (mostly marijuana) and sexual promiscuity from age 13 on.

Eric's criminal history dated back six years when, as a 9-year-old child, he stole a car, drove it 20 miles, and then ran it into a telephone pole. Since that time, he had been arrested multiple times for assault, shoplifting, petty larceny, trespassing, and possession of an illegal substance. He had been on probation nine times in four different states and had a history of being physically abusive toward his mother and sister. However, he knew how to feed psychologists and social workers what he believed they wanted to hear and got himself out of various predicaments by playing on the sympathy of others. While many adolescents express impractical notions, Eric, like most pre-criminals, was particularly unrealistic in discussing his future career aspirations. His stated goal was to become a professional football player, though he had never played a single down of organized football in his life.

In reviewing Eric's case, we see the importance of excitement and drama in pre-criminal behavior. If one were to inquire of Eric as to why he engages in crime, he would probably answer something to the effect that he enjoys the thrill and stimulation it provides him. The conflicts he has with adults, his use of alcohol and marijuana, sexual precocity, and physical appearance mirror a high degree of irresponsibility, self-indulgence, and nonconformity. His criminal acts also reflect the anger/rebellion (kicking another juvenile in the face with his foot, assaulting his mother and sister) and excitement/pleasure (joyriding, breaking into a house to watch TV) motives. Only time will tell whether Eric organizes these early juvenile patterns into a lifestyle of adult criminality.

seems destined to carry his life of criminality and predation into adulthood. However, there are a substantial number of adolescents who, like Eric, engage in a large number of serious juvenile offenses, but who never commit a major adult crime and never spend a day in an adult jail.

Early Criminal Stage

The early criminal stage extends from age 18 up through the mid- to late twenties. In entering the early criminal stage, the individual has made the decision to continue acting in ways that are more indicative of an adolescent level of adjustment than an adult one (Walters & White, 1989b). As we progress through this and later stages of criminal development, we notice that the number of subjects declines as a result of various attrition, selection, and mortality factors. Some persons select themselves out of the lifestyle process (see Greenwood & Zimring, 1985), while others are selected out by external factors like death and serious injury. Blumstein and Cohen (1987), for instance, observed a mild to moderate level of criminal attrition in the 20 to 30 age group, a span that covers much of the early stage of criminal development. A career line of criminality also begins to surface during this period of lifestyle development due in part to the fact that the offender finds himself in contact with new criminal associates, principally through confinement in jail or prison, and learns new criminal techniques while acquiring veteran status in the criminal world (Gibbs & Shelly, 1982).

One change that we see during the early criminal stage is that while the number of crimes decrease, the severity of individual offenses climbs. Langan and Farrington (1983) report that property crimes committed by adults were more serious than crimes committed by juveniles in terms of the value of the property stolen. Petersilia et al. (1978) and West and Farrington (1977) both found an increase in violent offenses as subjects moved from adolescence to adulthood. There is also a shift in the motivation for crime with passage into the early criminal stage of lifestyle development. Results from the Rand study (Petersilia et al., 1978) reveal that thrill-seeking, status acquisition, and peer acceptance decline, and the desire for money as a means to secure drugs and non-essential material goods expands as recidivistic offenders advance from a pre-criminal to an early criminal stage of development. The evolving life decision to lose in dramatic and destructive ways also begins to grow and expand into a self-reinforcing pattern of negative behavior as one moves through the early stage of criminal development.

Case History 5.2 demonstrates the changing motives of the early criminal. The subject of this case history, Art, is bright and articulate, yet he lacks the persistence to put these abilities to good use. Rather than move forward with his life, he has decided to remain at an adolescent stage of personal, social, and emotional development. Though Art's expressed motivation for crime may center more on greed and laziness than excitement and pleasure, he finds himself in the same negative situations as did Eric. Hence, delayed development and an ever-widening spiral of negative, self-destructive behavior characterize the criminal functioning at an early stage of lifestyle development.

Advanced Criminal Stage

The advanced stage of criminal development normally spans from the late twenties to the early forties. The act of voluntarily dropping out of crime is probably at its lowest point during this stage, as evidenced by data supplied by Blumstein and Cohen (1987). The impressionistic observations of Petersilia et al. (1978) further suggest that desistance is low during the fourth decade of life. This can probably be explained by the fact that at this stage in life, the individual has made a commitment to the criminal lifestyle, much like the noncriminal typically makes a commitment to his or her family and a particular vocation during the early to mid thirties (Levinson et al., 1978). Accordingly, the loser's life decision and primary organizing motive of fear are both at their height during this particular stage.

During the advanced stage of lifestyle criminal development, the individual's antisocial behavior appears driven and seemingly "out of control." As a means of compensating for this "out of control" feeling, the lifestyle criminal becomes increasingly concerned with gaining a sense of power and control over others. Consequently, the secondary organizing motive of power/control plays a prominent role in the behavior of the criminal who is functioning at an advanced stage of lifestyle development. The anger/rebellion motive is also quite influential during this particular period in the developmental sequence, although the excitement/pleasure motive drops precipitously during the advanced stage of lifestyle development. As I mentioned previously, the primary organizing motive of fear is a very strong motivator of behavior at this point in the criminal career (see Figure 5.1).

Case History 5.2: "Art"

Art is a 26-year-old divorced black male who is serving 15 years in a federal penitentiary for armed bank robbery. His arrest record is testimony to his desire to live on the criminal side of life. At the age of 14, he was referred to the juvenile court by his mother for stealing items from home, cutting school, expressing his anger by periodically assaulting his father and sisters, and bringing antisocial peers into the family home against the wishes of his parents. He began stealing items from family members at a relatively early age and had a particular affinity for jewelry. He accumulated juvenile arrests for petty larceny, burglary, and several probation violations. His parents were so concerned about this behavior that they sent Art to a psychiatrist, but the youngster terminated his contact with the therapist when he discovered that this psychiatrist was sharing information culled from their sessions with the mother.

Adulthood brought with it more opportunities for involvement in criminal activity. At the age of 18, Art was charged with resisting arrest and third degree assault, although both cases were dismissed. One year later, he was arrested for operating an unregistered motor vehicle without a license and breaking into a residence with the intent of stealing jewelry. The latter earned him one year in a county correctional center. Additional adult arrests for unlawful possession of a controlled substance, public drunkenness, third degree assault, and contempt of court are recorded in his file. The instant offense leading to his current incarceration involved robbing a bank in South Carolina. Not only did Art use his own automobile as the getaway car, but he was apprehended when his automobile, a Cadillac, collided with a patrol car following a high-speed chase that occurred subsequent to the robbery.

Somewhat of a "ladies' man," Art had fathered four children through two different relationships. Though he had previously provided financial support for these children, emotional support was usually not forthcoming since the subject was typically not at home. Art openly acknowledged a series of brief sexual liaisons with females he did not know well and seemed somewhat proud of his reputation as a "stud." Both his school and work records were poor due largely to a lack of initiative on his part. Art would normally only work a month or two until he quit or was fired. On one occasion, he misrepresented himself as a minister, and for several months was preaching to the congregation about the evils of sin while extolling the virtues of Christian living. Unbeknownst to the members of his congregation, however, he would often complete his sermon and then go to another part of town in order to do his robbing, stealing, and womanizing.

Besides possessing a fairly high need for excitement, Art was exceptionally greedy and self-centered. He enjoyed expensive jewelry, extravagant clothing, and luxurious automobiles. He was too lazy and impulsive to legitimately work for these possessions, yet too avaricious to lower his expectations. Consequently, he stole and robbed to support his lavish lifestyle and was now paying the price. Though he was fond of stating that he would never return to prison, he still believed that he could sham his way into the "good life." While incarcerated, Art quit his high-paying job in the institution textile factory for one that required less time and effort. Darting from one momentary conquest to the next, he would move from woman to woman and from job to job as he grew bored with what he had. The greed/laziness and excitement/pleasure motives would appear to lie behind much of Art's antisocial behavior.

Lest the reader think of Art in only negative terms, it is well to keep in mind that this individual is not without certain redeeming qualities. In addition to possessing outstanding social skills, Art exuded a charisma that had allowed him to pose as a minister for several months. In the penitentiary, he had been voted into a leadership position in one of the institutional religious groups, a feat quite uncommon for someone so young. As with many lifestyle criminals, however, Art needed to learn greater self-discipline in order to make better use of his many talents and turn these skills toward socially constructive activity.

Due chiefly to the driven quality of behaviors engaged in by the lifestyle criminal who is functioning at an advanced stage of offender development, these individuals can be quite dangerous to themselves and others. The case of a cocaine-intoxicated offender in Denver, Colorado, demonstrates the "out of control" nature of lawbreakers at this particular stage in the criminal development sequence. After murdering two women and sexually assaulting another, this individual secured himself in a condominium by taking an 18-year-old male hostage. When two police officers attempted to enter the dwelling, he wounded them, shot and injured the hostage, and then took his own life (Pankratz, Briggs, & Robinson, March 24, 1989). Although the convict described in Case History 5.3 fails to demonstrate the level of interpersonal dangerousness displayed by this Denver man, the drive to lose in a dramatic and self-destructive way exists nonetheless.

Criminal Burnout/Maturity Stage

The final stage of criminal development normally begins in the early forties and corresponds with the mid-life transition discussed by several developmental psychologists, most notably Levinson et al. (1978). This

Case History 5.3: "Bill"

A 32-year-old divorced black male, Bill was a state prisoner being boarded in the federal penitentiary. His state conviction was for burglary, possession of PCP with intent to sell, and carrying a pistol without a license, and his sentence ran from 3 to 10 years. The situation surrounding the possession of PCP charge is particularly illustrative of the loser's mentality that characterized much of this subject's behavior. Like a vendor hawking his wares at a baseball game, Bill had been walking up and down one of the busiest streets in Washington, DC, shouting "boat, boat, got that boat" (boat being a slang term for PCP). An undercover policeman purchased a small amount of the substance, which later tested out to be PCP, and arrested Bill on the scene. Bill's record in and out of prison was filled with similar episodes in which he figuratively "shot himself in the foot."

Although Bill's first recorded arrest did not take place until he was 20 years old, he had been experimenting with both drugs and crime in high school. By age 21, however, he had wholeheartedly embraced the criminal lifestyle, and over the next 10 years had accumulated a record of 17 arrests for such offenses as disorderly conduct, simple assault, armed robbery, armed burglary, and drug possession. Raised in a lower- to lower-middle-class home environment, both of Bill's parents worked and had owned their present home for many years. Furthermore, the record indicates that two of Bill's three brothers had never before been in trouble with the law. A high school graduate, Bill held several lower-level governmental jobs but either quit or was fired after a year to 3 years of service. He was fired from his longest running job (3 years) when he was found passed out in a drug stupor in one of the stalls in the office bathroom.

The author's first encounter with Bill came when he approached Psychology Service staff for a single-man cell. He spoke with each of the three psychologists and gave each one a different story. He shared with one psychologist that he just couldn't sleep when there was someone in the cell with him, and told another that he masturbated so often (seven times a day, according to the inmate) that this was creating a conflict for him with his current cell partner. Ever the entrepreneur, Bill had been running an illegal institutional "store" whereby he purchased various items at the prison commissary and then sold them to other inmates for a handsome profit. He ran into problems, however, when one dissatisfied customer stole several of Bill's "store" items. A fight ensued, and Bill spent the remainder of his stay at this particular institution in detention.

Serving a relatively short sentence, Bill prolonged his prison term by accumulating a rather large number of disciplinary reports. Though these rules violations were relatively minor (disobeying an order, lying to a staff member, failure to follow safety regulations, possession of intoxicants), they point to the self-defeating nature of many of Bill's actions. This would seem to suggest that not only did the subject set himself up for failure in the community, but he did so in prison as well. The evolving life decision to lose in dramatic and destructive ways seems to convey Bill's general demeanor, as does the primary organizing motive of fear. The secondary organizing motives of greed/laziness and power/control would also appear to be operating here.

stage, referred to by Walters and White (1989b) as the stage of criminal burnout, signals a turning point in many criminal careers and brings with it a high rate of termination from this lifestyle (Hirschi & Gottfredson, 1983). Blumstein and Cohen (1987) discovered that while cross-sectional data denote that the arrest rate declines dramatically after age 30, desistance from crime for many career criminals may occur 10 to 15 years after the drop in cross-sectional arrest data takes place. As a function of decreased physical strength, stamina, and activity, any criminal behavior engaged in during this stage will usually require negligible physical exertion but continued association with the criminal community. Such crimes might include illegal gambling, dealing in stolen property, or involvement in various confidence games. Petersilia et al. (1978) report that older criminals typically exhibit minimal interest in the type of crimes that appeal to most youthful offenders.

Walter Gove (1985) attributes the drop in criminality normally seen in career criminals during the fifth decade of life to changes occurring over the course of the adult life cycle. As a result of the mid-life transition thought to take place in males between the ages of 40 and 45, one becomes more introspective, less self-absorbed, and to a greater degree, concerned with such issues as the meaning of life (Levinson et al., 1978). The criminal offender is no exception in this regard, and research shows that the decision to give up crime is correlated with increased affiliation with others, less concern with material "success," and a growing awareness that crime is a "no win" proposition, at least where the criminal as an individual is concerned (Cusson & Pinsonneault, 1986; Irwin, 1970; Jolin & Gibbons, 1987; Meisenhelder, 1977; Shover, 1983). In addition, the fear of criminal sanctions, which most lifestyle criminals lose at a relatively early age, resurfaces in the form of a fear of growing old and dying in prison (Meisenhelder, 1977). Many of these issues are described in Case History 5.4.

One final bit of evidence demonstrating the demise of the criminal lifestyle during the fifth decade of life can be found in studies examining crime rates for different age groups. Langan and Greenfeld (1983), for instance, found

---

Case History 5.4: "Henry"

Henry is a 59-year-old divorced white male first incarcerated in 1949. He spent the next 40 years, less 15 months, locked in one of two penitentiaries, one state, the other federal. Initially arrested at age 15 for trespassing, Henry was convicted of burglary and theft at age 19. Then at age 20, he murdered a man and was sentenced to life in prison. Henry escaped from state custody twice, the first time after 12 months and the second time after 20 years. The second escape was actually a walk-away from a minimum-security state prison farm, and Henry picked up a federal sentence after he kidnapped a student nurse from a hospital parking lot in effecting his escape. Paroled twice, he remained in the community less than one year each time, violating his parole by engaging in new criminal acts (burglary, larceny).

The years have taken their toll on Henry. In addition to the wear and tear of a life of crime, Henry's medical history reads like an excerpt from *Ripley's Believe It Or Not*. Working several years in the institution soap plant without benefit of breathing protection, Henry suffered serious lung damage and had to have one of his lungs removed. While in the hospital recovering from this surgery, he was placed on a potent antibiotic one month too long and subsequently developed a serious and permanent hearing disability. Several years later, working in another part of the institution, he fell off a ladder and did serious damage to his back and one leg. In order to relieve the pain, an institutional physician severed a nerve running from the spinal cord to the leg. However, when Henry woke up from his surgery, he made a horrible discovery: The doctor had operated on the wrong leg.

Irresponsibility had always been a problem for Henry. Although he was considered a "model prisoner" by correctional staff, he had trouble behaving responsibly in the community. As long as he had someone looking over his shoulder, Henry did quite well in his jobs in the community. After work, however, he would stop by the liquor store and purchase two six-packs of beer and a fifth of whiskey. He would then spend his evenings drinking, watching television, and getting increasingly more bitter and frustrated. It wasn't long before he was breaking into houses for the purposes of burglary. Personal control had also never been one of Henry's strong suits, and he had been characterized in previous evaluations as impulsive and subject to low frustration tolerance. Henry wanted a change and, like many older offenders, reflected back on his life and saw the futility of criminality. However, he was still uncertain whether he would ever be able to fit into the mainstream of society.

For some years, Henry had been experiencing a reduced energy level, a condition that was being exacerbated by his various medical ailments. Although still somewhat of a nonconformist, Henry was no longer interested in "bucking the system" and had received no discipline reports for over five years. Mild depression was also beginning to set in as he thought about his life, and he was apprehensive, yet optimistic, about the prospect of returning to the community. Though the primary organizing motive of fear was of moderate intensity at the time of our interview, all of the secondary organizing motives, with the exception of anger/rebellion, had dropped to where they were barely discernible. An aging rebel without a cause, Henry waited for the day when he could give the "straight" life another chance.

the most populous group of offenders aged 40 and older confined in state prisons and penitentiaries to have no history of serious law violation during adolescence or early adulthood. Thus, while lifestyle criminals tend to be overrepresented in groups of younger felons, the composition of older prison populations is skewed toward non-lifestyle offenders. Similarly, Robert Hare, Leslie McPherson, and Adelle Forth (1988) report that psychopathic offenders, comparable in many ways to lifestyle criminals, display a high rate of lawlessness and incarceration during adolescence and early adulthood, but then their criminality drops off to where it equals the pace set by non-psychopathic offenders.

Although burnout and maturity often form a unit, they are not synonymous. Maturity entails a change in thinking, values, and motivation that frequently accompany the declining physical and mental energy characterizing criminal burnout. Thus, while nearly all offenders who live beyond the high-risk years enter the burnout phase, maturity may not be part of the process. Take, for instance, the case of an 82-year-old bank robber whose criminal record dates back to 1921, when he was placed in an Illinois reformitory for an unspecified crime. Discharged from prison in 1971, he apparently remained free of any serious legal problems until 1986, when he began robbing banks and supermarkets in central Colorado. He was eventually apprehended in March 1989, when he was spotted pedaling away from a bank robbery on a 10-speed bicycle (Garnass & Robinson, 1989). Destined to live out his years in a federal prison, we would be hard-pressed to conclude that he had achieved a state of maturity, or even burnout, though he had remained free of any formal legal difficulties for nearly 15 years.

It is important that we appreciate the difference between burnout and maturity. Although a number of lifestyle offenders mature out of their criminality, many more avoid serious criminality as they grow older, yet continue living on the "fringes" (generally irresponsible and self-indulgent but no longer intrusive). Still others, like our 82-year-old bank robber, continue violating the laws of society with impunity. Some authors take issue with the term *burnout* (see Hare et al., 1988), but there is evidence that criminality and its consequences (e.g., prison) do in fact wear upon the offender as he ages (Blumstein, Cohen, Roth, & Visher, 1986; Conrad, 1985). What's more, many offenders use this term themselves to describe the sense of fatigue that envelopes their actions as they grow older.

Conclusion

Returning to our school yard of 100 third-graders, I think we can state with a great deal more authority why only one or two of these children will evolve into lifestyle criminals. A principal factor is that the conditions involved in the development of this lifestyle occur in only a subsample of all persons. Furthermore, the decision to enter the preliminary stages of criminality, not to mention the decision to turn crime into a lifestyle, is made by only a smattering of persons exposed to the early developmental conditions associated with such criminality. This is because most people appreciate the self-defeating nature of habitual antisocial behavior, though it may take some longer to see this than others. The loser's life decision guides the thinking of the high-rate offenders and lifestyle criminals of the world. It is therefore understandable that out of all the possible recruits, only a handful enlist, and even fewer reenlist, for a career in crime.

According to the lifestyle theory presented in this chapter, recidivistic criminality has its foundation in the choices one makes relative to a specific set of life tasks and the fear of failing in the world at large. It is not these tasks or the fear, however, that is the cause of criminality, since these are developmental/existential phenomena we must all face. Instead, it is the manner in which the habitual lawbreaker resolves these tasks and the sense of inferiority we all experience as youngsters that sets into motion a ruinous chain of events, thoughts, and behaviors which I have come to call the criminal lifestyle. Instead of confronting our collective sense of inferiority and fear of failure, the evolving lifestyle criminal flees from his fears, as well as from his responsibilities, obligations, and commitments, and tacitly decides that if he is going to lose, then at least he is going to lose on his terms. In other words, he actively rejects society before it can reject him, and he seeks immediate gratification and momentary victories as substitutes for long-term happiness and meaningful success.

One might wonder why I have gone to the trouble of deriving a theory that delves into the criminal psyche when this behavior could be more parsimoniously explained through the use of various schedules of reinforcement. Although I find learning principles indispensable in understanding the criminal lifestyle, I also believe that we must go beyond a simple examination of reinforcement and punishment contingencies in an effort to understand why certain behaviors are reinforcing for some people but not to others. Framed somewhat differently, Why are certain conditions differentially reinforcing to lifestyle criminals and other conditions successful in deterring the antisocial inclinations of all but a handful of individuals? This is why I have devoted the better part of a chapter to exploring such internalized processes as the evolving life decision and primary organizing motive of fear—a discussion which, I hasten to add, is far from over.

Robert and Beverly Cairns (1986) state that a rapprochement needs to take place between interactionalists (social learning theorists), who are inclined to attribute changes occurring during childhood to such processes as observational learning, and developmentalists, who view childhood changes as the result of a maturation in cognitive functioning. As was conveyed to the reader in Chapter 1, such integration is a principal goal of this book. Aspects of this interactionalist-developmentalist integration will be particularly relevant when we take up the issue of criminal cognition. Hence, while decisions made relative to the life tasks and inferiority feelings of youth provide the criminal lifestyle with impetus, specific thinking patterns afford this lifestyle its substance. For this reason, the next chapter will probe the criminal thinking patterns of society's most recidivistic lawbreakers.

6. Cognitive Patterns

Conditions set the stage for choice, which in turn pave the way for cognition. Choice and thought are, of course, inextricably linked and to separate them portends a certain degree of artificiality. However, within the context of the criminal lifestyle, it is essential that we appreciate the sequence of events responsible for the rise of criminologic thought, a progression that commences with the early and later life tasks and the choices one makes relative to these tasks. Out of the morass of confusion generated by these interacting influences arises a cognitive system dedicated to supporting, buttressing, and perpetuating the irresponsibility and self-indulgence of adolescence. Learning eventually permits this thinking style to crystallize to the extent that the evolving lifestyle criminal finds shortsighted frivolity, unrestrained hedonism, intrusive action, and rulelessness more rewarding than accountability, self-discipline, interpersonal commitment, and social conformity.

Albert Ellis (1962) has spent the better part of four decades developing a cognitive model of human behavior and clinical psychopathology. Basing a number of his ideas on the earlier efforts of Alfred Adler (1927), Ellis contends that our actions and feelings follow from our thoughts and beliefs. As Figure 6.1 clearly illustrates, it is not the activating event or situation (A) that causes a specific consequent emotion or behavior (C), but the attitude or viewpoint (B) one holds toward this situation. There is a wealth of empirical evidence to suggest that our thoughts and feelings operate in just this way (Koriat, Melkman, Averill, & Lazarus, 1972; Schachter & Singer, 1962; Valins, 1966). Although several neo-cognitive theorists have arrived on the scene in recent years, Aaron Beck (1976), Michael Mahoney (1977), Maxie Maultsby (1975), Donald Meichenbaum (1977), and Walter Mischel (1973), to name but a few, Albert Ellis is responsible for having developed the first cognitive theory of deviance and treatment capable of generating a wide base of support from practitioners and academicians alike.

A fundamental premise of Ellis's (1962) perspective, also known as Rational Emotive Therapy (RET), is that previous conditioning and early

A → B → C

activating   belief   consequent
event   emotion

Figure 6.1. The ABCs of Human Emotion (Ellis, 1962)

influences have an impact on one's present circumstances only if one allows them to have an impact. One way people permit their pasts to influence their present circumstances is through irrational thinking. Ellis has derived a system of common irrational beliefs that get in the way of people leading happy, productive, anxiety-free lives. While the number of irrational beliefs has changed some over the years, three key irrational notions have stood the test of time. First, there is the belief that one must have the love and approval of all persons one views as significant. Second is the notion that one must prove to be thoroughly competent, achieving, and adequate at all times. Third is the presumption that we must see things as terrible, awful, or catastrophic if we are frustrated or perceive that we are being rejected or treated unfairly (Ellis & Harper, 1975).

Our focus in the present chapter will be on eight irrational beliefs held to be true by the lifestyle criminal, a system of self-talk that serves to fuel the irresponsible, self-indulgent, interpersonally intrusive, social rule breaking actions of the high rate offender. Before continuing with our examination of irrational thinking as the gateway to crime, I believe it is important that the reader appreciate the difference between logic and rationality. Logic is a system that considers the formal principles of deduction and inference, while rational analysis concerns itself with reason and the feasibility of a particular thought assessed against a specific set of criteria. Therefore, while the actions and feelings of the lifestyle criminal are logical in the sense that they follow deductively from the individual's thoughts, these thoughts are based on irrational, unfounded premises that lead the individual to engage in various self-defeating behaviors.

Although the process of criminal thought can be understood using Ellis's (1962) RET approach to human personality, the content of criminologic thought cannot. For this reason, Yochelson and Samenow's (1976) ground-breaking work on the criminal personality was invoked in an effort to better understand the content-related aspects of criminal ideation. As the reader may recall, Yochelson and Samenow identified 52 common thinking errors that they viewed as pathognomonic of the criminal personality, although several of these errors were actually more affective or behavioral than cognitive in nature. Commencing with five of Yochelson's and Samenow's more cognitively oriented errors, reconceptualizing and reorganizing several of these errors, and adding several terms of their own, psychologists at the United States Penitentiary in Leavenworth, Kansas, derived a system of criminologic thought comprised of eight primary cognitive errors/characteristics (see Walters & White, 1989c). These eight characteristics will be discussed at length in this chapter.

One issue often raised by many of the offenders I have worked with in therapy concerns the fact that nearly all of the patterns to be explicated in this chapter can also be observed in noncriminals. The difference appears to be largely one of degree since we all start out as self-centered, hedonistic infants. However, where most of us eventually redirect our thinking toward responsibility and self-control, the lifestyle criminal continues operating on the basis of early adolescent priorities: pleasure, immediacy, and self-justification being more important than accountability, delay, and self-discipline. While the noncriminal may occasionally experience sentimentality or attempt to justify his irresponsible actions, the lifestyle criminal erects a lifestyle around these characteristics. Even if individuals display one or more of these cognitive attributes on a fairly regular basis, they do not become truly criminogenic until they attach themselves to the wider life decision to lose in ways that are dramatic and self-defeating. Therefore, while some businessmen may express a strong sense of entitlement and an equally dynamic power orientation, these characteristics remain fairly circumscribed. In the recidivistic offender, however, these tendencies are liable to incite the other seven features to action in much the same way as a snowball gains momentum as it rolls downhill.

This excursion into the primary cognitive features of lifestyle criminality will be governed by theory-based conceptualizations, available research, and the published statements of a host of well-known criminals. As part of the latter, we will hear from the celebrated bank robber Willie "the Actor" Sutton (1953); thrill killers Nathan Leopold and Richard Loeb (Leopold, 1958); professional safe-cracker Harry King (1972); the architect of one of America's most infamous mass murders, Charles Manson (1986); and several others. In this chapter, we will also find ourselves examining portions of an interview that took place between psychologist Dr. James C. Dobson and condemned serial killer Ted Bundy only hours before Bundy was to be executed in the Florida electric chair. With these considerations in mind, we turn our attention to the first of eight primary cognitive patterns of relevance to the criminal lifestyle, that of mollification.

Mollification

Mollification has its roots in the rationalizations and self-justifications of adolescence. However, while most juveniles eventually learn to accept greater responsibility for their actions, the lifestyle criminal continues to focus on adolescent priorities and goals. In effect, the repeat offender attempts to justify and rationalize his criminal actions by pointing out the presence of unjust or inequitable conditions in the wider social environment. Though these conditions may, in fact, exist, the offender is overlooking two important factors. First, the entire notion of "fairness" is a subjective one for which there is no satisfactory resolution due to the fact that what one person finds "fair," another may find patently "unjust." Even more germane, however, is realizing that it is irrational to use environmental injustice to mollify, soften, or attentuate one's own irresponsible actions.

Gresham Sykes and David Matza (1970) identified a series of cognitive strategies used by delinquents to justify their antisocial actions and extinguish the guilt feelings many of them experience the first several times they violate another person's rights. These techniques of neutralization, the term used by Sykes and Matza to describe this process, are similar in form to mollification. Neutralization techniques, which include denying responsibility for delinquent acts, denigrating the plight of one's victims, and diverting attention away from one's negative behavior by questioning the motives of others (Sykes & Matza, 1970), all reflect the machinations of individuals who have learned to rely on mollification to diffuse responsibility for their own irresponsible actions. By focusing on external factors or minimizing the seriousness of one's actions, the lifestyle criminal attempts to mollify the significance of his intrusive, rule-breaking behavior.

There are several ways in which the mollification process can be expressed, one of which is to identify oneself as a victim of societal injustice or malevolence. Such an attitude underlies a statement offered by box man (a slang term meaning safe-cracker) Harry King (1972):

> As I said, I only received $10 when I got out. It didn't last me very long. Even in those days it wouldn't pay for meals and room for any length of time at all. So I had no alternative except to turn to crime. (p. 104)

Willie "the Actor" Sutton seems a little more aware of his efforts to mollify through self-pity:

> A man can always make excuses for himself and, of course, it didn't take me long to convince myself that I never had a decent chance. Had I been able to get

a good job after I had married Louise, I might never have done another dishonest thing the rest of my life. Society had forced me into crime—that's what I told myself anyhow. What criminal hasn't told himself that a hundred times? (Sutton, 1953, p. 116)

Mollification is also present when a person makes reference to various manifestations of unfairness and inequity as if doing so somehow justifies their irresponsibility. The criminal reasons that because there are police officers who take bribes, judges who overstep their bounds, and correctional officers who abuse their authority, this somehow attenuates the seriousness of their criminal pasts (Walters & White, 1989c). Mollification of this type appears to be prominent in the thinking of Harry King (1972):

There is no such thing as justice in criminal courts. If you've got the money you get the fix. If you haven't got the money, you don't get it. It's just that plain and simple. A woman set fire to her home in Portland and her father's extremely wealthy. Murder is not a bailable offense. While this woman was in jail they passed a law allowing murder to be bailed out. She was immediately bailed out and was turned loose by the jury. She deliberately set fire to her home and burned up two or three of her children. She admitted it. It was a premeditated crime, incidentally. But she was turned loose. How can you expect these guys and kids to believe that there is justice? You can't convince these kids of that when they go up there in these detention homes five or six times. Those things have to be changed. (p. 104)

Mollification can also be more specialized in the sense that the individual blames specific circumstances, events, or conditions for his or her criminal behavior rather than taking personal responsibility for these actions. The culprit might be any of the ones commonly ascribed to by society—poverty, drugs, one's parents—or it may be a more individualized malefactor. Take, for instance, the case of Ted Bundy. During his interview with Dr. James C. Dobson, Bundy seems to be trying to mollify his past criminal actions by pointing out the nefarious influence of hard core pornography on his behavior and those of others: "Pornography can reach out and snatch a kid out of any home today. It snatched me out of, it snatched me out of my home 20, 30 years ago" (Dobson, 1989).

An extremely destructive form of mollification involves blaming the victim. Martha Burt (1983) found that male rapists were more inclined to offer external explanations for rape behavior and attempt to justify such actions by blaming the victim (e.g., the woman must have done something to deserve being raped) than nonrapist male controls. Similar results were obtained when maximum security offenders were asked by Henderson and Hewstone (1984) to explain their violent behavior. It would appear, then, that many offenders attempt to divert responsibility for their violent and antisocial acts away from themselves by denigrating the victim or viewing the victim as deserving of his or her fate, the latter of which Lerner (1970) refers to as the "just world perspective." Mollification of this sort can be found in several statements offered by Jack Henry Abbott (1981), author of the book *In the Belly of the Beast*:

> Responsibility? I am not responsible for what the government—its systems of justice, its prisons—have done to me. I did not do this to myself. (p. 17)

> If I had not come under their influence, I probably would have gotten out of prison long ago. But I would have returned, over and over again. I would have been a thief or a jive-talking dope fiend who has no idea of anything else in life except singing the blues and paying his dues in prison. Why? Because that is what the government, the state reared me from childhood to be; that is what adjusting to prison does to a man. (p. 97)

> Tell America that as long as it permits the use of violence in its institutions—in the whole vast administrative system traditional to this country—men and women will always indulge in violence, will always yearn to achieve the cultural mantle of this society based on swindle and violence . . . .Tell America it is a cringing, back-stabbing coward because it cannot, has never tried to, exercise its will without violence. And because it is a coward, it does not respect reason. (pp. 107-108)

Since mollification involves an attempt by the individual to minimize or soften the seriousness of his criminal behavior, it is often conveyed in one's choice of words. In his interview with psychologist Dr. James Dobson (1989), Ted Bundy refers, not once, but twice, to the women he "has harmed," which seems a gargantuan understatement in light of the fact that he sexually abused, killed, and mutilated nearly all of his victims. In summary, mollification entails an effort by the lifestyle criminal to assuage, exonerate, or extenuate responsibility for his violent and antisocial activities by pointing out external considerations, which may or may not be true, but which have nothing to do with the individual's own behavior. Mollification is not only irrational and self-serving, but it also thwarts change by providing the lifestyle criminal with convenient, ready-made justifications and rationalizations for his past criminal behavior (Walters & White, 1989c).

Cutoff

A common misconception held by psychologists and psychiatrists 20 to 30 years ago was that the criminal does not learn from his past experiences and is largely unresponsive to deterrents (see Cleckley, 1976; Hare, 1970). Nothing could be further from the truth. The habitual lawbreaker is just as responsive to deterrents as anyone else, a fact attested to by the common observation that many offenders remain free of serious disciplinary problems while confined in prison or jail (see Flanagan, 1983). Unlike the noncriminal, however, the high-rate offender has at his disposal a cognitive mechanism, the cutoff, which is capable of eroding and rapidly eliminating the deterrents that prevent most of us from engaging in serious criminality (Yochelson & Samenow, 1976).

The cutoff is designed to eliminate the anxieties, worries, concerns, and fears that stand in the way of one committing a particular criminal act (Walters & White, 1989c). The criminal becomes very familiar with one or two preferred cutoffs, so much so that it becomes a nearly automatic response to environmental stress and frustration, similar to the way Beck (1976) conceives of negative self-talk as being automatic. It is essential to keep in mind, however, that the cutoff remains under the recalcitrant offender's voluntary control, for it is he who decides when to activate this mechanism. In fact, with time, many lifestyle criminals learn to eliminate or terminate the cutoff (see Yochelson & Samenow, 1976), as might happen in situations where the crime scene suddenly becomes significantly less conducive to the commission of a particular criminal act. There is preliminary evidence to suggest that a physiological mechanism may underlie the cutoff process. In a study directed by Robert Hare (1982), for instance, it was determined that the more psychopathic members of a group of Canadian criminals ignored various internal "warning signals" and other "irrelevant" cues in a manner that seemed physiologically mediated.

The most common cutoff I have observed in my years of clinical practice with recidivistic offenders involves a single word or phrase, the expression "fuck it" being particularly popular. This two-word phrase does an especially good job of capturing the anger that so often ignites the cutoff. This anger will frequently rise to a crescendo of emotion that rapidly purges one's mind of the type of concerns that normally prevent the individual from engaging in such activity. Once the antisocial act has been committed, the emotions that often trigger the cutoff response will typically subside just as quickly as they arose. Charles Manson (1986) demonstrates a cutoff fueled by mollification when he reflects on his thinking just prior to the Tate-LaBianca murders:

> All I could focus on was, "What the fuck is happening here? One by one this fucked-up society is stripping my love from me. I'll show them! They made animals out of us—I'll unleash these animals—I'll give them so much fucking fear the people will be afraid to come out of their houses!" These thoughts might sound like pure insanity, but every abuse, every rejection in my entire life flashed before me. Hatred, fury, insanity—I felt all of these things. (p. 199)

Although a word or phrase may be the most common form of cutoff, this is by no means the only type of cutoff mechanism available to the lifestyle criminal. Some will use visual images, while others implement a gradual building up of arguments against conventional behavior. One offender I interviewed recalled that he would hum a line of dramatic theme music to build up the gumption to enter a bank for the purposes of robbery. In the event an offender is unable to find an "internal" cutoff, there are a plethora of "external" cutoffs available to him. Alcohol and drugs are among the most frequently encountered "external" cutoffs. Ted Bundy attributes much of his negative behavior to alcohol and pornography. While one may take issue with his conclusions, both seemed to have served a cutoff function for him: "Alcohol reduced my inhibitions; at the same time the fantasy life that was fueled by pornography eroded them further" (Dobson, 1989).

As any criminal can tell you, one must eliminate anxiety and fear before effectively engaging in a major criminal act. No one knows this better than professional box man Harry King (1972):

> You just can't have any fear, that plugs up your mind. Your mind has to be open all the time. You have to be like an animal and be on your toes all the time prepared for danger that might arise. If you have a fear in you when you start, it plugs up part of your mind. (pp. 52-53)

Like all of the primary cognitive features of lifestyle criminality, the cutoff operates like a lubricant that not only facilitates the commission of particular criminal acts, but also creates the circumstances under which a large portion of serious criminality is committed each year. Without the cutoff, the offender would be unable to rapidly eliminate the deterrents that keep most of us from engaging in serious antisocial activity.

Entitlement

As Walters and White (1989c) assert, the lifestyle criminal has a strong sense of entitlement. Acting as if he were knighted by the queen or granted absolution by the pope, the lifestyle criminal callously infringes upon the rights of others and unceremoniously violates the laws of society. A number of robbers interviewed by Floyd Feeney (1986) expressed a clear sense of entitlement in sharing with him their motives for robbery:

> Another group did not think of themselves as trying to rob at all. They were attempting to recover money they claimed was either theirs or owed to them. Their motivation was to get what they thought belonged to them. A number had money with them or at home. (p. 59)

This sense of ownership plays a central role in the entitled sentiments of the average lifestyle criminal and is clearly evident in comments made by Charles Manson (1986) about not abiding by the laws of society:

> Asking me not to break the rules of society is like telling your kid not to eat candy because it's bad for him. The kid will continue to eat candy until you take it away, or until you prove why he shouldn't. You also need to provide substitutes for the candy you have denied that child. I was told often enough what was bad, but I was never given a substitute or the opportunity to try another world until I had already become so defiant and twisted, I no longer cared about someone else's right or wrong. (p. 63)

The reader should know that entitlement is comprised of three basic elements: ownership, uniqueness, and misidentification. An attitude of ownership was expressed by many of the subjects interviewed by Feeney (1986), while uniqueness relates to the fact that the lifestyle criminal fancies himself a special person for whom the rules and dictates of society generally do not apply. The backgrounds of many recidivistic offenders are filled with early messages from parents and significant others that the individual was special, unique, or different from others. Both ownership and uniqueness were explored in the original Walters and White (1989c) paper. The misidentification of wants as needs, however, is something that Walters and White failed to address in their article.

Over the past several months, I have become increasingly more cognizant of the prominent role that the misidentification of wants as needs plays in the evolution of the entitlement attitude. While in the community, the offender may express this attitude by telling himself he robs and steals because he needs a spacious home, nice car, fancy clothes, or expensive jewelry. While confined, he convinces himself that he violates institutional rules against stealing, using drugs, and gambling because he needs extra socks, cigarettes, a "lift," or the excitement of winning.

Lifestyle theory defines a need as a condition necessary for the preservation of one's life. Hence, air, water, food, and shelter qualify as needs, but control over others, a late model automobile, an expensive steak dinner, or fancy mansion in New England do not. Nevertheless, if we deceive ourselves into treating a desire as a need, we are, in effect, giving ourselves permission to pursue this "need" with vigor and a sense of urgency due to the fact that a need is something that is required for the preservation of life. Confusing one's desires with one's needs, in addition to several other reflections of entitlement, can be found in the words that George Jackson (1970) uses to describe his prison experience in the book *Soledad Brother*:

> I'm in regular adjustment center—segregation again. They have let me have my personal property, books, toilet articles, envelopes, that is minus 90 percent of it . . . . I'll need a few dollars to replace the necessary things (envelopes, dictionary, etc.) when you can afford it. (p. 119)

> I am charged to right the wrong, lift the burden from the backs of future generations. I will not shrink from my duties. (p. 70)

> I'm going to charge them for this, twenty-eight years without gratification. I'm going to charge them reparations in blood. I'm going to charge them like a maddened, wounded, rogue male elephant, ears flared, trumpet blaring. I'll do my dance on his chest, and the only thing he'll ever see in my eyes is a dagger to pierce his cruel heart. This is one nigger who is positively displeased. I'll never forgive, I'll never forget, and if I'm guilty of anything at all its of not leaning on them hard enough. War without terms. (p. 222)

It is likely that Nathan Leopold and Richard Loeb were experiencing an attitude of entitlement when they murdered 14-year-old Bobby Franks. Leopold, 19 years old at the time, and Loeb, one year his junior, both hailed from very wealthy Chicagoan families, as did young Franks. The two older boys, apparently looking to commit the "perfect crime," kidnapped Franks, murdered him, stuffed his body into a drainage pipe, and then constructed a ransom note in an effort to deceive the police into thinking the kidnapping was the work of a professional kidnapper. In reality, this crime was anything but perfect. One foible followed another, from Leopold leaving his glasses in the vicinity of the body to the use of a personal typewriter in constructing the ransom note, forming a trail that led officials directly to Leopold and Loeb. Defended by the renowned trial lawyer Clarence Darrow, the instigators of the "crime of the century" were sentenced to life plus 99 years, although more important for our purposes is Loeb's sense of entitlement as seen through his crime partner's eyes:

> But then there was that other side to him [Loeb]. In the crime, for instance, he didn't have a single scruple of any kind. He wasn't immoral, he was just plain amoral—unmoral that is. Right and wrong didn't exist. He'd do anything—anything. And it was all a game to him. He reminded me of an eight-year-old all wrapped up in a game of cops and robbers. (Leopold, 1958, p. 26)

Similar to the egocentricity expressed by the young child, entitlement begins with the belief that the world exists for one's personal benefit and pleasure (Walters & White, 1989c). Hook and Cook (1979) write that most children believe that they are entitled to whatever catches their fancy. Consequently, young children do not realize that their desires sometimes conflict with other people's plans, although with maturity most learn to become more realistic in appraising that to which they are entitled. The lifestyle criminal, on the other hand, continues to hold to his egocentric beliefs. If he does not attain that to which he feels entitled, he may respond in much the same manner as a child having a temper tantrum. Manipulation, intimidation, and physical violence are but a few of the techniques available to the lifestyle criminal intent upon exercising an attitude of privilege and prerogative.

As many of the offenders I have worked with in therapy are quick to point out, lifestyle criminals are not alone in experiencing ideas of entitlement. Most people articulate an attitude of entitlement about certain aspects of their lives, although the scope and intensity of these expressions of entitlement are very different in the criminal, as opposed to the majority of noncriminals. Where the entitlement beliefs of noncriminals are normally focused and circumscribed, the lifestyle criminal experiences a global sense of entitlement that encompasses a wide array of different contingencies. Additionally, since the entitlement exhibited by lifestyle criminals tends to be quite intense, such persons are much less likely to re-evaluate their "privileged status" in the face of new information than the average individual. Entitlement is therefore a necessary precursor for any criminal act since in the absence of prerogative, need, or ownership, the individual will likely refrain from the kinds of predatory activities observed in persons ensconced in the criminal way of life.

Power Orientation

The criminal is obsessed with gaining a sense of power and control over his environment, particularly other people. As we might predict from the delayed-adolescence interpretation of lifestyle development, the repeat offender has resisted the societal push for increased self-discipline through responsible, internalized action and remains at a point in his development where external control and influence are viewed as predominant. Consequently, the world view of most lifestyle criminals is immature, unsophisticated, and largely fatuous in that it focuses on a solitary dimension of human experience (strong versus weak). As part of this orientation to power, the lifestyle criminal may express irritation—even though he may not be feeling particularly angry—as a means of intimidating and controlling those around him. From the vantage point of an offender viewing life through power-oriented spectacles, the world is a chess board, he is the chess master, and everyone else is a pawn.

The power orientation is comprised of two primary elements, the power thrust and zero state (Yochelson & Samenow, 1976). Many lifestyle criminals vacillate between an image of themselves as all-powerful and one in which they are completely helpless and ineffective. Neither of these perceptions is very accurate, although they exert a profound impact on the behavior of these types of individuals. When the lifestyle criminal is on the low side of the power orientation teeter-totter, he is experiencing what Yochelson and Samenow (1976) call a zero state. An offender in the throes of a zero state believes that he is totally worthless because he has no control whatsoever over his environment. Nathan Leopold (1958) expressed such sentiments after finding himself about to be transferred from Stateville Prison to the Joliet Correctional Center because of his own irresponsibility:

> For me it was pretty tragic. This transfer meant leaving my work, leaving everyone I knew in prison, leaving my comfortable surroundings, and starting over again from the beginning. I didn't know whether I could take it.

Captain White—Sour Apples White, we called him—was to take me back to Joliet. He asked me before we set out whether I'd be more comfortable if he handcuffed me and pointed to the pistol in his holster. I answered that that wouldn't be necessary, but privately I thought, "If I could only be sure he'd kill me instantly, I'd run." But I was afraid of being paralyzed or permanently crippled. If I wanted to die, I'd better wait and do it myself, so that I could be sure. (pp. 183-184)

Leopold's desire to extricate himself from his situation not only reflects the inner workings of the zero state to the extent where he perceives himself as having little control over his situation, but also reflects an attempt on his part to power-thrust out of this zero state by taking symbolic control over the situation through suicidal fantasies.

The power thrust is often the offender's response to zero-state feelings. However, a power thrust can exist independently of the zero state, although the two are related in the sense that the power thrust and the zero state are at opposite ends of the power orientation continuum, existing in the form of complete control and total absence of control, respectively. One study, for instance, found retaliation, anger, and "saving face" to be important in explaining many forms of assaultive crime (Felson, 1982). Additional research suggests that power and control are compelling motives for sexual crimes (Groth & Hobson, 1983; Rada, 1978) as well as robbery (Feeney, 1986). Just the challenge of a criminal opportunity can be enough to stimulate the power orientation of most lifestyle criminals, as exemplified by bank robber Willie Sutton (1953):

Once, even though I had $30,000 in my pocket, I went by a bank, and I just had to meet its challenge. I took that bank all right, even though I didn't need the money. I just felt that I had to take that bank. I've felt that way about banks. (p. 28)

A central feature of the power thrust is elevating oneself above others in an effort to demonstrate one's superiority. In line with this, Luckenbill (1977) conceptualizes homicides as "character contests" in which participants endeavor to "save face" or gain the upper hand at their opponent's expense. In addition, there is an energizing component to the power thrust that seems almost self-generating (Walters & White, 1989c). As such, a disagreement between two lifestyle criminals can quite rapidly degenerate into a physical altercation since neither wants to back down for fear of being viewed as weak by the other or vulnerable by one's peers. The results of a study conducted by Porprine, Doherty, and Sawatsky (1987) reveal that a substantial number of killings taking place in penitentiaries are committed in full view of others, power apparently being more important than secrecy.

Although a fight, stabbing, or violent discord on the part of one or more lifestyle criminals nearly always reflects the control motive, power thrusts can also be indirect. Some criminals will power-thrust by talking in a pseudo-intellectual, stilted manner, although even the casual observer can usually see through this maneuver since such individuals often mispronounce many of the four-syllable terms they use to impress others (Walters & White, 1989c). Another nonviolent form of power thrusting is showing off the biggest car, most expensive home, fanciest clothes, or prettiest woman in the neighborhood. By capturing the attention of others, the lifestyle criminal has realized the primary goal of power thrusting: environmental control. Take as an example, the following dialogue offered by Charles Manson (1986):

A guy alone with car trouble can sit on the side of the road for a week and nobody will stop and give a hand, but let there be a girl and you can get plenty of help. With three girls, people are so anxious to stop and give you a hand that they have wrecks. Walking down a street or going into a party, restaurant, or nightclub, you immediately get some attention. And in the right spots, if you can play a little music and the girls join in, the party becomes yours. With things shaping up as they were, the party was mine everywhere we traveled. (p. 115)

As with all aspects of criminal thinking, the power orientation has its roots in development. From our discussion in Chapter 5, the reader may recall that the young child directs his attention to the external environment. With time and maturity, however, comes the dawning realization that self-control is the primary pathway to long-term success. The evolving lifestyle criminal, conversely, fails to appreciate the importance of self-control and continues centering his efforts on such superficial characteristics as charm in interacting with his environment. His is an extreme external orientation (Felson & Ribner, 1981; Henderson & Hewstone, 1984). This orientation brings with it a number of negative long-term consequences for the lifestyle criminal and subjugates him to the ravages of the zero state since no one can exert maximum control over their environment at all times. The lifestyle criminal endeavors to eliminate these zero state thoughts and feelings by power thrusting, although this is only a temporary solution to a problem that is chronic in nature.

In helping offenders change, it is important that we disrupt the zero state-power thrust cycle that the lifestyle criminal seems to enter into almost automatically. This is particularly challenging in working with incarcerated offenders since the prison environment is so conducive to power-oriented issues. There are constant reminders in any prison facility of an inmate's lack of control over his surroundings. The inmate is told when to rise in the morning, when to go to bed at night, when to eat, and is constantly subject to searches of his person and cell. This is certain to generate a great many zero state thoughts and feelings. What the high-rate offender needs to learn is to avoid power thrusting under such circumstances, even if these power thrusts are but thoughts, images, and fantasies. Once he has learned to cope with zero state feelings in ways other than power thrusting, the high-rate offender can start challenging other cognitive aspects of the criminal life-style. As he begins to place less value on external control and more of a premium on self-discipline, the individual will notice that zero state thoughts and feelings have less control over his behavior.

Sentimentality

Sentimentality, also known as the "Robin Hood syndrome" and "hell-of-a-fella fallacy," is a term initially coined by Yochelson and Samenow (1976) to describe the manner in which criminal personalities express tender feelings and aesthetic interests in a fickle and self-serving manner. The key to understanding sentimentality is realizing that we all have a need to view ourselves in a positive light and so tend to distort or gloss over the less desirable aspects of our behavior. Since the lifestyle criminal often has many more things to palliate than most people, his efforts in this regard will tend to galvanize around several different themes. He will engage in a variety of behaviors in an effort to convince both himself and others that he really is a "good person." Hence, he may buy ice cream cones for all the kids in the neighborhood or hand an old lady a few dollars as he flees a bank he just robbed, but these acts are more often a reflection of selfish motives than of genuine charity. Unlike love, which is other-centered and features sharing, sacrifice, and commitment, sentimentality is self-centered and geared toward making the individual feel good about himself (Walters & White, 1989c).

Those in the higher echelons of organized crime, particularly well-estab-lished groups like the Mafia or La Cosa Nostra, may not fit entirely within the framework of the criminal lifestyle since crime is treated by many of these persons as more of a business than a lifestyle. Such individuals do, nonethe-less, express a great deal of sentimentality as a means to defend against experiencing the full destructiveness of their illegal behavior. Take as an example several statements made by former Mafia hit man, turned federal informant, Jimmy "the Weasel" Fratianno (Demaris, 1981):

But you know Johnny [Roselli], I didn't bring it up—I could've reminded him (father), you know, that we could've done this together years ago. But I didn't want to embarrass him. He's an old man. (pp. 153-154)

I'm crazy about kids myself. They're so honest, you know, tell you exactly what they think, no bullshit. Everything's up front. (p. 168)

In fact, I even thought of clipping [killing] him. Then I thought, oh, Christ, this guy ain't worth it. I don't know, Johnny [Roselli]. I like his parents. Old-fashioned people, remind me of my mother and father. The old man talks Italian to me. (p. 279)

In an investigation into the thoughts of 80 white-collar criminals, Michael L. Benson (1985) discovered that normalcy and the denial of criminal intent, both of which reflect sentimentality, surfaced time and again. Normalcy was part of Ted Bundy's sentimental journey with interviewer James C. Dobson:

Basically I was a normal person. I wasn't some guy hanging out at bars or a bum or I wasn't a pervert in the sense that, you know, people look at somebody and say "I know there is something wrong with him, I can just tell." I was essentially a normal person. I had good friends; I lived a normal life; except for this one small, but very potent and very destructive segment of it, that I kept very secret and very close to myself and didn't let anybody know about it . . . . I wasn't perfect but, I want to be quite candid with you, I was OK. OK. I was. The basic humanity and basic spirit that God gave me was intact, but unfortunately it became overwhelmed at times. (Dobson, 1989)

Willie Sutton (1953) provides us with an example of sentimentality as a protestation of noninjury:

No matter what happened, we would never shoot anyone. If some rash employee did try to fight us, I'd shoot at him but purposely miss. I felt sure that one such shot would be enough to quiet the most courageous guard or clerk. After all, it was not their jewelry or their money they were protecting. In most cases, the boss himself wouldn't think of risking his life to protect property that was undoubtedly insured to the hilt. (pp. 116-117)

The reader should keep in mind that normalcy and statements of noninjury are designed to provide the lifestyle criminal with a positive view of himself. Other ways repeat offenders use sentimentality to feel good about themselves are by showing concern for their families; expressing tender emotions toward those who are helpless, hurt, or impaired (e.g., a small child, a dog with an injured leg); and sidetracking themselves with art, music, or literature (Walters &

White, 1989c). It is interesting how some convicts will spend hours profess-
ing love for their wives, girlfriends, and families when in fact most spent very
little time with these persons when they were living free in the community
and had the opportunity for unlimited contact. It is equally fascinating how
many offenders seem to lose interest in art or literature once they are released
from prison but then seemingly pick up right where they left off once they
return to the penitentiary. Sentimentality is clearly evident in several of
Charles Manson's (1986) remarks:

> Where the girls were concerned, I admit wanting to make it with anything that
> wore skirts, but not if it meant rape. For every girl I have ever made it with, there
> are ten times as many I have helped without thinking about sex . . . .I wasn't the
> culprit who lured them away, as everyone wants to believe. Never did I force
> anyone to join me, stay with me or succumb to my will. Things that were
> originally good and meant always to be good somehow turned around
> later . . . . Other than nailing a few under-age broads who were already giving
> their bodies to whoever they fancied, I kind of had the feeling of being a good
> samaritan because I was helping a lot of those kids on the streets. On more than
> a couple of occasions, if kids were down and out and had decided they would
> rather go back home, I took them back to their parents. (pp. 110-111)

In reading this section, one might well ask, "what's the harm in sentimentality? At least the offender is doing some good." The harm in sentimentality
is that it fosters continued violation of society's rules and the rights of others.
In other words, it is a necessary cognition for the perpetuation of the criminal
lifestyle since without sentimentality there would probably be no criminality.
This is based on the knowledge that if a person were to experience the true
destructiveness of their criminal lifestyle, they would be left with one of three
options: continued violation (which is unlikely given that even criminals are
bothered by actions that go against their principles), suicide, or change.
Because change requires time, practitioners need to be careful not to strip
away all vestiges of sentimentality before the offender is prepared to make
the necessary changes as this cognitive strategy does in fact serve a self-protective function. Only with proper intervention can sentimentality be con-
structively challenged and permanently put to rest.

Superoptimism

Superoptimism is an unrealistic appraisal of one's ability to achieve certain
criminal and noncriminal objectives (Yochelson & Samenow, 1976). As

Walters and White (1989c) assert, experience has taught the offender that he gets away with the vast majority of his criminal acts. Feeney (1986) describes the case of one, not so atypical, felon who owned but one conviction, though he had engaged in an excess of over one thousand arrestable crimes. Thus, while most lifestyle offenders realize that the law will eventually catch up with them should they continue their antisocial ways (Katz, 1979), they superoptimistically convince themselves that they will be able to evade capture "this time," for why else would they decide to commit the criminal act in the first place? Like all of the primary cognitive characteristics discussed in this chapter, superoptimism is a vital spoke in the wheel of events comprising the criminal lifestyle. Unlike a healthy attitude of confidence, which is geared toward establishing realistic goals, superoptimism allows the offender to function on the basis of his desires rather than on the basis of reality.

There is solid research evidence to suggest that high-rate offenders are less likely to consider apprehension a possibility than low-rate offenders or noncriminals (Henshel & Carey, 1975; Kraut, 1976; Teevan, 1975). Similarly, Peterson and Braiker (1980) found that recidivistic offenders recognize the risks associated with antisocial activity, but compared to noncriminals are more likely to overestimate their chances of eluding the authorities. Superoptimism is, in a sense, the criminal's Achilles' heel since it leaves him vulnerable to discovery and eventual arrest (Walters & White, 1989c). This was certainly the case with Richard Loeb and Nathan Leopold (1958) as represented in the words Loeb used to try to convince his crime partner of their invulnerability to apprehension:

> That'll be a snap, Nate. Nothing to it. You saw how smooth this all went off. Just like I told you over and over it would. Are you convinced now that it was easy as falling off a log? And the rest will be even easier. We don't have to get within a hundred yards of anybody. Just sit safe and snug in that alley and wait for them to toss us the dough. Those rubes have almost as much chance of catching up with us as a snowball in hell. What do you say, Butch, let's go out and have a few drinks after we make the phone call and mail the letter? (pp. 25-26)

As we know now, it wasn't as easy as Loeb made it out to be, and in the end they did get caught. However, it was superoptimism, as much as anything, that tripped them up.

The "just one more big score" fallacy also plays a role in superoptimism. Take, for instance, the following statement produced by Willie "the Actor" Sutton (1953):

Looking at the helpless child made me resolve that at least she would always have financial security. A few more real big jobs and I'd have enough money to take care of them for life. Was I being honest with myself? I don't know. (p. 116)

I would argue that Sutton was in fact basing his actions on a super-optimistic foundation. As is true of many aspects of the criminal lifestyle, the "just one more big score" notion is pure self-deception since there is always another job, scam, or bank more enticing than the last. Eventually, any criminal who thinks along such superoptimistic lines will find himself behind the eight ball, as did Willie Sutton shortly after he made the above statement.

Developmentally, we all possess a natural inclination toward the pursuit of pleasure and immediate gratification. In concert with this general orientation, the young child is preoccupied with fantasy and wish fulfillment, although maturity teaches us that in order to achieve something of value we must exert effort and make sacrifices. The lifestyle criminal fails to learn this particular lesson in life and finds the self-stimulation of superoptimism more rewarding than the long-term stability of a conventional lifestyle. He blocks rational alternatives, ignores personal obligations, and overlooks opportunities for establishing realistic goals, all in a self-indulgent effort to avoid responsibility for his actions. In fact, a study by Richard Siegel (1978) finds magical or superstitious logic to be a major characteristic of psychopathy in the sense that psychopathic criminals were less responsive to punishment than nonpsychopathic criminals and nonoffenders when the probability of punishment was uncertain (40% to 70%) but not when the probability became more certain (10% to 30% and 100%). This would seem to suggest that psychopaths, and possibly lifestyle criminals, are most prone to super-optimistic reactions in situations where the chances of detection and apprehension are uncertain or ambiguous.

Cognitive Indolence

Cognitive indolence captures the overall process of criminologic thought: lazy, easily bored, and undiscerning (Walters & White, 1989c). Hence, the lifestyle criminal is as lazy in thought as he is in action. Like water rolling downhill, he takes the path of least resistance, regardless of how self-defeating this path may be. In the words of Yochelson and Samenow (1976), the lifestyle criminal is more of a sprinter than a long-distance runner. It has been my experience that many lifestyle criminals spend the spoils of their criminal ventures with seeming abandon, in part because money acquired illegally holds less intrinsic value than income earned through hard work, but also because of their irresponsible, cognitively indolent thinking:

> The average box man doesn't save any money. I [Harry King] had a partner that anytime that we'd make a score, he'd fly to Reno and three days later he's broke. We're all suckers for somethin', I guess . . . . I know some box men that have to work every couple of weeks. Because they blow it in bars and stuff like that. Chicks. After making a score I may have planned a trip back East maybe . . . . (King, p. 40)

The lifestyle criminal seems to be continually searching for short-cuts designed to help him achieve unrealistic goals. Consequently, there is a fairly strong correlation between cognitive indolence and superoptimism, particularly in the "get rich quick" schemes dreamed up by some high-rate offenders (Walters & White, 1989c). However, these two features of criminal thinking need to be considered independently due to the fact that they touch upon two different, but related, aspects of a general trend in criminologic cognition. Another facet of cognitive indolence with ties to superoptimism arises when an offender with no prior entrepreneural experience states that his plans upon release from prison are to start up his own business. The ingenuousness of believing that one can count on opening up a successful business right out of prison with no prior experience in light of the fact that most new businesses fail within a year smacks of both superoptimism and cognitive indolence.

It has been hypothesized that the excitement-seeking tendencies of many repeat offenders are, in actuality, an attempt by the individual to compensate for an underactive internal world (Quay, 1977). In a study directed by Robert Hare (1982), it was determined that psychopathic offenders were less vigilant than nonpsychopathic offenders to conditioning when the experimental warning tone competed with the dialogue of a nightclub comic. This finding provides some support for the postulate that habitual criminals perform poorly on conditioning tasks because of an inability to filter out conflicting external stimuli which, in turn, may relate to weak cognitive control. It is therefore hypothesized that though the lifestyle criminal is capable of learning, he is so lacking in his ability to critically evaluate his own thinking that he often misses important learning opportunities.

Cognitive indolence can be expressed in a number of different ways but is often revealed in the general conversation of the lifestyle criminal. For example, the repeat offender is inclined to speak in broad, global terms as a means of avoiding the accountability that comes with specificity. Such individuals will avoid particulars, responding instead with vague generalities that serve to both frustrate and confuse the listener. Cognitive indolence is a major impediment to long-term change in that it fosters a sense of laziness that interferes with the lifestyle offender's ability to challenge irresponsible and irrational thoughts. It also leaves the lifestyle criminal vulnerable to detection and eventual arrest. Malcolm Braly (1976) discusses how cognitive indolence led to the first of his five incarcerations:

> I went back to the hotel. My suitcase was full of stolen clothes, some still in laundry wrappers. I considered getting rid of them. I considered leaving town, heading north into the woods and logging camps. Right then. Instead I went to sleep. . . . The sheriff woke me in the morning. He thought my story of a man who sat in hotel lobbies and spoke Latin was ridiculous and while this man, however unlikely, was real enough, when the sheriff turned out my suitcases the point became academic. He had his burglar. (pp. 35-36)

Cognitive indolence is also operating when criminals sidestep their responsibilities as if they never existed, preferring the easy way out of a personal obligation. Several of the offenders I have worked with in treatment have simply terminated their therapy sessions without a word to me as their therapist, acting as if I possessed the ability to know their intentions. This is similar to the way many of these same individuals handled the responsibilities of holding a job in the community, often quitting without notice. Frequently the only hint an employer has of the lifestyle criminal's intent to terminate employment is that the individual stops coming to work. Cognitive indolence of this type can be seen in Willie Sutton's (1953) approach to his mother and father's apparent disapproval of his criminal lifestyle:

> I hadn't seen my parents for some time. I'd stay away purposely because I had always found it impossible to lie to my mother. If she had asked me, "where are you working my son?" I would have found it almost impossible to give her a convincing answer. I thought it would be easier for me if I just stayed away from them. (p. 79)

Werner (1957) has hypothesized that a child's thinking goes from global, to differentiated, to integrated over the course of several years. Walters and White (1989c) speculate that the thinking of the typical lifestyle criminal remains at a fairly global level; while there may be some differentiation, full-fledged integration rarely takes place. I remind the reader, however, that this developmental anomaly is not typically the result of inferior intelligence but mirrors the criminal's choice to remain cognitively immature and avoid the responsibilities of adult life. However, what initially appears gratifying eventually creates a major problem for the offender. In the case of cognitive indolence, the lifestyle criminal becomes a victim of his own lazy, irresponsible thinking, which removes him even further from meaningful goal attainment and directs him toward fulfilling the evolving life decision to lose in ways that are dramatic and destructive to himself and others.

Discontinuity

Discontinuity refers to the fact that the lifestyle criminal fails to follow through on commitments and intentions over time. This particular cognitive characteristic is what leads to the fluctuations commonly observed in the lifestyle criminal's train of thought and activity that occur in concert with various environmental changes. Such vacillation can be observed in the writings of box man Harry King (1972):

> I have a terrific animosity towards the type of people they hire in these penitentiaries. They pay them the lowest salary there is and get the lowest type labor. . . . They gamble a great deal in the penitentiary to pass the time and they use cigarettes as a means of exchange, exclusively. I understand that they have changed to Pall Malls—it used to be Camels. But I was talking to a guy a while back, he told me that they smoke Pall Malls, and I never use Pall Malls. Why I don't know. (p. 125)

As the reader can see, King starts with a discussion of prison staff, which leads to an examination of the type of cigarettes available in prison, and ends with a highly personalized soliloquy. Unlike the ramblings of a psychotic or schizophrenic person, however, there are interconnections between the thoughts expressed by the average lifestyle criminal, though these linkages are arbitrary and largely idiosyncratic. It is important, then, that persons working clinically with criminal offenders note the difference between discontinuity and psychosis and take pains not to confuse them.

Discontinuity, while related to Yochelson's and Samenow's (1976) notion of fragmentation, differs from the latter in the sense that it is a more general term that I believe more adequately captures the lack of persistence, consistency, and realistic goal-setting seen in abundance in lifestyle criminals. Marks and Glaser (1980) report that criminal offenders contrast with "surfers," "hippies," and "straights" in being less dedicated to a particular life path and less realistic in appraising the future direction of their lives. One ex-offender informed these researchers that during adolescence he was "too involved with immediate survival to think ahead" (Marks & Glaser, 1980, p. 189). Although this attitude may be observed in many noncriminal youth, the lifestyle offender is unique in the sense that he refuses to respond to the societal demand for increased responsibility and accountability with increased age and continues to operate on the basis of adolescent exigencies well into adulthood.

The inconsistencies generated by discontinuity make both problem-solving and goal attainment difficult. Discontinuity interferes with problem-solving by focusing the individual on irrelevant concerns at the expense of the more salient aspects of a situation. Discontinuity also interferes with one's ability to attain goals by forming so many possibilities in a person's mind that he/she finds it difficult to follow up on any single alternative. Charles Manson (1986) describes the inconsistency that characterized his life: "I always had too many irons in the fire and never wanted to miss out on anything. It was my nature to start something with a ton of enthusiasm and drop it as soon as something else attracted my attention" (p. 184).

Inconsistency, along with an external orientation and compartmentalization tendencies, form a triumvirate of ruling influences in the discontinuity observed in the average lifestyle criminal. The external orientation displayed by high-rate offenders is as important to discontinuity as it is to cognitive indolence and the power orientation. Since the behavior of most lifestyle criminals is guided more by external, than internal, considerations, their actions will tend to fluctuate in response to changes occurring within the environment, much like a willow tree undulating in a strong wind. Although research on the internal-external orientation of criminal offenders is largely inconclusive (see Ross & Fabiano, 1985), there is at least a modicum of support for the notion that habitual offenders tend to be more externally, rather than internally, oriented (Buikhuisen, Bontekoe, Plas-Korenhoff, & van Buuren, 1984; Dean, 1979; Felson & Ribner, 1981). It follows therefore that the proposed external orientation of the lifestyle criminal has a great deal to do with the discontinuity of thought observed in such individuals.

A third major feature of discontinuity involves the developing ability to compartmentalize thoughts, feelings, and actions. Consequently, the lifestyle criminal handles the inconsistency in his own thoughts and actions by forcing these contradictory aspects of his experience into separate mental compartments. It would appear that compartmentalization played a protective role in Leopold's (1958) life following the murder of young Bobby Franks:

> This lateness of emotional maturing must be what made it possible for me to compartmentalize my mind and to shut the horror of what I had done into a

separate mental chamber where it would not influence my ordinary daily thoughts and actions. It seemed unreal then, not a part of my life at all. (p. 33)

Over time, however, this initially protective function of compartmentalization is replaced by a more insidious process whereby one begins to rely on discontinuity to function in an anxiety-free way. However, like so many of the cognitive features of lifestyle criminality, it reinforces the destructive aspects of the criminal lifestyle. Take as a case in point the thinking of serial murderer Ted Bundy:

The unique thing about how this worked Dr. Dobson is that I still felt, in my regular life, the full range of guilt and remorse about other things, and regret. . . . This compartmentalized, very well focused, very sharply focused, area where I, it was like a black hole. It was like, you know, like a crack and everything that fell into that crack just disappeared. (Dobson, 1989)

As Walters and White (1989c) mentioned in their original paper on criminal cognition, discontinuity appears to be the glue that holds the eight-part criminal thinking style together. Therefore, while I think it is essential that we stop short of elevating this feature to a position of predominance over the other seven factors, it is equally important that we appreciate the cohesive function that discontinuity serves within the framework of criminal thinking. In other words, this particular cognitive characteristic of high-rate criminality does a better job of perpetuating the criminal lifestyle than any of the other seven attributes. Discontinuity is also what makes intervening with the lifestyle criminal so difficult in the sense that it frequently interferes with one's ability to make good on initially positive intentions. Finally, discontinuity is most prominent in situations where environmental structure is low, and least problematic when environmental structure is high. Hence, while many offenders are able to maintain control over their discontinuity while confined in jail or prison, these tendencies become more conspicuous once the offender returns to the community.

Conclusion

Throughout this chapter, I have made reference to the irrationality of criminal thought, but how can we be so confident that these eight thinking patterns are in fact irrational? To examine this possibility, I will call upon an approach initially developed by Maxie Maultsby (1975), a procedure that

TABLE 6.1: Challenging the Eight Primary Cognitive Features of Lifestyle Criminality

| | Rational Challenge | | | | |
	Criterion 1	Criterion 2	Criterion 3	Criterion 4	Criterion 5
Mollification	No	No	No	No	No
Cutoff	N/A	No	No	No	No
Entitlement	No	No	Yes/No	No	No
Power Orientation	No	No	Yes/No	No	No
Sentimentality	No	N/A	No	No	Yes
Superoptimism	No	No	No	No	Yes
Cognitive Indolence	No	Yes/No	No	No	Yes/No
Discontinuity	No	No	No	No	No

Note: The five criteria read as follows: 1. Does it meet with objective reality? 2. Does it lead one to protect one's life and health? 3. Does it assist one in achieving one's long- and short-term goals? 4. Does it help one avoid conflict with others? 5. Does it make one feel the way one wants to feel?
Yes = satisfies criterion
No = fails to satisfy criterion
N/A = criterion not applicable to this particular thought pattern

makes use of five fundamental rules or criteria: (1) Does the thought meet with objective reality (is it based on verifiable facts)? (2) Does the thought lead one to protect one's life and health? (3) Does the thought assist one in achieving one's long- and short-term goals? (4) Does the thought help one avoid conflict with others? (5) Does the thought make one feel the way one wants to feel?

To be considered rational, the thought or thinking pattern must satisfy at least three of the five rules of rational thinking delineated above. We will therefore subject the eight criminologic thinking patterns to a rational analysis by asking these five questions of each pattern.

Beginning with mollification (see Table 6.1), we find that this cognitive pattern fails to satisfy a single one of the five criteria. Though some of the perceptions that feed into the mollification process may in fact be accurate, the overall attitude, the essential ingredient of mollification, that life should be fair and that unfairness justifies or mitigates one's own responsibility for certain criminal actions, is in violation of the objective reality criterion. Such an attitude is also likely to bring one into conflict with society (Criterion #4) and generate anger and resentment, which in turn may endanger one's health (Criterion #2) and emotional well-being (Criterion #5). Furthermore, by centering in on inequity and unfairness, the lifestyle criminal has little time to pursue his own goals, thereby falling short on Criterion #3 as well.

The cutoff is difficult to evaluate in terms of objective reality and is therefore scored N/A. However, there is little doubt that the cutoff violates the other four criteria in such a way as to lead us to the unequivocal conclusion that the cutoff is based on an irrational premise. As we saw in our discussion of the cutoff earlier in this chapter, the cognitive operation of rapidly eliminating deterrents to criminal action places one's life and physical health in jeopardy due to the fact that it allows one to engage in behaviors that are against one's better judgment. It also fails to make us feel the way we want (Criterion #5) since we are using the cutoff to trick ourselves into engaging in these criminal actions. The cutoff will most assuredly lead us into conflict with others (Criterion #4) and remove us further from nearly all of our long-term goals and a substantial portion of our short-term ones (Criterion #3).

Unlike the cutoff, entitlement would appear to aid us in our quest for personal goals since it allows us to adopt an attitude of privilege relative to those things we desire most. However, while entitlement may foster the achievement of short-term aims, it would seem to interfere with the realization of long-range goals. Entitlement therefore provides the lifestyle criminal with immediate gratification but is no more effective in procuring long-term satisfaction than either mollification or the cutoff. Moreover, the notion that one is entitled to violate the laws of society or infringe upon the personal rights of others in order to obtain immediate gratification—not to mention the belief that one "needs" certain luxuries in life—falls far short of satisfying the objective reality rule. This thinking pattern is also likely to bring one into conflict with others (Criterion #4) and is more self-destructive than self-protective (Criterion #2). In addition, entitlement does not lead the lifestyle criminal to feel the way he wants because he is so frequently thwarted in his efforts to realize his sense of prerogative.

Like entitlement, the power orientation is reasonably conducive to short-term gratification but frustrates one in the pursuit of long-range goals. In a related vein, the philosophical underpinnings of the power orientation (e.g., people are either strong or weak; strength is an exclusively physical phenomenon) are oversimplified, if not infantile, and certainly incongruent with objective reality. The power orientation is similar to the cutoff in that it generates angry feelings; so, like the cutoff, it neither protects our health (Criterion #2) nor makes us feel the way we want to feel (Criterion #5). To this last point I would like to add that the zero state, a common by-product of the power orientation, is perceived by nearly all lifestyle criminals as an extremely aversive experience. Almost by definition, the power orientation brings the lifestyle criminal into regular conflict with others (Criterion #4).

Sentimentality provides us with our first unequivocal "yes" response to any of the five criteria. Since sentimentality is a self-centered attempt by the high-rate offender to think well of himself despite his irresponsible, intrusive actions, the individual does, in fact, feel the way he wants to feel. As such, Criterion #5 is clearly satisfied. By the same token, this belief system is highly inconsistent with objective reality in the sense that the lifestyle criminal is not the nice guy he tries to portray through various sentimental maneuvers (Criterion #1). Moreover, sentimentality is antithetical to the development of realistic goals (Criterion #3) and is liable to bring one into conflict with others (Criterion #4) since it perpetuates the criminal lifestyle by deceiving the individual into believing that there is no need to change his behavior. The protection of life and health (Criterion #2) does not appear to be a relevant rule within the context of sentimentality.

Superoptimism probably violates the criterion of objective reality more than any of the other seven criminal thinking patterns. By believing that he can do and get away with just about anything and everything, the lifestyle criminal defies the laws of reality, reason, and good sense. Such an attitude not only fails to satisfy the objective reality criterion, but it will likely place one's physical safety in jeopardy (Criterion #2), not to mention the fact that it creates a great deal of conflict with others (Criterion #4). Furthermore, rather than prepare one for success, superoptimism sets one up for failure since the goals it establishes are unrealistic and generally unattainable (Criterion #3). Like sentimentality, however, superoptimism provides the criminal with immediate pleasure and so satisfies Criterion #5 to the extent that sentimentality is largely a reflection of hedonistic self-involvement.

Turning our attention to cognitive indolence, we see that it receives equivocal ratings on two criteria (#2 and #5). Thus, while the lazy, noncritical mentation associated with cognitive indolence may lead the lifestyle criminal to protect his life and feel the way he wants to in the short run, it also tends to put his physical health at risk while engendering uncomfortable consequences for the individual over the long haul in much the same manner as entitlement and the power orientation receive equivocal ratings on Criterion #3. In the end, however, cognitive indolence scores out as irrational since there is no evidence that it is consonant with objective reality in the sense that it is a philosophy based more on opinion than verifiable fact; strong evidence indicates that it interferes with goal attainment; and there is every likelihood that it will bring the person into conflict with others.

Discontinuity would appear to flunk the five rules for rational thinking across the board. First, the premise upon which this thinking pattern is based has no foundation in objective reality and so fails the first criterion miserably. Instead of leading a person to protect his or her life and health, discontinuity would likely place one's physical well-being in jeopardy to the extent that this thinking pattern interferes with one's ability to avoid the same self-destructive predicaments that the individual has fallen victim to time and again. Discontinuity is by definition inimical to effective problem-solving and the development of meaningful goals (Criterion #3) and, like all of the thinking characteristics, is liable to bring one into conflict with others, as well as society (Criterion #4). Finally, discontinuity creates confusion, conflict, and frustration for the individual, which is certainly not how most people want to feel (Criterion #5).

In comparing the eight criminologic thinking patterns against the five rules for rational thinking, it should be obvious that none of the eight is based on a rational understanding. Rather, they are subjective, poorly organized, and geared toward immediate gratification at the expense of long-term success and satisfaction. Accordingly, this eight-part thinking style serves to fulfill the lifestyle criminal's loser's life decision. In fact, it is a perfect formula for such an outcome since what else but failure should we anticipate from someone whose thinking is unrealistic, self-justifying, fragmented, and geared toward immediate gratification? It is hoped that this discussion will help the reader understand how the thinking style associated with lifestyle criminality consummates a process that began with the choices the individual made relative to various life conditions, a decision that has serious repercussions for the individual as well as society.

Before concluding this section on theory, I believe it is critical that the interrelatedness of the three Cs be made more explicit. Throughout this section, I have highlighted the role of the condition-choice-cognition sequence in the development of lifestyle criminality, and certainly this would appear to be an accurate portrayal from a purely theoretical standpoint. In reality, however, while it follows the decisions one makes relative to the early life tasks, the incipient thinking style effects and colors some of the decisions and choices one makes within the context of the later life tasks. Moreover, thought, no matter how primitive, plays a central role in behavior from about the age of two on and so is a necessary prerequisite for choice. Consequently, we are left with a mass of interacting effects that culminate in a thinking style that furthers the criminal lifestyle in a manner that is both dramatic and self-defeating. In the next chapter, we will explore how the lifestyle of crime, and the thinking errors that subserve it, can be identified, evaluated, and changed.

7. Assessment and Change

Developing and understanding an idea is one thing, but applying that idea in ways that are coherent, consistent, and meaningful is quite another matter. I have noticed in the group sessions I have conducted with chronic offenders that while many can understand the concepts, very few are able to effectively apply the principles. Application is difficult enough when one is attempting to assemble a child's bicycle from a confusing set of instructions, solve a complicated word problem with a foundational mathematical equation, or communicate with the denizens of Tijuana on the basis of knowledge gleaned through an entry-level course in Spanish. Application-spectrum problems increase two- or three-fold when the subject of application is oneself and the behavior we are targeting for change has existed for 20 or 30 years. The principal focus of this chapter will be on the issues of assessment and change as they relate directly to the criminal lifestyle.

Assessment

Assessment involves an evaluation of individuals, usually by means of procedures that describe behavior with the aid of a numerical scale or category system (Cronbach, 1970). Assessment, considered along either scientific or practical lines, rests on the assumption that people exhibit reasonably consistent and enduring patterns of behavior, sometimes referred to as traits. This is an assumption that has been challenged rather vehemently by scholars within, as well as outside, the field of psychology. Walter Mischel (1968), a psychology professor at Stanford University, calls into question personality constructs and the measurement of these constructs. He is more inclined to look at the situational context of behavior and what he calls person variables. This outlook is very much like the position adopted in this book, in which criminal behavior is viewed as a consequence of the dynamic interaction taking place between a myriad of person and situation variables.

What we are doing when we conduct an evaluation on an individual criminal offender, then, is measuring the residual outcome of the person × situation interaction and the choices the individual makes relative to this interaction.

Mischel's point is well taken and one that is probably quite popular with sociologically minded scholars. Clinical psychologists, on the whole, tend to overlook the importance of the situational context in administering their psychological tests. It behooves us to consider this context since in my own clinical work with criminal offenders, I have come to realize that there exist behaviors, which if observed in the community would be indicative of severe psychopathology, yet when seen inside the walls of a penitentiary, are more the norm than the exception. The situational context can have a more direct bearing on behavior as suggested by the observation that criminal offenders normally respond best in more highly structured milieus. Environmental assessment should therefore be an integral part of our evaluation, although with a few notable exceptions (i.e., Moos, 1975), this is an area that has been underinvestigated. With this in mind, we shall examine three procedures and a general model that may hold promise of assisting us in our efforts to assess persons who approach crime as a lifestyle, although we must always be mindful of the contextual features of our evaluation.

Minnesota Multiphasic Personality Inventory

The Minnesota Multiphasic Personality Inventory (MMPI) is the most widely investigated objective measure of personality currently available to clinicians and researchers (Lubin, Larsen, Matarazzo, & Seever, 1985). Starting with a sample of over 1,000 true-false items, Hathaway and McKinley (1940) constructed the MMPI by contrasting various groups of psychiatric patients with a control group of 724 friends and relatives of patients at the University Hospitals in Minneapolis. In the end, Hathaway and McKinley had an inventory comprised of four validity [*?* (Cannot Say), *L* (Lie), *F* (False), and *K* (Defensiveness)] and nine clinical [*1* (Hypochondriasis: Hs), *2* (Depression: D), *3* (Hysteria: Hy), *4* (Psychopathic Deviate: Pd), *5* (Masculinity-Femininity: Mf), *6* (Paranoia: Pa), *7* (Psychasthenia: Pt), *8* (Schizophrenia: Sc), and *9* (Hypomania: Ma)] scales plotted using *T*-scores with a mean of 50 and standard deviation of 10. Several years later, Scale *0* (Social Introversion: Si: Evans & McConnell, 1941) was added to the standard MMPI profile. Hundreds of studies and research investigations are published each year on the MMPI, the results of which frequently lend support to the utility of this procedure for clinical, as well as research, purposes (Dahlstrom, Welsh, & Dahlstrom, 1972; Graham, 1987; Greene, 1980).

Scale 4 (Pd) was normed on a group of male and female delinquents, and it should therefore come as no surprise that it also happens to be routinely elevated on the MMPI records of adult and juvenile offenders. In a large scale follow-up of adolescents originally administered the MMPI in the ninth grade, Hathaway and Monachesi (1963) discovered that boys with subsequent histories of criminal involvement scored significantly higher on Scales 4 (Pd), 8 (Sc), and 9 (Ma) and significantly lower on Scales 2 (D), 5 (Mf), and 0 (Si) relative to noncriminal boys. James Panton (1958) examined over 1,300 MMPI profiles of offenders confined in the North Carolina penal system and ascertained a mean profile, as well as many individual profiles, with Scale 4 scores elevated above a T-score of 70[1]. However, there were no MMPI differences when subjects were broken down by crime category (white collar, aggravated assault, robbery/burglary, property theft, sexual perversion, sexual assault), a finding subsequently replicated by Quinsey, Arnold, and Pruesse (1980).

Although Scale 4 does not appear to differentiate between crime categories, it is nonetheless effective in making other types of determinations. Walters (1985), for instance, notes that young, male military prisoners satisfying the Psychiatric Diagnostic Interview (PDI: Othmer, Penick, & Powell, 1981) criteria for a diagnosis of Antisocial Personality achieved significantly higher scores on Scale 4, the only moderating effect being that property offenders achieved higher scores on this MMPI scale than individuals serving sentences for more violent crimes. Likewise, Hare (1985) witnessed a moderately strong correlation between scores on Scale 4, on the one hand, and a DSM-III diagnosis of Antisocial Personality Disorder and checklist rating of psychopathy on the other. Holland, Beckett, and Levi (1981) discerned a modest, but significant, elevation on Scale 4 in violent offenders, while Erikson and Roberts (1966) report that inmates with poor records of institutional adjustment achieved significantly higher Scale 4 scores than inmates exhibiting good institutional adjustment. Though much of the research on Scale 4 has been conducted using white samples, Elion (1974) found this scale to be effective in discriminating between delinquent and nondelinquent black subjects as well. Finally, the cross-national validity of the Scale 4-criminality connection is corroborated by the results of one study in which Scale 4 elevations were commonplace on the MMPI protocols of a group of Japanese delinquents (Ono, 1980).

It is common practice for clinical psychologists to interpret the two most highly elevated MMPI scales on a profile in combination. As one might anticipate, Scale 4 plays a prominent role in all of the high-point combinations associated with serious criminality. A spike 4 profile exists as a conspicuous peak on Scale 4, with all of the other clinical scales being below a T-score of 70. Greene (1980) characterizes persons achieving this profile type as impulsive, rebellious, egocentric, and lacking in insight. Research conducted on Veterans' Administration inpatients reveals that one-half of the subjects achieving a spike 4 profile exhibited seriously assaultive behavior, and 65% were heavy consumers of alcohol (Gilberstadt & Duker, 1965). In a factor analysis of MMPIs generated by a large sample of federal inmates, the group achieving the spike 4 profile evidenced a propensity toward hedonism and relatively poor institutional adjustment (Megargee & Bohn, 1979). Finally, King and Kelley (1977) observed legal problems in college students achieving the spike 4 profile, with arrests for shoplifting, possession of a controlled substance, grand larceny, assault, and murder being noted.

MMPI profiles characterized by simultaneous elevations on Scales 4 (Pd) and 3 (Hy), particularly when Scale 4 exceeds Scale 3, reveal a pattern of denial and rigid overcontrol (Walters, Greene, & Solomon, 1982). Davis and Sines (1971) found this high-point pair in the more violent, acting-out members of state hospital, university-based medical center, and state prison populations. Persons and Marks (1971) observed hostility and violence in the behavior of subjects obtaining the 4-3 pattern, although Buck and Graham (1978) were unable to replicate these findings. The relationship between the 4-3 high-point pattern and Megargee, Cook, and Mendelsohn's (1967) Over-controlled-Hostility (O-H) scale has been a topic of some research investigation, the results of which suggest a strong degree of correlation between the two (Walters, Greene, & Solomon, 1982; Walters, Solomon, & Greene, 1982).

A third high-point combination frequently observed in persons owning records of serious criminality involves the dual elevation of MMPI Scales 4 (Pd) and 8 (Sc). Since Scale 8 tends to measure cognitive confusion and bizarre mentation, it is not surprising that persons achieving the 4-8/8-4 high-point pair combination typically engage in crimes that are poorly planned and often bizarre or violent in nature (Greene, 1980). Sexual acting out is frequently part of the picture when offenders obtaining the 4-8 pattern are studied (Dahlstrom et al., 1972; Erickson, Luxenberg, Walbek, & Seeley, 1987). Hence, this high-point pair has been observed in child molesters (McCreary, 1975; Hall, Maiuro, Vitaliano, & Proctor, 1986), rapists (Armentrout & Hauer, 1978; Rader, 1977), and exhibitionists (Moncrieff & Pearson, 1979; Rader, 1977). Forgac and Michaels (1982) mention that exhibitionists who commit crimes in addition to exposure score significantly higher on Scales

F, 4, and *8* than exhibitionists arrested for exposure exclusively, although a multivariate analysis of the data from this study failed to identify a significant overall MMPI difference between subjects in these two groups.

A final MMPI high-point pair observed with a fair degree of regularity in offender populations shows simultaneous peaks on Scales *4* (Pd) and *9* (Ma). The *4-9/9-4* high-point combination is nearly always associated with acting out in ways that bring the individual into conflict with his or her environment (Carson, 1969). Marks, Seeman, and Haller (1974) found a history of juvenile delinquency, substance abuse, and sexual promiscuity and current indications of immaturity, hostility, and manipulativeness in psychiatric patients exhibiting the *4-9/9-4* pattern. Both Marks et al. (1974) and Gilberstadt and Duker (1965) witnessed a modal diagnosis of Antisocial Personality/Sociopathy in individuals achieving this particular high-point combination. The *4-9/9-4* composite has been observed in persons displaying marital conflict and child abuse difficulties (Paulson, Afifi, Thomason, & Chaleff, 1974), chronic drug and alcohol abuse problems (Loper, Kammeier, & Hoffmann, 1973), and delinquent patterns of adjustment (McCreary, 1975).

Lifestyle Criminality Screening Form

The Lifestyle Criminality Screening Form (LCSF: Walters, White, & Denney, in press) was developed in an effort to derive a reliable and valid measure of the theoretical construct, lifestyle criminality. The 14 items comprising this scale (see Figure 7.1) were selected on the basis of their presumed ability to tap the four primary behavioral dimensions of the criminal lifestyle (i.e., irresponsibility, self-indulgence, interpersonal intrusiveness, social rule breaking). In the initial cross-validation of this scale, the LCSF successfully discriminated between two groups of offenders hypothesized to contain differing percentages of lifestyle criminals—25 prisoners incarcerated in a maximum-security federal penitentiary (high percentage of lifestyle criminals) and 25 inmates housed in a minimum-security federal prison camp (low percentage of lifestyle criminals)—with a high degree of accuracy ($R^2 = .82$: Walters et al., in press). The internal consistency of this instrument seems adequate (alpha coefficient = .84: Walters et al., in press), and the inter-rater agreement (total score: range = 0 to 22) was found to be adequate in two separate investigations (.96 in Walters et al., in press; .93 in Walters, Revella, & Baltrusaitis, 1990).

One of the guiding tenets of the lifestyle theory of criminal behavior is that habitual felons function with the least amount of difficulty when

Directions: After reviewing a subject's background, complete this form by inserting the appropriate number (in parentheses next to the box) for responses suggested by information in the subject's file. If there is no information available for a particular question, then leave the boxes blank, although more than one unanswered question per section may result in unreliable results. Once the evaluator has completed this form, numbers should be totaled for each of the four sections. A total section score of 2 indicates a *probable* diagnosis and a score of *3* a *definite* diagnosis of the lifestyle characteristic (i.e., irresponsibility, self-indulgence, interpersonal intrusiveness, social rule breaking) being measured by that particular section.

Section I. *Irresponsibility*

A. Failed to provide support for at least one biological child.
- Yes   ☐ (1)
- No   ☐ (0)

B. Terminated formal education prior to graduating from high school.
- Yes   ☐ (1)
- No   ☐ (0)

C. Longest job ever held.
- Less than six months   ☐ (2)
- At least 6 months but less than 2 years   ☐ (1)
- Two or more years   ☐ (0)

D. Terminated from job for irresponsibility or quit for no apparent reason.
- Two or more times   ☐ (2)
- Once   ☐ (1)
- None reported   ☐ (0)

Total Irresponsibility   ☐

Section II. *Self-Indulgence*

A. History of drug or alcohol abuse.
- Yes   ☐ (2)
- No   ☐ (0)

B. Marital background
- Two or more prior divorces   ☐ (2)
- One prior divorce/more than 1 separation   ☐ (1)
- Single but with illegitimate child   ☐ (1)
- Married, but no divorces/single, no children   ☐ (0)

C. Physical appearance (check only one box).
- Tattoos on face or neck   ☐ (2)
- Tattoos up and down arms   ☐ (2)

Figure 7.1. The Lifestyle Criminality Screening Form

Presence of one or several tattoos
    If black   ☐ (2)
    If white   ☐ (1)
    No tattoos   ☐ (0)

Total Self-Indulgence   ☐

Section III. *Interpersonal Intrusiveness*
  A. Confining offense.
    Intrusive (e.g., murder, rape, robbery, breaking & entering, assault)   ☐ (1)
    Nonintrusive (e.g., drugs, embezzlement)   ☐ (0)
  B. History of prior arrests for intrusive behavior (excluding the confining offense).
    Three or more   ☐ (2)
    One or two   ☐ (1)
    None   ☐ (0)
  C. Use of weapon or threatened use of weapon during commission of confining offense.
    Yes   ☐ (1)
    No   ☐ (0)
  D. Physical abuse of significant others (primarily family members).
    Yes   ☐ (1)
    No   ☐ (0)

Total Interpersonal Intrusiveness   ☐

Section IV. *Social Rule Breaking*
  A. Prior arrests (excluding confining offense).
    Five or more   ☐ (2)
    Two to four   ☐ (1)
    One or none   ☐ (0)
  B. Age at time of first arrest.
    14 years of age or younger   ☐ (2)
    Older than 14 by younger than 19   ☐ (1)
    19 years of age or older   ☐ (0)
  C. History of being a behavioral/management problem at school.
    Yes   ☐ (1)
    No   ☐ (0)

Total Social Rule Breaking   ☐

Figure 7.1. (continued)

environmental structure is at its highest. It would stand to reason that the possibility of a relationship between lifestyle criminality and institutional adjustment might be moderated by such factors as environmental structure. In testing this hypothesis, Walters (1989) ascertained that the congruence between lifestyle patterns of criminality and disciplinary adjustment approached zero in a highly structured setting (maximum-security federal penitentiary), but that high LCSF scores were associated with poor institutional adjustment when examined in a less structured milieu (minimum-security federal prison camp).

If lifestyle criminals have problems adjusting in loosely structured situations, it follows that they should have particular difficulty functioning problem-free in the community. This is exactly what Walters et al. (1990) discovered when they examined the community adjustment of 79 federal parolees and probationers over a period of one year. Not only did the LCSF successfully predict future technical and criminal violations ($r = .36$), but it did so at a rate that was independent of the individual contributions of such traditional indices as age and marital status. Viewed side-by-side, the results of Walters et al. (1990) combined with Walters's (1989) earlier findings would seem to suggest that persons achieving high LCSF ratings experience problems with self-control and self-discipline that are most clearly evident when the person is placed in environments that are less than maximally structured.

Problem Oriented Survey

The Problem Oriented Survey (POS) consists of five conflict situations (see Figure 7.2) designed to elicit the eight primary cognitive features of lifestyle criminality: mollification, cutoff, entitlement, power orientation, sentimentality, superoptimism, cognitive indolence, and discontinuity. Once the subject formulates his or her response to a question, the examiner poses a follow-up question (from a pool of two or three possible queries), the intent being to evoke more information about the individual's particular style of thinking. Although still at a conceptual level of development, the POS may be capable of providing us with increased insight into the thinking of persons who have chosen the criminal way of life.

Although at this point, the POS is nothing more than an interesting idea in search of verification, a review of the type of responses it elicits in groups of habitual offenders shows that it is a technique worthy of further exploration.

INSTRUCTIONS: Please respond to each of these situations as you believe you would in real life. In addition to reporting what it is you believe you would do, be sure to discuss what you believe you would be thinking in each particular situation.

1. Imagine for the moment that you and your young son, age 4, are at a local park. Your son is playing on a set of monkey bars, and you are sitting on a park bench approximately 40 yards away. Imagine next that your attention is drawn to a shabby-looking individual who approaches your son. You get up and walk toward the monkey bars but before you can reach your son, this stranger tries to abduct (take away by force) your son. In the struggle, your son falls to the ground. You are now within 10 yards of both the stranger and your son, and you notice that your son is injured, possibly unconscious. The stranger, seeing you approach, starts to flee. **What are you going to do?**

2. Imagine you are taking a college course with an eventual goal of earning a bachelor's degree. The course is not all that exciting, and you don't particularly like the instructor. However, you need this course to graduate. Imagine further than you are several weeks behind in your reading assignments and that your employer informs you that you will have to work late (until 2:00 A.M.) tonight, and tomorrow night you promised some friends you would help them out with a party they had been planning for some time. **What are you going to do?**

3. Imagine you are at work and notice a coworker stealing money from the cash register. Several days later, your boss calls you into his office and accuses you of taking the money. He states that unless the money is returned by the next day, you are fired. **What are you going to do?**

4. Imagine you are drinking at a local tavern or bar and get more drunk or intoxicated than you had planned on. You get into your car and a half-mile down the road you hit an elderly man as he is walking across the street. There is no one else around. **What are you going to do?**

5. Imagine you are waiting in line in a grocery store with your wife or girlfriend. You are already late for a dinner engagement with friends. Just then, a big, burly individual pushes his way into line directly in front of you. **What are you going to do?**

Figure 7.2. The Problem Oriented Survey

Power orientation, superoptimism, and discontinuity are clearly present in the response of one felon to Question #1:

The guy starts to run? I would break his neck. I used to run track. I would run him down and break his neck. No joking or jiving. I would put his neck in my arms and break it. If I couldn't get his neck, I'd break his arm first. (Follow-up question: "What happens if after 50 yards you catch up to him and he turns around and pulls a knife on you?"): If I had a jacket on, I'd wrap it around my left hand. If I have a gun on me, I'd shoot him. If not, I'd wrap the coat around my arm and go for him. I don't know if you know about martial arts, but most people don't know how to hold a knife in their hand.

Cognitive indolence and mollification can be observed in a second offender's reaction to Question #4:

Well, first I'd take all this into view. See if he dented my car. If he dented up the car, I'd probably stay behind and see if he's alright, see if he's alive. If he is, then I'd call the ambulance. Then I'd remove the beer and alcohol out of the car. If he didn't dent up the car, I'd keep going. Shouldn't have been walking in the street, anyway. Shouldn't have jumped out there like that. Another one bites the dust, that's the way it goes. (Follow-up question: "What if later on you learn that this man dies and leaves a wife and invalid mother without any means of support?"): By then I'd probably have forgot all about it and don't even worry about it.

Though these responses demonstrate the potential utility of the POS for both research and clinical purposes, there is a need for research into the reliability, validity, and correlates of this performance measure of criminal ideation.

The Lifestyle Model of Assessment

In presenting their ideas on assessment, Walters and White (in press) discuss three systems of evaluation: lifestyle analysis, developmental assessment, and cognitive profiling. These three systems comprise the lifestyle model of assessment and will be discussed in turn.

Lifestyle Analysis: The initial step in the assessment sequence is the lifestyle analysis, which asks whether our subject satisfies the four primary behavioral characteristics of lifestyle criminality: irresponsibility, self-indulgence, interpersonal intrusiveness, and social rule breaking. It would seem prudent of the evaluator to begin with the LCSF since this instrument was originally conceived, developed, and normed on a group of offenders who clearly approached crime as a lifestyle. A score of 6 or higher on the LCSF suggests the possibility of lifestyle criminality, while a score of 10 or higher indicates probable lifestyle criminality. The offender should also attain a score of at least 1 on each of the four LCSF subscales (Irresponsibility, Self-Indulgence, Interpersonal Intrusiveness, Social Rule Breaking) since the theory postulates that all four characteristics are present in lifestyle criminals.

Unfortunately, written sources of information are sometimes so incomplete that we must rely on behavioral observation and self-report data, in addition to the LCSF, in conducting a lifestyle analysis.

Developmental Assessment: Once it has been established that our client fits the behavioral criteria for a diagnosis of lifestyle criminality, the next step in the sequence is to place him within the developmental scheme presented in Chapter 5. As the reader may recall, there are four stages in the development of the criminal lifestyle: the pre-criminal stage, early criminal stage, advanced criminal stage, and burnout/maturity stage. In gauging an offender's developmental status, we consider not only his age, but also the pattern of primary and secondary organizing motives as expressed in his current actions. As Walters and White (in press) mention, accounting for the subject's skills and personal deficits in various areas (educational, occupational, social) and developing them into an integrated program of rehabilitation should also be part of the developmental assessment.

Cognitive Profiling: Although it is hypothesized that habitual lawbreakers possess all eight of the primary cognitive features of lifestyle criminality, there are differences in the overall pattern of these characteristics. Thus, the power orientation may be predominant in the thinking of one offender, while cognitive indolence is central to the cognitions of a second felon. There are several ways by which we might construct a cognitive profile, the simplest being to informally rate our subjects on the eight criminal thinking patterns. The POS is also designed to provide a cognitive profile of sorts, although this instrument is still in a preliminary stage of development. In light of the fact that the POS does not properly survey all eight of the primary cognitive characteristics of lifestyle criminality, a four-choice, 32-item personality inventory designed to yield a more complete cognitive profile (and provide scores on all eight characteristics) is currently being developed.

The "single pill dilemma" is a therapy technique that may be useful in generating a cognitive profile. The therapist using this technique will casually inform the offenders in his or her group that a gas, poisonous only to lifestyle criminals, has just been released through the air ducts and that all lifestyle criminals in the room have but one hour to live. The therapist goes on to advise the group that he or she has an antidote, but only enough for one person, and so solicits input from the group as to who should receive this "single pill." The type of responses this exercise elicits are fascinating and often provide a wealth of insight into how individual offenders structure their thinking around the eight primary cognitive features of lifestyle criminality. Perhaps it goes without saying, but before implementing such a procedure, the therapist should have established a reasonable degree of trust with group members and should refrain from using this exercise with subjects who are actively delusional and may truly believe that a poisonous gas has been released into the room.

Change

If we were to expand the 3 Cs by one, our fourth C would most assuredly be change. Relative to our present discussion, change involves a shift in behavior away from the irresponsibility, self-indulgence, interpersonal intrusiveness, and chronic rule breaking that characterize the criminal lifestyle. This is a truly challenging task for someone who has spent the better part of 20 plus years thinking and acting in ways that are antagonistic to the conventional social order. As such, the thinking style arising from the lifestyle criminal's decision to reject the norms and conventions of society is a prime target for intervention. Even though this thinking pattern occurs subsequent to the choices one makes relative to the various life conditions, they mediate the lifestyle criminal's daily behavior and will be referred to frequently in our discussions on change.

"Nothing Works:" Fact or Fiction

Robert Martinson became a controversial figure in criminal science circles with his assertion that there was no good evidence for the efficacy of various educational, vocational, and treatment programs in reducing recidivism. In summarizing the results of a 1,400-page manuscript commissioned by the New York State Governor's Committee on Criminal Offenders which he co-authored with Douglas Lipton and Judith Wilks, Martinson (1974) concluded that "it may be . . . that there is a more radical flaw in our present strategies—that education, at its best, or that psychotherapy at its best, cannot overcome or ever appreciably reduce, the powerful tendency for offenders to continue in criminal behavior" (p. 46). After acknowledging the serious methodological errors extant in available research on the rehabilitation issue, Martinson proceeds to inform us that there is no evidence that educational/vocational training, individual and group counseling, environmental manipulations, medical treatment, or parole/probation supervision are effective in reducing recidivism. What is left unsaid, however, is that there is no good evidence against the efficacy of rehabilitation, either. Five years later,

Martinson (1979) denounced the "nothing works" argument and acknowledged that under specific circumstances, successful rehabilitation was possible.

The literature reviewed by Martinson and his colleagues was incontrovertibly replete with methodological shortcomings. In a review of 236 post-1975 studies surveying the characteristics of various correctional programs, Bernstein (1975) noticed that only 59% of the studies employed randomized samples, only 25% utilized experimental or quasi-experimental research designs, and only 35% reported the results of statistical analyses. Gendreau and Ross (1979) examined research published between 1973 and 1978 and restricted their review to studies that employed an experimental or quasi-experimental design, reported the outcome of data analyses, and included a follow-up period of at least 6 months. The results of this review led Gendreau and Ross to conclude that rehabilitative programs could, in fact, lower the rate of recidivism for a number of criminal groups. These same two investigators (Gendreau & Ross, 1987) probed the literature published between 1981 and 1987 and again found support for the efficacy of a variety of different procedures with delinquents, sex offenders, and drug abusing felons, although research examining intervention programs with violent, habitual offenders, the group whose actions most closely parallel the behavior of the typical lifestyle criminal, is mixed.

In their 1987 publication, Gendreau and Ross surveyed the results of several meta-analyses. A meta-analysis consists of a quantitative analysis of a body of research and is viewed by some as a major methodological advance in that it forces the investigator to evaluate the literature more carefully than is often the case with qualitative reviews (Fiske, 1983; Glass, McGraw, & Smith, 1981). Davidson, Gottschalk, Gensheimer, and Mayer (1984) found small, yet significant, effect sizes in a meta-analysis of rehabilitative research on delinquents, while Garrett's (1985) meta-analysis, which considered 111 studies, ascertained somewhat larger effect sizes—behavioral, cognitive, and family interventions yielding better outcomes than psychodynamic and life skills approaches. In what is probably the most comprehensive meta-analysis of juvenile rehabilitative programs to date, Lipsey (1986) uncovered results that were largely consistent with the findings attained by Davidson et al. and Garrett. Whether the data are examined qualitatively (standard review) or quantitatively (meta-analysis), there appears to be little support for the pessimistic conclusion that "nothing works."

Despite the problems with Martinson's original conclusion, there is still value in his review. One issue brought to light by this review is that several of the negative results Martinson and his colleagues observed may have been more a function of the manner in which the programs were implemented than a direct outcome of the programs themselves. Martinson cites a study directed by Zivan (1966) in which staff hostility toward a vocational/occupational training program appeared to sabotage the outcome before the program ever got off the ground. In an investigation of an adult vocational training program, Gearhart, Keith, and Clemmons (1967) observed a lack of overall relationship between vocational training and recidivism but added that when trainees found a job related to their training, a counter-recidivism effect was noted. In addressing this issue, Martinson (1974) concedes that some skill development programs may fail "because what they teach bears so little relationship to an offender's subsequent life outside the prison" (p. 27).

An additional issue raised by the Martinson review is that offenders judged by their therapists/counselors to be "successfully treated" (Persons, 1967) or "amenable to treatment" (Adams, 1961) experienced better outcomes than no-treatment controls, although the inclusion of "unsuccessfully treated" and "unamenable" subjects in these data analyses tended to confound the results to the point where there appeared to be no treatment effect whatsoever. This is an issue that needs to be considered in future research examining rehabilitative programs and recidivism. At this point in time, however, the overwhelming preponderance of evidence suggests that when training/rehabilitative programs are properly implemented, stocked with motivated subjects, and dedicated to teaching relevant skills/attitudes, the conclusion that "nothing works" has been greatly exaggerated and is largely inconsistent with available data.

Stimulating the Change Process

Confronted with a cup of water filled to the mid-point, a pessimist will tend to view the cup as half empty, while an optimist will see it as half full. When it comes to inspecting recidivism rates, the pessimist will take heed of the fact that approximately 62% of all offenders are rearrested on felony or serious misdemeanor charges within three years of their release from prison (Beck & Shipley, 1989). The optimist is quick to point out, however, that this means 38% of all offenders remain free of serious legal entanglements for three years and, in many cases, longer. The latter attitude is essential for effective application of change methodologies and finds support in the fact that some forms of treatment reduce recidivism by as much as 30% to 74%, with outcomes that may last as long as 15 years post-treatment (see Ross, Fabiano, & Ewles, 1988). Ergo, while we cannot force someone to change against his or her will, we can most certainly stimulate or facilitate the change process through implementation of certain programs. We will explore three such programs here.

In introducing their model of treatment intervention, Yochelson and Samenow (1985) emphasized modification of the 52 thinking errors they observed with a high degree of regularity in their sample of "criminal personalities." Wolfgarth (1976) also sees the value of taking a cognitive approach in working with habitual criminals, and Ruby (1984) advocates the use of Rational Behavior Therapy (RBT: Maultsby, 1975) principles with a wide spectrum of criminal offenders. Implementation of one cognitive training program, the Reasoning and Rehabilitation Project, with "high risk for recidivism" probationers met with very encouraging results (Ross et al., 1988). This program instructs offenders in problem-solving, perspective taking, assertiveness, social skills, rational thinking, and critical analysis. Outcome measures revealed that rearrest and incarceration rates were substantially lower in subjects exposed to this cognitive program compared to subjects enrolled in regular probation or life skills training. Overall recidivism after 9 months was 69.5% in the probation group, 47.5% in the life skills group, and 18.1% in the cognitive group (Ross et al., 1988).

Gary Field (1986) provides a 5×3 matrix of various cognitive skill deficits that seems relevant to our discussion on cognitively oriented intervention procedures. Field argues that there are five personal deficits—excessive need for stimulation, low frustration tolerance, rigid thinking, compartmentalized (distorted) thinking, poor ability to process affect (emotions)—and five corollary interpersonal deficits—intolerance of boredom, impatience/impulsivity, poor decision-making, irresponsibility, inability to express or manage affect—that characterize the overall adjustment of recidivistic criminal offenders. He goes on to state that each of these five personal-interpersonal deficit combinations correlate with specific treatment needs. These would include learning to live with reduced sensory stimulation, acquiring self-monitoring skills, developing effective decision-making abilities, procuring basic life skills, and achieving better affective (particularly anger) control, respectively.

Behavioral techniques are a second class of intervention strategies that have been found effective for use with habitual criminal offenders. Contingency management, whereby the individual is reinforced or rewarded for certain pro-social behaviors and punished for engaging in antisocial activity, has been particularly successful with delinquent youth and criminal adults. Davidson and Robinson (1975) implemented a community-based behavior modification program with a group of "hard core" juvenile offenders. The results of a time series analysis revealed that program participants demonstrated increased school attendance, better academic test scores, and decreased rates of rearrest relative to a group of control subjects. Douds, Engelesjord, and Collingwood (1977) used contingency management and behavioral contracting to reduce recidivism by 31% and improve behavior at school as well as at home. The fact that learning and reinforcement are considered by lifestyle theory to be important in the development of the criminal lifestyle lends further credence to the use of contingency management techniques with this group of often seemingly unmanageable individuals.

Blending behavioral and moralist considerations has been the bailiwick of such luminaries as Victor Frankl (1963) and O. H. Mowrer (1964). However, William Glasser's (1965) Reality Therapy approach to intervention is probably the most popular behavioral-moralist strategy for use with violent, recalcitrant criminal offenders. Involvement, a focus on current behavior, goal-clarification, planning, and commitment are seen as the five primary steps to be taken by a therapist following a Reality Therapy script (Cohen & Sordo, 1984), and this procedure has been found to be moderately successful in curbing the criminal inclinations of juvenile delinquents and adult offenders (see Goldstein & Stein, 1975). Gad Czudner (1985) introduced a five-stage cognitive-moral approach for use with violent and recidivistic offenders that centers on fostering responsibility through nonacceptance of the excuses the individual makes for his or her behavior, developing increased self-awareness, instilling within the person a sense of guilt and remorse, encouraging long-term commitments, and involving the offender in activities that are incompatible with crime.

There appear to be at least three major points of overlap between the cognitive, behavioral, and moralistic approaches to intervention with high-rate offenders. The first point of integration concerns the foundational prerequisites for change. The cognitive perspective addresses the importance of avoiding excuses for one's behavior, the behaviorists consider the role of contracts, and the moralists try to instill a sense of guilt and remorse for one's past criminal deeds. A second point of commonality centers around awareness. The cognitive perspective focuses on understanding one's thinking as a means to increased self-control; behaviorists talk about gaining insight into the reinforcers that motivate one's actions; and the moralist viewpoint emphasizes awareness of the pain suffered by those exposed to one's criminal ways. A third point around which the cognitive, behavioral, and moralistic approaches seem to converge involves commitment to action. The cognitive approach stresses application of cognitive principles learned in therapy to

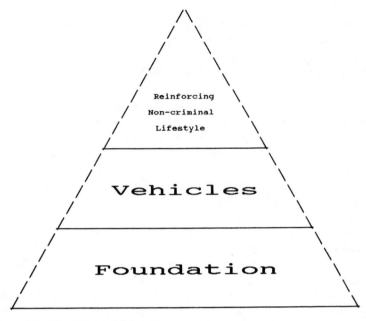

Figure 7.3. The Lifestyle Model of Intervention

everyday situations; behaviorists concern themselves with the development of a program of self-reinforcement; and the moralists concentrate on encouraging the individual's participation in actions incompatible with crime.

The Lifestyle Model of Intervention

Employing the three points of integration discussed above (i.e., foundation, awareness, commitment), a three-stage approach to working with lifestyle criminals is proposed. This model considers three steps or stages: the foundation, vehicles, and reinforcing noncriminal lifestyle (Walters & White, in press). The hierarchical structure of these three stages is pictured in Figure 7.3. Although an offender may be working on two different levels simultaneously, it is a fundamental premise of the lifestyle theory of intervention that lower levels need to be negotiated before lasting progress can be made at higher levels. Consequently, one would have problems finding a reinforcing noncriminal lifestyle in the absence of a solid foundation. The hope is that the treated individual will move up this three-tiered triangle over time. However, if the individual does not continue to reinforce his or her foundation, it is just as easy to move down the triangle as it is to go upward.

Level 1: The Foundation: Some therapists have come to conclude that psychopaths and criminals do not experience any guilt about their negative behavior (Cleckley, 1976). Taking a different perspective, Hammer and Ross (1977) point out that offenders may, in fact, suffer guilt, though they have learned to ward off such feelings with the aid of the cognitive strategies discussed in Chapter 6 (e.g., mollification, sentimentality, discontinuity). Taking a hint from cognitive-moralist thinkers, the lifestyle theory of intervention features the development of a foundation for change. However, rather than try to instill feelings of guilt, the lifestyle model of intervention centers on helping the individual establish a sense of disgust with his past criminal activity and current criminal thinking. Like a house with no foundation, the lifestyle criminal without a sense of disgust is subject to the push and pull of various environmental forces and is liable to succumb to one temptation or another, just like the foundationless house will most assuredly fall down in response to the first strong wind (Walters & White, in press).

One of the most insidious aspects of criminality for the individual offender is that it is so immediately reinforcing. The foundation of disgust is therefore necessary to combat the immediate gratification that crime can provide, while at the same time furnishing the high-rate offender with the structure he requires to resist criminal temptation and opportunity. The foundation is similar to taking a moral inventory of one's life in the manner proposed by Yochelson and Samenow (1985) in their work on the criminal personality. Whether one conjures up images of lost opportunities for lasting success, the suffering one's behavior has brought to persons who have tried to assist one in the past, or the terror and heartbreak one's intrusive actions have elicited in persons victimized by one's assorted criminal acts, the foundation of disgust can serve to motivate the lifestyle criminal for change by helping him direct and maintain his focus of attention.

In negotiating the transition from the foundational stage of treatment to the vehicle stage, it is important that we confront the offender's defenses. Step by step, the old defense structure is gradually shown to be invalid and, it is hoped, will be replaced with a growing sense of personal responsibility. It is vital, however, that we proceed cautiously since this defense structure conceals a great many negative feelings—fear, guilt, and anxiety in particular—and the rapid release of such feelings can be very frightening to the individual and potentially dangerous to those around him. It is also significant that guilt and disgust are thought to be helpful in building empathy for others (Czudner & Mueller, 1987), an attribute most lifestyle criminals have in short supply (see Chapter 5). In sum, then, the foundation revolves around the development of a sense of disgust with one's past criminal actions and current criminal thoughts, a challenging and reorganization of one's defenses, and establishing feelings of empathy for others.

Level 2: Vehicles: Once a solid foundation has been laid, the lifestyle offender can begin to develop a system of vehicles designed to change his criminologic thinking. A vehicle in its most basic form is a means of carrying or transporting something from point A to point B. In the therapeutic sense, a vehicle transports the habitual offender from a lifestyle of crime to one that is significantly less predatory, and, it is hoped, more successful. It follows, then, that vehicles are often seen as the essence or substance of therapeutic interventions with criminal offenders, although it is important that the individual possess a reasonably strong foundation before preceding to this middle stage in the change process. Vehicles should be tailored to the individual needs of the offender and can run the full gamut, ranging, for example, from a genuine interest in religion to forcing oneself to remain in a "boring" job as an avenue to developing a greater sense of responsibility. There are several vehicles that seem to be particularly effective in changing certain specific criminal beliefs. A synopsis of several such techniques can be found in Table 7.1

I have found group therapy sessions to be a particularly powerful vehicle in identifying and confronting the antisocial thinking patterns that subserve the criminal lifestyle. This is because habitual offenders are better able to cut through the deception and lies that enfold the criminal lifestyle than can a therapist, no matter how well trained. In an effort to keep the deceit and game playing to a minimum, I have established as a fundamental ground rule of my groups that participants receive nothing for their involvement other than the personal satisfaction that accompanies self-understanding and meaningful long-term change. The practice of not handing out certificates or making parole recommendations contingent upon participation in these groups not only cuts down on the game playing, but it also forms an emerging sense of cognitive dissonance in the minds of many offenders since they soon come to realize there are no external incentives for their participation, though they continue attending the group sessions. A number of such individuals resolve this growing sense of dissonance by concluding that treatment must be worthwhile and respond by investing renewed energy, interest, and commitment in the therapy process.

In negotiating the transition from vehicle stage issues to the development of a reinforcing noncriminal lifestyle, it is critical that the offender abandon his sense of entitlement that has carried him through many a criminal venture. It is also vital that he realize the implications of compliance versus noncompliance when it comes to violating societal norms. This is a point with which

TABLE 7.1: Vehicles Useful in Confronting the Eight Criminologic Thinking Patterns

Thinking Pattern	Vehicle
Mollification	Rational Challenge: challenging the irrational belief that life should be fair and that unfairness in the world justifies one's own irresponsibility.
Cutoff	Stress Management: Anger Control (Novaco, 1975).
Entitlement	Rational Challenge: challenging notion that one is privileged or entitled; proper identification of and effective discrimination between one's needs and wants.
Power Orientation	Rational Challenge: challenging notion that a meaningful life goal is control over others; renewed interest in self-discipline and control; Response Prevention: avoiding the power thrust when confronted with zero state feelings.
Sentimentality	Rational Challenge: challenging the "good guy/Robin Hood" perception the offender has of himself; objective review of how criminal has hurt self and others through his illegal actions.
Superoptimism	Objective review of how individual has set himself up to lose time and again.
Cognitive Indolence	Problem-solving: teaching the offender how to better structure his experience, set goals, and work toward productive aims; Critical Thinking Training (Ross & Fabiano, 1985).
Discontinuity	Moral Inventory (Yochelson & Samenow, 1985); self-montiroing of behavior.

many inmates take exception, arguing that I am advocating a passive stance in the way one deals with the world. Nothing could be farther from the truth. I believe there is a place for social change, as well as social disobedience. However, society, or certain segments of society, promulgate the rules, and we can either abide by these rules or violate them. If we choose to violate the rules, then we must also be willing to accept the consequences of our choices, just as our forefathers were prepared to accept the consequences of their rebellion against the British monarchy. Far from being a high-minded revolutionary, a prototypic lifestyle criminal violates societal norms (as well as the rights of others) for self-indulgent, short-term aims, thereby setting himself up for failure in the process—hardly what I would call a modern-day Thomas Jefferson.

Level 3: Reinforcing Noncriminal Lifestyle: A founding premise of the lifestyle theory of criminal conduct is that offenders engage in criminal action because such behavior is rewarded. The antisocial deeds of the average lifestyle criminal are reinforcing, in part, because they fulfill the criminal's image of himself as a loser. Even if the offender comes to appreciate the "no win" nature of the criminal lifestyle and begins to understand that he can do better, he must replace these old negative behavior patterns with something. This is where the reinforcing noncriminal lifestyle comes into play. During the final stage of treatment, the high rate offender must find the noncriminal way of life intrinsically rewarding or he is destined to return to the self- and other-destructiveness of the criminal lifestyle. It should be noted that our focus in working with the lifestyle criminal is on stimulating the natural process of maturity/burnout that most offenders attain with age. In working with this group of offenders, we are, in effect, encouraging them to move forward into the burnout/maturity developmental stage that occurs naturally in most offenders as a result of certain physical and psychological changes taking place during the mid-life stage of adult male development (see Chapter 5).

The reinforcement contingent upon living a noncriminal existence might be found in relationship with one's family, a sense of satisfaction with legitimate employment, or just the knowledge that one is free to go from place to place without a pass or under the watchful eye of a prison guard. As part of this third level of treatment, I will sometimes ask group participants whether working in a car wash or busing tables at a restaurant would be enough to keep them out of legal difficulty if these were the only jobs available to them. Provided the offender is being honest with the therapist, as well as with himself, such a question holds the potential of providing insight into an offender's priorities and is sometimes helpful in prognosticating the possibilities for change. In effect, what we are asking when we pose such a question is what is more important to the individual, having a late model automobile and a pocketful of cash or remaining free in the community? If it is the former, then it is likely that the individual will eventually return to a criminal way of life upon being discharged from prison. If it is the latter, then he must find a noncriminal existence as rewarding as he once found his life of lawlessness or he is almost assured of repeating his criminal past.

Conclusion

The fact that we are even considering the issue of application suggests that I am crediting criminals with the capacity for change. The reader should note that I make no claims concerning the ease with which this change process might be implemented, only that it is possible. It is understandably difficult to change a behavioral pattern that has existed for many years, although such change remains a possibility if we can agree that thought precedes action and that we control the way we think except in cases where one is suffering from a debilitating brain disorder, crippling psychosis, or severe mental retardation. Logically, if we control our thinking and if it is our thoughts that cause us to act in certain ways, then we are fully capable of changing our behavior. When we speak of change, what we are referencing is the process of relearning; when we assist the lifestyle criminal in making certain changes in his life, what we are doing, in effect, is teaching him a new (and more socially appropriate) set of responses to his environment.

The relearning process involves at least three steps: attention, education, and practice. Attention is the first step and involves focusing on information relevant to the relearning scenario. Stated somewhat differently, we must prepare ourselves for change before it can become a reality. Consequently, the offender must not only desire change, but assume full responsibility for his past criminal actions as well. In addition to taking greater responsibility for his behavior, the lifestyle criminal must stop making excuses for his past criminal conduct and current criminal thinking. This nonacceptance of excuses serves as the cornerstone, not only of this system, but also of several of the more popular behavioral and moralistic systems of intervention (see Czudner, 1985; Glasser, 1965; Mowrer, 1964). Personal responsibility therefore lays the groundwork for behavioral change, a necessary, but not sufficient, condition for the maturity that accompanies such change.

Once the lifestyle offender accepts full responsibility for past transgressions, the next step is for him to challenge the criminologic beliefs that subserve these activities. The eventual goal of this second step in the relearning process is to think in ways that are appreciably more rational, realistic, and responsible than before. We must educate the lifestyle criminal regarding the error of his thinking, being sure to point out that as long as he continues thinking this way, he will persist in setting himself up to lose in ways that are destructive to himself and others. The therapist or counselor therefore takes a largely educational role in the treatment process, although personal sensitivity, timing, and the therapeutic alliance are just as important as they are with more traditional psychotherapies. A counselor utilizing a lifestyle approach to stimulate the change process must be thoroughly familiar with the basic tenets of the underlying theory, as well as the major treatment issues discussed in this chapter.

Practice is the final stage in the relearning sequence. Though one may have a proper attitude and be exposed to useful information, new behavioral patterns must be rehearsed if change is to become a permanent part of one's behavioral repertoire. Since the thinking pattern supporting the criminal lifestyle develops over many years, it is unrealistic to expect that it will disappear simply because we would like it to do so. It is of utmost importance that both the therapist and offender realize that the application and rehearsal of principles enunciated during the middle (educational) stage in the relearning sequence take place inside, as well as outside, prison walls. Inmates often overlook opportunities for personal growth while incarcerated and placate themselves with the false belief that change can only be effected following their release from confinement. It has been my experience, however, that if the individual waits until after he is discharged to modify his thinking and behavior, he probably won't remain in the community very long.

Just because this chapter has focused on individual solutions to the problem of serious criminality does not mean that certain environmental solutions are not also possible. There is a great deal that can be done at the familial, community, and societal levels to stem the tide of serious criminality that seems to be sweeping the nation. It is our responsibility as a society to find innovative answers to the problem of lifestyle criminality. U.S. society can ill-afford complacency in its approach to criminal justice issues nor should it settle for simple, pat answers to the complex question of crime. We owe it to the offender, the offender's future victims, and ourselves as a society to explore these issues in depth. Thus, while I am steadfast in my belief that offenders cannot legitimately use societal injustice as an excuse for their criminal actions, neither can we as a society realistically escape our responsibilities by putting everything off on the offender.

NOTE

1. Scores at this level are normally interpreted as being clinically significant.

8. Working Hypothesis Revisited

As of this writing, the working hypothesis is alive and well; it continues to serve a vital function in the development of the theory that crime can be conceptualized in lifestyle terms. Just because articles have been written and books published does not mean that this model is complete—far from it. If working with criminal offenders has taught me anything, it is how little we actually understand about crime and its causation. Instead of serving as a source of frustration, however, this knowledge has caused me to work that much harder to develop a model of criminal conduct that might be useful in explaining one particular subcategory of lawbreaking behavior—offenders who approach crime as a lifestyle. I would argue that without a continually updated working hypothesis, the model of lifestyle criminality presented in this book will gradually lose its vitality. That we should continue examining the criminal lifestyle with the aid of a working hypothesis approach to theory building would seem advisable.

It appears self-evident that the working hypothesis will need to incorporate new information as such knowledge is brought to light. Besides pursuing the development of this hypothesis, we also need to determine the boundaries of the associated theory. In short, we must ascertain where the theory of lifestyle criminality ends and where nonlifestyle forms of criminal conduct begin. Consequently, the parameters of the lifestyle theory of criminal involvement and the lifestyle theory of criminal events will need to be probed and specified. We might well ask ourselves whether these models apply where juveniles, females, blacks, or so-called "successful criminals" are concerned. These and other questions will be addressed in this, the final, chapter of a book on crime as a lifestyle.

Moderator Variables

Moderator variables modify or regulate the nexus between two or more other variables. Take for instance, the example of caloric intake and weight gain. If the association between the number of calories one consumes in a

24-hour time period and subsequent weight gain is higher for males than for females, sex would be playing a moderating role in the calorie-weight gain relationship due to the fact that the correlation between these two variables differs as a function of the subject's gender. The three moderator variables with the greatest potential relevance to the lifestyle theory of criminal behavior are age, gender, and race.

Age

It has been discerned that age exerts an important moderating effect on criminal justice data (Wilson & Herrnstein, 1985). In fact, the crime-age relationship (rising precipitously during the mid- to late teens, falling sharply as one proceeds through the third decade of life, and stabilizing at a low rate at about age 40) has been shown to vary little as a function of history, culture, or offense type (Hirschi & Gottfredson, 1983). It would seem sensible, then, that we explore the moderating influence of age on the criminal lifestyle. Being a developmental theory of deviance, however, the lifestyle model of criminal involvement does, in fact, account for the interactive effect of age on criminal conduct. There is, nonetheless, a need for greater clarification of the pre-criminal features of criminal development and the drawing of a finer distinction between burnout and maturation as the termination point in the criminal career.

Gender

The lifestyle theory of criminal behavior was conceived, derived, and validated on an all-male group of recidivistic felons. This, rather than chauvinism, is my rationale for identifying the lifestyle criminal with the pronoun "he." The astute reader might well ask whether lifestyle concepts apply to female offenders. The data on this issue unfortunately are inconclusive at this time. Outcomes observed in several studies signal the presence of significant male-female differences, not only in the rate of crime, but also in the types of crimes committed and the general characteristics of offenders (Hindelang, Hirschi, & Weis, 1979; Ward, Jackson, & Ward, 1969). There is evidence, however, that a small portion of the female offender population does, in fact, exhibit several of the same behavioral and cognitive attributes normally associated with lifestyle criminality in males (see Steffensmeier & Cobb, 1981).

Marguerite Q. Warren and Jill Rosenbaum (1986) studied a group of female offenders who had spent time in a detention facility during adolescence. It was observed that nearly half of the women in this sample were subsequently arrested as adults for offenses that fell into the high-severity range (e.g., armed robbery, murder, kidnapping, and selling weapons or "hard" drugs). Warren and Rosenbaum discerned that a quarter of their sample had accrued ten or more adult arrests, and three of five had experienced some form of adult incarceration. Using a modified Haapenen/Jesness Scale (1982), these authors determined that 64% of their sample displayed a chronic pattern of violent aggressive, violent economic, or property criminality. Results such as these would seem to suggest that the lifestyle model of criminal conduct holds relevance with at least a subsample of female offenders. In point of fact, Douglas A. Smith and Raymond Paternoster (1987) probed the explanatory power of four major theories of criminal behavior (strain, social control, differential association, deterrence) originally designed to explain male criminality and found them to be equally effective in accounting for drug use among males and females.

Race

Perhaps the most salient moderator variable effect is that of the race or ethnic status of the offender in question. The literature on black-white comparisons communicates the presence of a clear racial effect for several criminal science and lifestyle variables. To begin with, blacks tend to commit more crimes than whites (Elliott & Ageton, 1980; Kelly, 1977), even when the socioeconomic status of offenders is controlled (Wolfgang, Figlio, & Sellin, 1972). These racial effects tend to shrink, however, when we redirect our attention to self-reported criminality. In a comparison of black and white adolescent high school males, Chambliss and Nagasawa (1969) witnessed the existence of higher arrest rates for blacks, but with the corollary finding that these differences dropped to near zero when self-reported delinquency was probed. However, self-report studies tend to be weighted heavily on the side of relatively minor, nuisance crimes, and Hindelang et al. (1979) note that when they restricted their analyses to self-report data on serious criminality, black-white differentials rose in a fashion similar to the ones found with official arrest rates.

Efforts have been made to expound on the theoretical significance of black-white differences in criminal involvement. Although black-white variations occur even in samples matched on socioeconomic status (Wolfgang et al., 1972), social/economic factors may still be at work since being raised in a black ghetto is not the same as growing up in a poor white neighborhood. It has also been argued that many blacks may engage in crime as a way of venting their anger toward society for years of oppression, prejudice, and segregation, although Elijah Anderson (1978) noticed that the black patrons of a popular South Chicago bar spent more time admiring "successful" black criminals than expressing hatred for "powerful" whites. In a similar vein, Harris and Lewis (1974) ascertained that the black inmates in their study seemed to view crime as enhancing their self-worth, while criminal identification and self-esteem were inversely correlated in a group of white inmates. There would appear to be a fundamental difference in how blacks and whites organize their thinking around crime and the formation of self-esteem, a fact which, along with sociocultural/early environmental findings, may help explain why more blacks than whites seem to engage in criminal activity.

Race would appear to play a moderating role in the relationship presumed to exist between self-image and lifestyle criminality. The negative self-evaluations thought to be so central to the development of lifestyle patterns of criminal conduct (see Chapter 5) appear to be more characteristic of white than of black offenders. Blacks seem to view crime as enhancing their self-worth by providing them with external verification of success, while whites are more likely to see themselves as being unsuccessful relative to their criminal careers. Once the individual—black or white—has spent any time in the lifestyle of crime, however, he or she usually realizes the no-win nature of the criminal lifestyle. Likewise, the self-appraisals emanating from the self-image and role identity life tasks are multidimensional, and several of these dimensions (e.g., "I'm it") appear to be indistinguishable when blacks and whites are compared. Consequently, while race may moderate the self-image and role identity aspects of lifestyle criminality, it does not necessarily invalidate lifestyle theory for use with nonwhite offenders.

Variations on the Lifestyle Theme

There are four criteria that must be met before we are justified in rendering a diagnosis of lifestyle criminality. These core characteristics, as the reader should know, include a global state of irresponsibility, blatant expressions of self-indulgence, a limpid pattern of interpersonally intrusive behavior, and chronic violation of societal rules, norms, and mores. There are other characteristics (corollary features) which, while they may not be pathognomonic of lifestyle criminality, are commonly observed in the behavior of many high-rate offenders. These would include an early age of onset in rule-breaking behavior, a high degree of predatory activity, and a clear pattern of failure in criminal, as well as noncriminal, ventures. In this section, we will consider the possibility that a person could violate one or more of the corollary features of high-rate criminality yet still satisfy the primary behavioral criteria for a diagnosis of lifestyle criminality.

Late Onset Criminal Conduct

It is common for persons falling under the lifestyle criminal umbrella to exhibit a pattern of violation dating back many years—all the way back, in fact, to early or mid-adolescence. There are, however, exceptions to the developmental continuity normally observed with lifestyle patterns of criminal conduct. In a television movie entitled *In the Line of Duty: The F.B.I. Murders*, the story of two south Florida bank robbers is recounted. Operating in true advanced-stage lifestyle fashion, these two desperadoes drove themselves down the path of self-destruction and were responsible for the deaths of three persons (an armored truck guard and two FBI officers) before ending their own lives in a furious gun battle with federal agents. At the conclusion of the show, we are informed that a review of the backgrounds of these two individuals revealed that neither had ever been arrested for a violent criminal offense prior to the crime spree portrayed in the movie. Such a finding would appear to present some problems for a theory that holds that crime can be conceptualized as a lifestyle with its roots in early development.

In addressing the seeming inconsistency of advanced-stage criminal behavior in an individual who doesn't appear to have progressed through earlier stages of criminal development, I think it is imperative that we distinguish between luck and true post-adolescent onset criminality. As the data show, criminals normally get away with the majority of their criminal acts. Consequently, there are some individuals who, despite having engaged in semi-regular lawlessness since adolescence, have no record of juvenile arrest (or in some cases have had their juvenile record expunged). In contrast to this group of "lucky" offenders, the genuine "late bloomer" rarely engages in criminal action during adolescence, although we could hardly call such a person's early years idyllic. What is often found in the backgrounds of these "late bloomers" is a history of strong external control (e.g., religion, domineering mother) that gradually weakens as the individual grows older. The seeds of criminality were sown early in the life of the violent offender profiled in Case History 8.1, although religion helped keep these antisocial tendencies in check until early adulthood.

As this case history illustrates, David used the structure of his religious upbringing to maintain control over a criminologic attitude. Accordingly, once he started robbing banks, he did so with the abandon and drive of an

Case History 8.1: "David"

A 28-year-old single white male, David was raised in an upper-middle-class home environment. The middle child in a family of three children, his parents were highly religious, and David followed suit. His father took an authoritarian approach to child-rearing and worked as a college professor during the better part of David's school-age years. A C+ student in school, David was referred to a school psychologist because he was not achieving his academic potential according to the expectations of his family and school. The psychologist concluded that David suffered from severe self-criticism, high anxiety, and poor motivation, fueled by a negative self-appraisal, the result of having been unable to compete with a high-achieving older brother. A school counselor remarked that this older brother was very popular with teachers and other students and that David attempted to focus attention on himself in less socially desirable ways (e.g., drinking alcohol and associating with peers who regularly got into trouble with the law and/or school officials).

After graduating from high school, David spent two years working as a missionary for his church in a foreign country. He describes himself as fulfilling the role of "religious zealot" during his tour with the foreign ministry, but acknowledges that he gradually became disillusioned with the church when he observed hypocritical behavior on the part of certain church officials. He came across wide-spread graft, corruption, and closed-mindedness on the part of these church leaders, all of which seemed highly incompatible with the teachings he had been exposed to in church and Sunday School. He subsequently returned to the United States, where he joined the military and spent several months working as a recruiter. Following a one-year stint in the military, David enrolled in the university in which his father taught. Following the spring semester of his freshman year, he hopped onto his motorcycle and moved West. In the tradition of Jesse James and Billy the Kid, David went on a bank-robbing spree that landed him in serious trouble with legal authorities and two separate incarcerations.

David's first arrest took place when he was 22, an unquestionably late start for a lifestyle criminal. Once he began, however, David pursued crime with a gusto that would have made John Dillinger jealous. Over the course of just two years (three-quarters of which was spent in a state prison), David robbed several banks and, on one occasion, outran a squad of FBI agents who seemingly had him cornered. During the commission of the instant offense, the subject, wielding a sawed-off shotgun, disarmed the bank guard and then proceeded to rob the tellers of nearly $7,000. Leaving the scene of the robbery at a high rate of speed, David and his crime partner were rammed by a pickup truck, and it was observed that David fired several shots at the driver. In effecting his escape, David kidnapped a man and his infant daughter at gunpoint and ordered the man to drive him out of town. Upon exiting the vehicle, the subject wiped down the backseat and thanked the driver for his cooperation.

Despite the fact that he began his criminal career relatively late in life, David still displays all four characteristics of lifestyle criminality. Irresponsibility and self-indulgence appear to be of only mild to moderate severity, but David's high-intensity intrusive rule-breaking actions more than make up for this. In light of the fact that this individual clearly meets the criteria for a diagnosis of lifestyle criminality, a logical question might be why he waited so long to put this lifestyle into action. The answer can quite naturally be found in the external control provided by the subject's religious teachings, as well as the fact that he grew up in a rural environment and thus had fewer opportunities for criminal involvement compared to someone raised in an urban area. The hold David's religious upbringing had on his behavior ended once he became disillusioned with his religion and disappointed with the leaders of his church. With the external authority over his behavior removed, there was very little to control his actions since, like most lifestyle criminals, self-discipline was something David had never taken the time to develop.

advanced stage lifestyle criminal, although he had no prior history of serious criminal involvement. The foundation for this criminal lifestyle had been implanted at a relatively early age, although the behavior lay dormant until David became disillusioned with his church and its teachings. For much the same reason, many lifestyle criminals function surprisingly well in the highly structured milieu of a maximum-security penitentiary but then encounter difficulty when released into the community, which, of course, is much less structured than prison. It should also be understood that late onset criminality may reflect more than just luck or the presence of a "late bloomer." The individual may, in fact, not fit the lifestyle criteria, although this can only be determined through an analysis of the four primary behavioral characteristics delineated earlier.

Low Predatory Criminal Behavior

Interpersonal intrusiveness is a defining property of the lifestyle pattern of criminal conduct. Consequently, predatory behavior of one type or another will be found in the backgrounds of all lifestyle criminals, although important individual differences may exist. At the high end of the spectrum we find individuals for whom predation is their primary form of human interaction, even if it isn't instrumental in obtaining anything other than a sense of power and control over others. Situated at the low end of the spectrum are persons who engage in actions that are sufficiently predatory so as to satisfy the intrusiveness criterion yet not so rapacious as to totally disregard the rights of others. These individuals still fit the lifestyle pattern even though they diverge from the prototypic picture of the lifestyle offender as predacious and exploitive in their interpersonal relationships. Society often views the low predatory habitual criminal as less dangerous than the more violent members of the lifestyle genre, although both must substantially modify their thinking if they are to have much chance at lasting success in the community.

The pattern of Mike's behavior suggests a lifestyle offender who has, for the most part, avoided violent, predatory solutions to his problems. He has, however, engaged in a sufficient level of interpersonally intrusive conduct to qualify as a lifestyle criminal. The lifestyle facets of this individual's behavior and thinking are plainly evident in his background (see Case History 8.2), as is the losing nature of his criminal adventures. If we had been unable to demonstrate interpersonally intrusive trends in Mike's demeanor, we would not have legitimately been able to offer a diagnosis of lifestyle criminality. Take, for instance, the example of a heroin addict who has engaged in a wide assortment of criminal offenses as a means of securing funds for the express purpose of purchasing narcotics. Arrests may be present for shoplifting, drugs, and larceny, but without evidence of interpersonally intrusive action, our subject cannot be classified within the lifestyle grouping. He may, however, fit another category of criminal conduct. Interpersonal intrusiveness is, therefore, a defining behavioral characteristic of the criminal lifestyle, although it tends to vary widely, from the recurring predatory actions of the "mainstream" lifestyle felon to the isolated, but nonetheless significant, intrusive acts of an offender like Mike.

The Successful Criminal

According to the theory of criminality espoused in this book, success and high-rate, recidivistic criminality are incompatible. The lifestyle criminal is someone who presumably sets himself up for failure and in the process sabotages his chances for long-term success. There are individuals who exhibit lifestyle characteristics, yet seem to have achieved a measured level of success by way of their involvement in criminal activity. One such example is Al Capone. With a juvenile and early adult arrest record that would have made any lifestyle criminal proud, Capone commanded a criminal

Case History 8.2: "Mike"

Mike is a 41-year-old divorced white male serving a 13-year sentence for possession of cocaine, with intent to distribute. The subject was known to deal in large quantities of marijuana and cocaine. Mike states that as a youngster he always wanted to be the tough guy, but didn't really get involved in crime and various quasi-legal ventures until after he witnessed the unethical practices of two large corporations he worked for during his early twenties. He was first arrested at the age of 12 for breaking and entering and was placed on probation. However, he remained free of any serious legal trouble until the age of 32, when he was arrested for conspiracy to present a live sex show, a charge for which he was eventually found not guilty. Several months later, he was arrested for transporting obscene materials as part of an interstate pornography ring, although he was subsequently acquitted on these charges as well.

Mike initially started using cocaine in his late twenties and began selling it when he was about 34. It was within the context of his involvement in the drug trade that Mike engaged in the majority of his intrusive actions. For instance, he and several of his drug associates were suspected by police of attempted murder in the case of another group member thought to have stolen a quantity of cocaine from the group. Though he was arrested several times on drug-related charges, our subject was able to elude prosecution until the age of 39. It is noteworthy that when pursued by police just prior to his arrest for the instant offense, Mike had a loaded pistol in his possession, which he jettisoned out a car window as arrest became inevitable. Once apprehended, Mike resisted arrest by kicking the arresting officer in the face with his foot. Therefore, while predatory behavior is not this individual's typical modus operandi, he has exhibited sufficiently intrusive action to be classified a lifestyle criminal.

Mike was an only child, raised by his mother. His father was rarely at home and is described as a highly irresponsible individual who worked a variety of low-paying jobs, consumed large quantities of alcohol, and gambled excessively—hardly a proper role model for young Mike. The subject indicates that he quit school in the tenth grade in order to find a job and support his family. Prior to this, he had been an average student in school but was thought to possess above-average academic potential. Though not particularly rebellious, Mike did get himself into fights with other juveniles on numerous occasions and is said to have been suspended from school at least twice. Shortly after quitting high school, the subject joined the military wherein he obtained his GED and an honorable discharge. After his release from the military, Mike went to work for two large corporations but became disenchanted and eventually got involved in several quasi-legal ventures that entailed making pornographic films and running various adult book stores.

He was quite successful in the pornography business and reports an annual income in the $125,000 to $150,000 range.

In examining the four behavioral characteristics of lifestyle criminality, we find evidence of mild to moderate intrusiveness and moderate levels of irresponsibility and social rule breaking. Although there are examples of responsible behavior in this individual's background (good work record, working to support his family), he became increasingly more irresponsible and willing to violate the norms, rules, and mores of society as he grew older— particularly as he got more heavily involved in the personal use of cocaine. He would employ mollification, for instance, to argue that the government had no right to prosecute him for selling drugs since there were "respectable" companies (such as the two he had worked for previously) that were "legally robbing" people of their hard-earned money. Despite the role of irresponsibility, interpersonal intrusiveness, and social rule breaking in Mike's difficulties, self-indulgence was the characteristic that contributed most to his downfall as a successful entrepreneur. His use of cocaine—a clear sign of self-indulgence—was so extensive that it brought into focus criminal thinking patterns that previously either lay dormant or were relatively weak in intensity. Superoptimism, sentimentality, and power-oriented thoughts flourished in light of increased cocaine usage, and Mike would stroke his ego to the point where his thinking became increasingly more fragmented and discontinuous. In the end, he couldn't manage himself, let alone a business, and readily admits that getting arrested probably saved his life.

empire that at its zenith employed over 1,000 thugs and had a weekly payroll of nearly $300,000. What we sometimes overlook, however, is that Capone's reign lasted only five years, and in the end he contributed to his own demise due to overconfidence and inattention to the actual running of his organization. It should be remembered that there are many juvenile offenders who cease their criminal activity upon entering adulthood, others who continue with this pattern into adulthood, but very few who abandon the criminal lifestyle in favor of successful criminal ventures. Case History 8.3 portrays yet another example of short-lived success by an enterprising, but nevertheless lifestyle, criminal.

Success in crime breeds overconfidence, superoptimism, and an emerging sense of invulnerability, which in the end led to Chuck's downfall. Had Chuck disbanded his operation after legal authorities showed signs of closing in on his organization, or refrained from further drug involvement upon entering prison, we would be hard pressed to classify him a lifestyle criminal. However, the fact that he continued his losing ways in prison, knowing full

Case History 8.3: "Chuck"

Chuck is a 45-year-old Hispanic male serving a 15-year sentence for two separate narcotics violations. An intelligent, streetwise individual, Chuck was raised in the Spanish Harlem section of New York City, where he saw criminal acts taking place on a daily basis. He grew up in an environment where drug dealers and pimps were viewed as heroes and the police were treated with suspicion. The record reflects that Chuck dropped out of high school in the tenth grade despite average to above-average ability. The subject's work record is also spotty and suggests that while he has held a number of jobs, he rarely remained on a job longer than several months at a time. Chuck would often quit a job without giving notice or without having another job lined up. On one occasion, he had an argument with his father, for whom he was working at the time, and quit the job on the spot, exiting his father's truck as it came to a stop at a cross street.

Chuck's first documented arrest took place at age 16, although he had been breaking the law long before that time. Juvenile arrests were for a variety of offenses, but auto theft, burglary, and narcotics violations were most prominent. Early adult arrests followed this same general pattern, although they brought with them more serious consequences for Chuck. As a juvenile, the subject spent several months in a county workhouse, but this appeared to have had no effect on our subject other than to eliminate any fear he may have had concerning the legal sanctions society imposes upon its lawbreakers. As an adult, Chuck became well acquainted with the inside of a prison, receiving two separate state sentences, succeeded by a 15-year federal sentence.

After serving the second of two state sentences, Chuck decided that he would do things differently "this time." He went about forming a drug organization with himself at the helm. Chuck imposed a management structure on his organization that resembled a small-sized corporation. At its height, this organization had a staff of 80 persons and was doing $175,000 worth of business in cocaine and heroin each week. Since a substantial portion of this figure was profit, it does not take an accountant to figure out that this drug organization netted Chuck a tidy sum over the four years it was in operation. As with all ventures headed by a lifestyle criminal, however, Chuck's drug empire came tumbling down in the face of legal scrutiny, and Chuck was sentenced to 15 years in a federal penitentiary.

In understanding the demise of Chuck's drug organization, it should be pointed out that the legal authorities were wise to the subject's machinations long before they were able to do anything about it. Chuck had quite ingeniously worked a number of safeguards into his system, and for a while they seemed reasonably effective in warding off serious legal complications. As time progressed, however, the subject became less careful and superoptimism set in. Eventually, this led to

Chuck's arrest and the disintegration of his once-successful drug organization. Several years later, he was caught attempting to smuggle narcotics into a federal penitentiary, for which he received an additional federal sentence. Apparently, he hadn't learned that success in the drug business (particularly for someone who already has a record of such activity) usually is fleeting.

well that the odds against success were heavy, simply adds credence to our impression of Chuck as a lifestyle offender. Genuinely successful criminals perpetrate their crimes within the structure and framework of society, engaging in unethical/illegal acts that have a high potential yield, low rate of detection, and relatively lenient sanctions attached to them. This is just the opposite of how the lifestyle offender approaches crime. It bears repeating that the principal intent of the lifestyle criminal is not eluding capture, but losing in ways that are dramatic and self-destructive. This is the reason why we find an over-abundance of lifestyle offenders and a scarcity of genuinely successful criminals in U.S. maximum-security prisons and penitentiaries.

Other Patterns

In addition to the outlying patterns of lifestyle criminality discussed in the previous section, there are several patterns that do not reflect the inner workings of the criminal lifestyle, in part or whole. These individuals may engage in a variety of criminal, irresponsible, and self-defeating behaviors, but they cannot legitimately be considered lifestyle criminals, as the term has been defined in this book. Among the patterns to be discussed in this section are the nonlifestyle criminal and noncriminal "loser."

Nonlifestyle Criminal

Research suggests that habitual criminal conduct is characteristic of only a small percentage of all offender groups (Shannon, 1982; Wolfgang et al., 1972). It follows, then, that most lawbreakers do not exhibit features of lifestyle criminality. One such individual is John List, accused of murdering his mother, wife, and three children (see Example 8.1). With the aid of the television show, *America's Most Wanted,* List was identified and arrested in Richmond, Virginia. The fact that he had remained free of legal arrest for over 17 years argues against his being a lifestyle criminal. Just the same, there are indications that List set himself up for failure in the sense that he

Example 8.1

On June 1, 1989, alleged killer John Emil List was taken into custody by FBI agents on the basis of tips made by persons who had tuned into a recent episode of the television program *America's Most Wanted*. The murders, which occurred in 1971, shook the quiet, upper-middle class suburb of Westfield, New Jersey, where List and his family had been residents. The victims were List's wife, mother, daughter (age 16), and two sons (ages 13 and 15). All had been shot to death with a .22-caliber or 9mm automatic pistol that List had purchased several weeks before the murders. In reconstructing the crime scene, police believe that List systematically executed each family member; except for the mother, who was found stuffed in a clothes closet, he had lined the bodies up on the floor of the ballroom, which sat in the middle of the 18-room mansion List had purchased for $50,000 and mortgaged three times. The subject not only meticulously cleaned up most of the blood, but he took pains to cover his tracks by writing notes providing explanations for the family's absence to the children's teachers, the post office, and the milkman (*Star Ledger*, June 2, 1989).

It was not until one month after the murders that the bodies were discovered. Police officers state that when they finally entered the dwelling, they were greeted by the corpses in the ballroom and a radio hauntingly playing liturgical music. Following the murders, List abandoned his 1963 blue Chevrolet at the John F. Kennedy International Airport in New York City, and it was speculated that he may have fled to Europe or South America. The FBI has been unable to document List's whereabouts for several years after the murders, although he did surface in Denver, Colorado, some six years later under the alias Robert P. Clark. It was not long after this that he met the woman who was to become his second wife at a Lutheran church event. After dating eight years, they were married and eventually moved to a suburban neighborhood in the Richmond, Virginia, area. His new neighbors and coworkers characterized him as a quiet, rather conventional individual who was known to have displayed a Fraternal Order of Police sticker on his car. As before the murders, List worked as an accountant and was heavily involved in church activities (*Star Ledger*, June 2, 1989).

People have characterized John List as a very rigid individual. Two letters written by the alleged perpetrator of New Jersey's most notorious mass murder shortly after the crime suggest that a primary motive in the killings was power/control. List apparently believed that family members, particularly his wife and daughter, were going down the wrong path in life and that he was losing his authority over them. He had also gotten himself into financial difficulty and had presumably misappropriated nearly $200,000 from his mother's estate over a period of several years. An interview with a close friend of List's second wife

> revealed that they were suffering from many of the same problems List had
> experienced in his first marriage and that a major reason for these financial woes
> was List's tendency to purchase items he could not afford (*Star Ledger,* June 4,
> 1989). Though List may have set himself up for failure, to consider him a lifestyle
> criminal would be to stretch the term to the point of unrecognizability.

encountered serious financial problems before, as well as after, the murders
and that this was a result of his own financial mismanagement and poor
decisions.

In making lifestyle-nonlifestyle determinations, we are safest if we employ
the four behavioral characteristics of lifestyle criminality (i.e., irresponsibility, self-indulgence, interpersonal intrusiveness, social rule breaking) as our
guide. Development of the LCSF makes our job that much easier, although
it must be remembered that the LCSF is a screening instrument that provides
only a cursory lifestyle analysis with a moderately high false-negative rate.
If we were to conduct a complete lifestyle analysis and were to find no
evidence of one or more of the four primary behavioral characteristics, we
could be reasonably confident that while we may be dealing with a criminal,
it is probably not of the lifestyle variety. As the criminal actions of John List
imply, there are persons who commit serious offenses that seem out of step
with their general character. Though these nonlifestyle patterns of criminal
conduct may be worthy of further investigation, our focus here has been on
persons who engage in crime as part of a wider lifestyle.

Noncriminal "Losers"

Although the loser's mentality assumes a prominent position in the behavior of lifestyle criminals, crime is only one means of failure or losing.
Alcohol/drug abuse, family conflict, poor occupational adjustment, and
dissatisfying relationships with others may all occur in the absence of serious
criminal action. This was certainly evident in several of the people interviewed by Hyatt and Gottlieb (1988) in their study on major career failure.
The case of a lawyer who apparently lacked the initiative and personal drive
to succeed in the work world is delineated in Example 8.2.

The case of the apathetic attorney represents the role of losing and failure
in the life of a person who had never been in trouble with the law. He is but
one example of a relatively large number of people who have learned to live
with failure because it is easier than aspiring for success and the possibility
of not realizing one's goals. Like the lifestyle criminal, such individuals

Example 8.2

A lawyer interviewed by Carole Hyatt and Linda Gottlieb for their book *When Smart People Fail* and printed as an excerpt in *Reader's Digest* (Hyatt & Gottlieb, 1988), illustrates a noncriminal form of losing or failure. The authors state that this attorney had learned to shield himself from failure by putting forth less than maximal effort. Therefore, if he did fail, he could feel secure in the knowledge that he never actually had a chance because he never really tried. By his own volition and lack of initiative, the subject set himself up for outcomes which, on the surface, he would argue he had been trying to avoid. Surely, someone bright enough to graduate from law school would have more insight into his behavior than this? Apparently not, according to the results obtained by Hyatt and Gottlieb.

Following his graduation from a prestigious eastern law school, the subject accepted employment with a large legal firm located on the West coast, where he hoped to specialize in entertainment law. His plans never materialized, and he returned to the eastern United States, where he joined another law firm. However, he was asked to resign from this firm after only six months due to an apparent lack of motivation. The subject rationalized this action by stating, "It didn't bother me, I didn't like the firm anyway" (Hyatt & Gottlieb, 1988, p. 71). From here he went back to entertainment law but continued to exhibit an angry, resentful disposition: "Let's face it, this is the minor leagues" (Hyatt & Gottlieb, 1988, p. 71).

The fear of failure, which seems to be a predominant theme in this attorney's thinking, is similar in many ways to the primary organizing motive of fear seen in the lifestyle criminal, despite the fact that Hyatt and Gottlieb report no evidence of serious criminality in this person's background. This would seem to suggest that a losing lifestyle need not result in serious criminality. However, similar to the behavior exhibited by the average lifestyle offender, the subject of Hyatt and Gottlieb's analysis displays fear, low self-esteem, and a tendency to set himself up for failure. The commonalities that appear to tie together various losing lifestyles would seem to be worthy of further investigation.

sabotage their efforts by setting themselves up to lose, but on their own terms; in so doing, they do not have to face the prospect of failing at something in which they are truly invested. The lifestyle criminal's mode of failure is much more dramatic and other-destructive than most forms of life failure and clearly separates this group of individuals from others who set themselves up to lose. It follows, then, that while all lifestyle criminals demonstrate a losing pattern of environmental adjustment, not all losing life patterns reflect the criminal lifestyle.

Conclusion

In closing, I would like to return to a theme expressed in the opening chapter, namely that research provides a theory with its foundation and practice provides its utility. A solid bedrock of empirical research support demonstrates that a theory is based on relationships that are meaningful, robust, and verifiable. Attempting to construct a theory in the absence of a sound research base is akin to building castles in the sand, since both will eventually topple into nonexistence. With nothing more than formal research support, however, a theory is frivolous, trite, and shallow. It is crucial, then, that we understand how this theory applies to individual offenders. This is where practical application of theoretical principles comes into play. Without the prospect of practical application, a theory, no matter how eloquent, is a hollow shell of principles and postulates with little substance. Consequently, a solid research base, as well as practical applicability, are both necessary for a theory to contribute significantly to a particular field of thought.

The working hypothesis approach to theory building offers an avenue through which one might achieve both research support and practical utility. In presenting an interactional theory of delinquency, Terence Thornberry (1987) states that criminal action should be viewed within a wider causal network and that such action is not only affected by social factors, but also exerts its own influence over these same social factors. The working hypothesis provides us with the opportunity to examine these interacting influences in greater detail than is possible with several of the more traditional approaches to theory building. From the research and clinical data we collect on offenders, we could construct a personalized library of experiences which, when compared between investigators, might form a composite sketch of a particular group of offenders. This information might then be used to derive a meaningful typology of criminal behavior. Only through a cogent synthesis of research and clinical data will the criminal science field ever be able to live up to its vast potential and answer such questions as the one posed to me by that middle-aged inmate over six years ago.

As we approach the end of this book, I hope the reader finds him- or herself looking forward rather than back. This future-oriented attitude will help guide us in the proper use of the working hypothesis because it conveys the understanding that acquiring knowledge is a never-ending process. As we know from the field of physics and the thinking of such scientists as Albert Einstein and Werner Heisenberg, knowledge is relative and may change depending upon how it is measured. Thus, even before this book goes to print, there will be sections that could be revised, although I have confidence in the basic stability of the overall model. Nevertheless, there is always the possibility that this theory or any of its underlying assumptions will be shown to be untenable as new information is brought to light. We can ill-afford to permit the prospect of disconfirmation to deter us from further exploring the working hypothesis, no matter what this might mean for our intuitively based notions, pet theories, or even this book. A science unwilling to offer challenge to its basic hypotheses, contemplate the limitations of its investigative methods, or entertain the possibility of its own obsolescence is no science at all.

References

Abbott, J. H. (1981). *In the belly of the beast: Letters from prison.* New York: Random House.

Adams, S. (1961). *Effectiveness of interview therapy with older youth authority wards: An interim evaluation of the PICO project* (Research Report No. 20). California Youth Authority.

Adler, A. (1927). *The practice and theory of individual psychology.* New York: Harcourt, Brace, & World.

Ageton, S., & Elliott, D. S. (1974). The effect of legal processing on delinquent orientations. *Social Problems, 22,* 87-100.

Aichhorn, A. (1935). *Wayward youth.* New York: Viking Press.

Ainsworth, M. D. S. (1979). Inmate-mother attachment. *American Psychologist, 34,* 932-937.

Akers, R. L. (1977). *Deviant behavior: A social learning approach.* Belmont, CA: Wadsworth.

Alexander, F., & Staub, H. (1931). *The criminal, the judge, and the public.* New York: Macmillan.

Amdur, R. L. (1989). Testing causal models of delinquency: A methodological critique. *Criminal Justice and Behavior, 16,* 35-62.

Anderson, E. (1978). *A place on the corner.* Chicago: University of Chicago Press.

Andrews, D. A. (1980). Some experimental investigations of the principles of differential association through deliberate manipulations of the structure of service systems. *American Sociological Review, 45,* 448-462.

Anglin, M. D., & Speckart, G. (1988). Narcotics use and crime: A multisample, multimethod analysis. *Criminology, 26,* 197-233.

Armentrout, J. A., & Hauer, A. L. (1978). MMPIs of rapists of adults, rapists of children, and non-rapist sex offenders. *Journal of Clinical Psychology, 34,* 330-332.

Austin, R. L. (1977). Commitment, neutralization, and delinquency. In T. N. Ferdinand (Ed.), *Juvenile delinquency: Little brother grows up* (pp. 121-137). Beverly Hills, CA: Sage.

Bachman, J. G., & O'Malley, P. M. (1978). *Youth in transition, Volume VI: Adolescence to adulthood: Change and stability in the lives of young men.* Ann Arbor: University of Michigan Press.

Bahr, S. J. (1979). Family determinants and effects of deviance. In W. R. Burr, R. Hill, F. I. Nye, & I. L. Reiss (Eds.), *Contemporary theories about the family: Research-based theories, Vol. I.* New York: Free Press.

Baker, B. L. (1969). Symptom treatment and symptom substitution in enuresis. *Journal of Abnormal Psychology, 74,* 42-49.

Balsh, R. (1972). *Negative reactions to delinquent labels in a junior high school.* Unpublished doctoral dissertation, University of Oregon, Eugene.

Beck, A. (1976). *Cognitive therapy and the emotional disorders.* New York: International Universities Press.

Beck, A. J., & Shipley, B. E. (1987). Recidivism of young parolees. *Bureau of Justice Statistics: Special Report.* NCJ-104916. Washington, DC: Bureau of Justice Statistics.

Beck, A. J., & Shipley, B. E. (1989). Recidivism of prisoners released in 1983. *Bureau of Justice Statistics: Special Report.* NCJ-116261. Washington, DC: Bureau of Justice Statistics.

Becker, G. S. (1968). Crime and punishment: An economic approach. *Journal of Political Economy, 76,* 169-217.

Becker, H. S. (1953). Becoming a marijuana user. *American Journal of Sociology, 59,* 235-243.

Bell, R. Q. (1979). Parent, child, and reciprocal influences. *American Psychologist, 34,* 821-826.

Bem, D. J., & Funder, D. C. (1978). Predicting more of the people more of the time: Assessing the personality of situations. *Psychological Review, 85,* 485-501.

Bennahum, D. A. (1971). Tattoos of heroin addicts in New Mexico. *Rocky Mountain Medical Journal, 68,* 63-66.

Benson, M. L. (1985). Denying the guilty mind: Accounting for involvement in a white-collar crime. *Criminology, 23,* 583-607.

Bernard, T. J. (1987a). Structure and control: Reconsidering Hirschi's concept of commitment. *Justice Quarterly, 4,* 409-424.

Bernard, T. J. (1987b). Testing structural strain theories. *Journal of Research in Crime and Delinquency, 24,* 262-280.

Berne, E. (1961). *Transactional analysis in psychotherapy.* New York: Grove Press.

Bernstein, I. N. (1975). Evaluation research in corrections: Status and prospects revisited. *Federal Probation, 39,* 56-57.

Bernstein, I. N., Kelly, W. R., & Doyle, P. A. (1977). *Labeling and sanctioning: The differential processing of criminal defendants.* Paper presented at the meeting of the American Sociological Association, Chicago, IL.

Binswanger, L. (1963). *Being-in-the-world* (J. Needleman, Trans.). New York: Basic Books.

Blackburn, R. (1978). Psychopathy, arousal, and the need for stimulation: In R. D. Hare & D. Schalling (Eds.), *Psychopathic behavior: Approaches to research.* Chichester, England: Wiley.

Blumstein, A., & Cohen, J. (1979). Estimation of individual crime rates from arrest records. *Journal of Criminal Law and Criminology, 70,* 561-585.

Blumstein, A., & Cohen, J. (1987). Characterizing criminal careers. *Science, 237,* 985-991.

Blumstein, A., Cohen, J., & Hsieh, P. (1982). *The direction of adult criminal careers.* Washington, DC: U.S. Department of Justice.

Blumstein, A., Cohen, J., & Nagin, D. (Eds.). (1978). *Deterrence and incapacitation: Estimating the effect of criminal sanctions on crime rates.* Washington, DC: National Academy of Sciences.

Blumstein, A., Cohen, J., Roth, J. A., & Visher, C. A. (Eds.). (1986). *Criminal careers and "career criminals"* (Vol. I). Washington, DC: National Academy Press.

Bolton, F. (1983). *When bonding fails: Clinical assessment of high-risk families.* Beverly Hills, CA: Sage.

Bowlby, J. (1946). *Forty-four juvenile thieves: Their character and home-life.* London: Bailliere Tindall & Cox.

Bowlby, J. (1969). *Attachment and loss: Vol. 1. Attachment.* New York: Basic Books.

Braithwaite, J. (1981). The myth of social class and criminality reconsidered. *American Sociological Review, 46,* 36-57.

Braly, M. (1976). *False starts.* Boston: Little, Brown.

Brennan, T., & Huizinga, D. (1975). *Theory validation and aggregate national data* (Integration Report of the Office of Youth Opportunity Research, FY 1975). Boulder, CO: Behavioral Research Institute.

Brier, S. S., & Fienberg, S. E. (1980). Recent econometric modelling of crime and punishment: Support for the deterrence hypothesis. *Evaluation Review, 4*, 147-191.

Buck, J. A., & Graham, J. R. (1978). The 4-3 MMPI profile type: A failure to replicate. *Journal of Consulting and Clinical Psychology, 46*, 344.

Buikhuisen, W., Bontekoe, E. H., Plas-Korenhoff, C., & van Buuren, S. (1984). Characteristics of criminals: The privileged offender. *International Journal of Law and Psychiatry, 7*, 301-313.

Buikhuisen, W., & Dijksterhuss, P. H. (1971). Delinquency and stigmatization. *British Journal of Criminology, 11*, 185-187.

Bureau of Justice Statistics. (1988). *Criminal victimization in the United States, 1986.* NCJ-111456. Washington, DC: Author.

Bureau of the Census. (1981). *Statistical abstract of the United States.* Washington, DC: U.S. Government Printing Office.

Bursik, R. (1980). The dynamics of specialization in juvenile offenses. *Social Forces, 58*, 851-864.

Burt, M. R. (1983). Justifying personal violence: A comparison of rapists and the general public. *Victimology, 8*, 131-150.

Cairns, R. B., & Cairns, B. D. (1986). The developmental-interactional view of social behavior: Four issues of adolescent aggression. In D. Olweus, J. Block, & M. Radke-Yarrow (Eds.), *Development of antisocial and prosocial behavior: Research, theories, and issues* (pp. 315-342). New York: Academic Press.

Carroll, J. S. (1978). A psychological approach to deterrence: The evaluation of crime opportunities. *Journal of Personality and Social Psychology, 36*, 1512-1520.

Carson, R. C. (1969). Interpretative manual to the MMPI. In J. Butcher (Ed.), *MMPI: Research developments and clinical applications* (pp. 279-296). New York: McGraw-Hill.

Cernkovich, S. (1978). Evaluating two models of delinquency causation. *Criminology, 16*, 335-352.

Cernkovich, S., & Giordano, P. (1979). Delinquency, opportunity, and gender. *Journal of Criminal Law and Criminology, 70*, 145-151.

Chaiken, J., & Chaiken, M. (1982). *Varieties of criminal behavior.* Santa Monica, CA: Rand Corporation.

Chambliss, W., & Nagasawa, R. (1969). On the validity of official statistics: A comparative study of white, black and Japanese high school boys. *Journal of Research in Crime and Delinquency, 6*, 71-77.

Cimler, E., & Beach, L. R. (1981). Factors involved in juveniles' decisions about crime. *Criminal Justice and Behavior, 8*, 275-286.

Cleckley, H. (1976). *The mask of sanity* (5th ed.). St. Louis: Mosby.

Clinard, M. B., & Abbott, D. J. (1973). *Crime in developing countries: A comparative perspective.* New York: Wiley.

Cloward, R. A., & Ohlin, L. E. (1960). *Delinquency and opportunity.* New York: Free Press.

Cohen, A. K. (1955). *Delinquent boys.* New York: Free Press.

Cohen, A. K. (1983). Sociological theories. In S. H. Kadish (Ed.), *Encyclopedia of Crime and Justice* (Vol. I, pp. 342-353). New York: Free Press.

Cohen, A. K., Lindesmith, A., & Schuessler, K. (1956). *The Sutherland papers.* Bloomington, IN: Indiana University Press.

Cohen, B-Z., & Sordo, I. (1984). Using reality therapy with adult offenders. *Journal of Offender Counseling, Services, and Rehabilitation, 8*, 25-39.

Collins, J. J. (1976, November). *Chronic offender careers.* Paper presented at the annual meeting of the American Society of Criminology, Tucson, AZ.

Colvin, M., & Pauly, J. (1983). A critique of criminology: Toward an integrated structural Marxist theory of delinquent production. *American Journal of Sociology, 89,* 513-551.

Conger, J. J., & Miller, W. L. (1966). *Personality, social class, and delinquency.* New York: Wiley.

Conrad, J. P. (1985). *The dangerous and the endangered.* Lexington, MA: Lexington Books.

Cook, P. J. (1980). Research on criminal deterrence: Laying the groundwork for the second decade. In N. Morris & M. Tonry (Eds.), *Crime and justice: An annual review of research* (Vol. 2, pp. 211-268). Chicago: University of Chicago Press.

Cooper, H. H. A. (1971). Crime, criminals, and prisons in Peru. *International Journal of Offender Therapy and Comparative Criminology, 15,* 135-148.

Corbin, R. M. (1980). Decisions that might not get made. In T. S. Wallsten (Ed.), *Cognitive processes in choice and decision behavior* (pp. 47-67). Hillsdale, NJ: Erlbaum.

Cornish, D. B., & Clarke, R. V. (Eds.). (1986). *The reasoning criminal: Rational choice perspectives on offending.* New York: Springer-Verlag.

Cressey, D. R. (1960). Epidemiology and individual conduct: A case from criminology. *Pacific Sociological Review, 3,* 47-58.

Cronbach, L. J. (1970). *Essentials of psychological testing* (3rd ed.). New York: Harper & Row.

Cusson, M., & Pinsonneault, P. (1986). The decision to give up crime. In D. Cornish & R. Clarke (Eds.), *The reasoning criminal: Rational choice perspectives on offending* (pp. 72-82). New York: Springer-Verlag.

Czudner, G. (1985). Changing the criminal. *Federal Probation, 49,* 64-66.

Czudner, G., & Mueller, R. (1987). The role of guilt and its implication in the treatment of criminals. *International Journal of Offender Therapy and Comparative Criminology, 31,* 71-78.

Dahlstrom, W. G., Welsh, G. S., & Dahlstrom, L. E. (1972). *An MMPI handbook: Vol. I. Clinical interpretation* (rev. ed.). Minneapolis: University of Minnesota Press.

Davidson, W. S., Gottschalk, R., Gensheimer, L., & Mayer, J. (1984). *Interventions with juvenile delinquents: A meta-analysis of treatment efficacy.* Washington, DC: National Institute of Juvenile Justice and Delinquency Prevention.

Davidson, W. S., & Robinson, M. J. (1975). Community psychology and behavior modification: A community based program for the prevention of delinquency. *Corrective and Social Psychiatry, 21,* 1-12.

Davis, K. R., & Sines, J. O. (1971). An antisocial behavior pattern associated with a specific MMPI profile. *Journal of Consulting and Clinical Psychology, 36,* 229-234.

Davis, N. J. (1972). Labeling theory in deviance research: A critique and reconsideration. *Sociological Quarterly, 13,* 447-474.

Dean, D. (1979). Some correlates of social insight in adult incarcerated males. *Offender Rehabilitation, 3,* 257-270.

Demaris, O. (1981). *The last Mafioso: The treacherous world of Jimmy Fratianno.* New York: Times Books.

DeMyer-Gapin, S., & Scott, T. J. (1977). Effect of stimulus novelty on stimulation seeking in antisocial and neurotic children. *Journal of Abnormal Psychology, 86,* 96-98.

DeRen, G., Diligent, M. B., & Petiet, G. (1973). The tattoo and the personality of the tattooed. *Medical Legal Dommage Corporation, 6,* 309.

Devine, J. A., Sheley, J. F., & Smith, M. D. (1988). Microeconomic and social-control policy influences on crime rate changes, 1948-1985. *American Sociological Review, 53,* 407-420.

Dinitz, S., Scarpitti, F. R., & Reckless, W. C. (1962). Delinquency vulnerability: A cross group and longitudinal analysis. *American Sociological Review, 27,* 515-517.

Dixon, D. J. (1986). On the criminal mind: An imaginary lecture by Sigmund Freud. *International Journal of Offender Therapy and Comparative Criminology, 30,* 101-109.

Dobson, J. C. (1989). *Fatal addiction: Ted Bundy's final interview* [Film]. Pomona, CA: Focus on the Family.

Doren, D. M. (1987). *Understanding and treating the psychopath.* New York: Wiley.

Douds, A. F., Engelesjord, M., & Collingwood, T. R. (1977). Behavior contracting with youthful offenders and their parents. *Child Welfare, 56,* 409-417.

Douglas, J. D. (Ed.). (1970). *Observations of deviance.* New York: Random House.

Durkheim, E. (1938). *The rules of sociological method* (S. A. Solovay & J. H. Mueller, Trans.). New York: The Free Press.

Edwards, W. (1955). The prediction of decision among bets. *Journal of Experimental Psychology, 50,* 201-214.

Einhorn, H. J., & Hogarth, R. M. (1978). Confidence in judgment: Persistence in the illusion of validity. *Psychological Review, 85,* 395-416.

Elion, V. H. (1974). The validity of the MMPI as a discriminator of social deviance among black males. *FCI Research Reports* (Tallahasee, FL), *6,* 1-18.

Elliott, D. S., & Ageton, S. S. (1980). Reconciling race and class differences in self-reported and official estimates of delinquency. *American Sociological Review, 45,* 95-110.

Elliott, D. S., Ageton, S. S., & Canter, R. J. (1979). An integrated theoretical perspective on delinquent behavior. *Journal of Research in Crime and Delinquency, 16,* 3-27.

Elliott, D. S., & Voss, H. (1974). *Delinquency and dropout.* Lexington, MA: D.C. Heath.

Ellis, A. (1962). *Reason and emotion in psychotherapy.* Secaucus, NJ: Lyle Stuart.

Ellis, A., & Harper, R. A. (1975). *A new guide to rational living.* Englewood Cliffs, NJ: Prentice-Hall.

Enyon, T. G., & Reckless, W. C. (1961). Companionships at delinquency onset. *British Journal of Criminology, 2,* 167-168.

Erez, E. (1980). Planning of crime and the criminal career: Official and hidden offenses. *Journal of Criminal Law and Criminology, 71,* 73-76.

Erickson, W. D., Luxenberg, M. G., Walbek, N. H., & Seeley, R. K. (1987). Frequency of MMPI two-point code types among sex offenders. *Journal of Consulting and Clinical Psychology, 55,* 566-570.

Erikson, R. V., & Roberts, A. H. (1966). An MMPI comparison of two groups of institutionalized delinquents. *Journal of Projective Techniques and Personality Assessment, 30,* 163-166.

Erlanger, H. S. (1980). The allocation of status within occupations: The case of the legal profession. *Social Forces, 58,* 882-903.

Evans, C., & McConnell, T. R. (1941). A new measure of introversion-extroversion. *Journal of Psychology, 12,* 111-124.

Fairweather, G. W. (1953). *Serial rate learning by psychopathic, neurotic, and normal criminals under three incentive conditions.* Unpublished doctoral dissertation, University of Illinois, Urbana.

Farley, F. H., & Cox, O. (1971). Stimulus-seeking motivation in adolescents as a function of age and sex. *Adolescence, 6,* 207-218.

Farley, F. H., & Farley, S. V. (1972). Stimulus-seeking motivation and delinquent behavior among institutionalized delinquent girls. *Journal of Consulting and Clinical Psychology, 39,* 94-97.

Farley, F. H., & Sewell, T. (1976). Test of an arousal theory of delinquency: Stimulation-seeking in delinquent and nondelinquent black adolescents. *Criminal Justice and Behavior, 3,* 315-320.

Farnworth, M., & Leiber, M. J. (1989). Strain theory revisited: Economic goals, educational means, and delinquency. *American Sociological Review, 54,* 263-274.

Farrington, D. P. (1982). Longitudinal analyses of criminal violence. In M. E. Wolfgang & N. A. Weiner (Eds.), *Criminal violence.* Beverly Hills, CA: Sage.

Federal Bureau of Investigation. (1984). *Crime in the United States, 1983.* Washington, DC: U.S. Government Printing Office.

Feeney, F. (1986). Robbers as decision-makers. In D. Cornish & R. Clarke (Eds.), *The reasoning criminal: Rational choice perspectives on offending* (pp. 53-71). New York: Springer-Verlag.

Felson, R. (1982). Impression management and the escalation of aggression and violence. *Social Psychology Quarterly, 45,* 245-253.

Felson, R., & Ribner, B. (1981). An attributional approach to accounts and sanctions for criminal violence. *Social Psychology Quarterly, 44,* 137-142.

Fenz, W. D. (1971). Heart rate responses to a stressor: A comparison between primary and secondary psychopaths and normal controls. *Journal of Experimental Research in Personality, 5,* 7-13.

Field, G. (1986). The psychological deficits and treatment needs of chronic criminality. *Federal Probation, 50,* 60-66.

Figgie Corporation. (1988). *The Figgie report, Part VI. The business of crime: The criminal perspective.* Richmond, VA: Figgie International Incorporated.

Figlio, R. (1981). Delinquency careers as a simple Markov process. In J. Fox (Ed.), *Models of quantitative criminology* (pp. 25-37). New York: Academic Press.

Fiske, D. W. (1983). The meta-analytic revolution in outcome research. *Journal of Consulting and Clinical Psychology, 51,* 65-70.

Fitts, W. H., & Hammer, W. T. (1969). *The self-concept and delinquency* (Research Monograph No. 1). Nashville, TN: Nashville Mental Health Centre.

Flanagan, T. (1983). Correlates of institutional misconduct among state prisoners. *Criminology, 21,* 29-39.

Forgac, G. E., & Michaels, E. J. (1982). Personality characteristics of two types of male exhibitionists. *Journal of Abnormal Psychology, 91,* 287-293.

Foster, J. D., Dinitz, S., & Reckless, W. C. (1972). Perceptions of stigma following public intervention for delinquent behavior. *Social Problems, 20,* 202-209.

Fox, R., & Lippert, W. (1963). Spontaneous GSR and anxiety level in sociopathic delinquents. *Journal of Consulting Psychology, 27,* 368.

Frankl, V. (1963). Existential dynamics and neurotic escapism. *Journal of Existential Psychiatry. 4,* 27-42.

Freeman, R. B. (1983). Crime and unemployment. In J. Q. Wilson (Ed.), *Crime and public policy* (pp. 89-106). San Francisco: Institute for Contemporary Studies.

Freud, S. (1957). Some character types met with in psychoanalytic work. In J. Strachey (Ed.), *Standard edition of the complete psychological works of Sigmund Freud* (Vol. 14, pp. 311-333). London: Hogarth Press and the Institute of Psycho-Analysis.

Freud, S. (1963). Introductory lectures on psycho-analysis. In J. Strachey (Ed.), *Standard edition of the complete psychological works of Sigmund Freud* (Vol. 15-16, pp. 9-496). London: Hogarth Press and the Institute of Psycho-Analysis.

Gacono, C. B., & Meloy, J. R. (1988). The relationship between cognitive style and defensive process in the psychopath. *Criminal Justice and Behavior, 15,* 472-483.

Garnass, S., & Robinson, M. (1989, March 30). Salt-pepper suspect has 68-year record. *Denver Post,* pp. 1, 14.

Garrett, C. J. (1985). Effects of residual treatment on adjudicated delinquents: A meta-analysis. *Journal of Research in Crime and Delinquency, 22,* 287-308.

Gearhart, J. W., Keith, H. L., & Clemmons, G. (1967). *An analysis of the vocational training program in the Washington state adult correctional institutions* (Research Review No. 23). State of Washington, Department of Institutions.

Gendreau, P., & Ross, R. R. (1979). Effective correctional treatment: Bibliotherapy for cynics. *Crime and Delinquency, 25,* 463-489.

Gendreau, P., & Ross, R. R. (1987). Revivification of rehabilitation: Evidence from the 1980s. *Justice Quarterly, 4,* 349-407.

Gibbons, D. C. (1971). Observations on the study of crime causation. *American Journal of Sociology, 77,* 262-278.

Gibbs, J. J., & Shelly, P. L. (1982). Life in the fast lane: A retrospective view by commercial thieves. *Journal of Research in Crime and Delinquency, 19,* 299-330.

Gibbs, J. P., & Erickson, M. L. (1975). Major developments in the sociological study of deviance. *Annual Review of Sociology, 1,* 21-42.

Gilberstadt, H., & Duker, J. (1965). *A handbook for clinical and actuarial MMPI interpretation.* Philadelphia: Saunders.

Glaser, D. (1960). Differential association and criminological prediction. *Social Problems, 8,* 6-14.

Glass, G. V., McGraw, B., & Smith, M. L. (1981). *Meta-analysis in social research.* Beverly Hills, CA: Sage.

Glasser, W. (1965). *Reality therapy.* New York: Harper & Row.

Glover, E. (1960). *The roots of crime: Selected papers on psychoanalysis* (Vol. II). London: Imago.

Gluck, G. H. (1989, June 2). Accused mass killer netted after years on the run. *Star Ledger,* pp. 1, 17.

Gluck, G. H. (1989, June 4). Denver neighbor had nagging doubts. *Star Ledger,* p. 28.

Glueck, S., & Glueck, E. T. (1968). *Delinquents and nondelinquents in perspective.* Cambridge, MA: Harvard University Press.

Gold, M., & Williams, J. R. (1969). National study of the aftermath of apprehension. *Prospectus, 3,* 3-12.

Goldstein, A. P., & Stein, N. (1975). *Prescriptive psychotherapies.* Englewood Cliffs, NJ: Prentice-Hall.

Gove, W. (1985). The effect of age and gender on deviant behavior: A biopsychological approach. In A. Rossi (Ed.), *Gender and the life course* (pp. 115-144). Washington, DC: American Sociological Association.

Graham, J. R. (1987). *The MMPI: A practical guide* (2nd ed.). New York: Oxford University Press.

Greene, R. L. (1980). *The MMPI: An interpretive manual.* New York: Grune & Stratton.

Greenwood, P. W. (1983). Controlling the crime rate through imprisonment. In J. Q. Wilson (Ed.), *Crime and public policy* (pp. 251-269). New Brunswick, NJ: Transaction Books.

Greenwood, P. W., & Zimring, F. (1985). *One more chance: The role of rehabilitation in reducing the criminality of chronic serious juvenile offenders* (Rand Report R-3214-OJJDP). Santa Monica, CA: Rand Corporation.

Groth, A. N., & Hobson, W. F. (1983). The dynamics of sexual assault. In L. B. Schlesinger & E. Revitch (Eds.), *Sexual dynamics of anti-social behavior* (pp. 159-172). Springfield, IL: Charles C Thomas.

Gurr, T. R. (Ed.). (1989). *Violence in America: Vol. 1. The history of crime.* Newbury Park, CA: Sage.

Haapenen, R. A., & Jesness, D. F. (1982). *Early identification of the chronic offender.* Sacramento, CA: California Youth Authority.

Hagan, F. E. (1986). *Introduction to criminology: Theories, methods, and criminal behavior.* Chicago: Nelson-Hall.

Hall, G. C. N., Maiuro, R. D., Vitaliano, P. P., & Proctor, W. C. (1986). The utility of the MMPI with men who have sexually assaulted children. *Journal of Consulting and Clinical Psychology, 54,* 493-496.

Hammer, M., & Ross, M. (1977). Psychological needs of imprisoned adult females with high and low conscience development. *Corrective and Social Psychiatry and Journal of Behavioural Technology Methods and Theory, 23,* 73-78.

Hamparian, D. M., Schuster, R., Dinitz, S., & Conrad, J. P. (1978). *The violent few.* Lexington, MA: Lexington/D.C. Heath.

Hanson, C. L., Henggeler, S. W., Haefele, W. F., & Rodick, J. D. (1984). Demographic, individual, and family relationship correlates of serious and repeated crime among adolescents and their siblings. *Journal of Consulting and Clinical Psychology, 52,* 528-538.

Haran, W. F., & Martin, J. M. (1984). The armed urban bank robber: A profile. *Federal Probation, 48,* 47-53.

Hare, R. D. (1970). *Psychopathology: Theory and research.* New York: Wiley.

Hare, R. D. (1978). Electrodermal and cardiovascular correlates of psychopathy. In R. D. Hare & D. Schalling (Eds.), *Psychopathic behavior: Approaches to research* (pp. 107-144). Chichester, England: Wiley.

Hare, R. D. (1982). Psychopathy and physiological activity during anticipation of an aversive stimulus in a distraction paradigm. *Psychophysiology, 19,* 266-271.

Hare, R. D. (1985). Comparison of procedures for the assessment of psychopathy. *Journal of Consulting and Clinical Psychology, 53,* 7-16.

Hare, R. D., & Craigen, D. (1974). Psychopathy and physiological activity in a mixed-motive game situation. *Psychophysiology, 11,* 197-206.

Hare, R. D., McPherson, L. M., & Forth, A. E. (1988). Male psychopaths and their criminal careers. *Journal of Consulting and Clinical Psychology, 56,* 710-714.

Hare, R. D., & Quinn, M. J. (1971). Psychopathy and autonomic conditioning. *Journal of Abnormal Psychology, 77,* 223-235.

Harris, A. R., & Lewis, M. (1974). *Race and criminal deviance: A study of youthful offenders.* Paper presented at the annual meeting of the American Sociological Association.

Hathaway, S. R., & McKinley, J. C. (1940). A multiphasic personality schedule (Minnesota): I. Construction of the schedule. *Journal of Psychology, 10,* 249-254.

Hathaway, S. R., & Monachesi, E. D. (1963). *Adolescent personality and behavior: MMPI patterns of normal, delinquent, dropout, and other outcomes.* Minneapolis: University of Minnesota Press.

Hebb, D. O. (1972). *Textbook of psychology* (3rd ed.). Philadelphia: Saunders.

Henderson, M., & Hewstone, M. (1984). Prison inmates' explanations for interpersonal violence: Accounts and attributions. *Journal of Consulting and Clinical Psychology, 52,* 789-794.

Henshel, R. L., & Carey, S. (1975). Deviance, deterrence and knowledge of sanctions. In R. L. Henshel & R. A. Silverman (Eds.), *Perceptions in criminology* (pp. 54-73). New York: Columbia University Press.

Hepburn, J. R. (1976). Criminology: Testing alternative models of delinquent causation. *Journal of Criminal Law and Criminology, 67,* 450-460.

Heron, W. (1957). The pathology of boredom. *Scientific American, 196,* 52-56.

Hershey, J. C., & Schoemaker, P. J. H. (1980). Risk taking and problem context in the domain of losses: An expected utility analysis. *Journal of Risk and Insurance, 47,* 111-132.

Hewitt, J. (1970). *Social stratification and deviant behavior.* New York: Random House.

Hindelang, M. J. (1971). The social versus solitary nature of delinquent involvements. *British Journal of Criminology, 11,* 167-175.

Hindelang, M. J. (1973). Causes of delinquency: A partial replication and extension. *Social Problems, 20,* 471-487.

Hindelang, M. J., Gottfredson, M., & Garofalo, J. (1978). *Victims of personal crime: An empirical foundation for a theory of personal victimization.* Cambridge, MA: Ballinger.

Hindelang, M. J., Hirschi, T., & Weis, J. G. (1979). Correlates of delinquency: The illusion of discrepancy between self-report and official measures. *American Sociological Review, 44,* 995-1014.

Hindelang, M. J., Hirschi, T., & Weis, J. G. (1981). *Measuring delinquency.* Beverly Hills, CA: Sage.

Hirschi, T. (1969). *Causes of delinquency.* Berkeley, CA: University of California Press.

Hirschi, T., & Gottfredson, M. (1983). Age and the explanation of crime. *American Journal of Sociology, 89,* 552-584.

Hirschi, T., & Hindelang, M. J. (1977). Intelligence and delinquency: A revisionist view. *American Sociological Review, 42,* 571-587.

Hofer, P. (1988). Prisonization and recidivism: A psychological perspective. *International Journal of Offender Therapy and Comparative Criminology, 32,* 95-106.

Holden, C. (1986). Growing focus on criminal careers. *Science, 233,* 1377-1378.

Holland, T. R., Beckett, G. E., & Levi, M. (1981). Intelligence, personality, and criminal violence: A multivariate analysis. *Journal of Consulting and Clinical Psychology, 49,* 106-111.

Holland, T. R., & McGarvey, B. (1984). Crime specialization, seriousness progression, and Markov chains. *Journal of Consulting and Clinical Psychology, 52,* 837-840.

Hook, J. G., & Cook, T. D. (1979). Equity theory and the cognitive ability of children. *Psychological Bulletin, 86,* 429-445.

Hyatt, C., & Gottlieb, L. (1988). Why smart people fail. *Readers Digest, 132,* pp. 69-73.

Irwin, J. (1970). *The felon.* Englewood Cliffs, NJ: Prentice-Hall.

Jackson, E. F., Tittle, C. R., & Burke, M. J. (1986). Offense-specific models of the differential association process. *Social Problems, 33,* 335-356.

Jackson, G. (1970). *Soledad brother.* New York: Coward-McCann.

Jamieson, K. M., & Flanagan, T. J. (1987). *Sourcebook of criminal justice statistics—1986.* Washington, DC: U.S. Department of Justice, Bureau of Statistics.

Jensen, G. F. (1972). Parents, peers, and delinquent action: A test of the differential association perspective. *American Journal of Sociology, 78,* 562-575.

Jensen, G. F., & Eve, R. (1976). Sex differences in delinquency. *Criminology, 13,* 427-448.

Johnson, R. E. (1979). *Juvenile delinquency and its origin.* Cambridge: Cambridge University Press.

Jolin, A., & Gibbons, D. C. (1987). Age patterns in criminal involvement. *International Journal of Offender Therapy and Comparative Criminology, 31*, 237-260.

Kahneman, D., & Tversky, A. (1979). Prospect theory: An analysis of decision under risk. *Econometrica, 47*, 263-291.

Kaplan, H. (1976). Self-attitudes and deviance response. *Social Forces, 54*, 788-801.

Katz, J. (1979). Concerted ignorance: The social construction of a cover-up. *Urban Life, 8*, 295-316.

Kazdin, A. (October, 1987). Personal communication cited in Magid & McKelvey (1987, p. 33).

Kellam, S. G., Adams, R. G., Brown, H. C., & Ensminger, M. E. (1982). The long-term evolution of the family structure of teenage and older mothers. *Journal of Marriage and the Family, 44*, 539-554.

Kelly, D. H. (1977). Labeling and the consequences of wearing a delinquent label in a school setting. *Education, 97*, 371-380.

Kempf, K. L. (1987). Specialization and the criminal career. *Criminology, 25*, 399-420.

Kerlinger, F. N. (1973). *Foundations of behavioral research* (2nd ed.). New York: Holt, Rinehart, & Winston.

King, G. D., & Kelley, C. K. (1977). Behavioral correlates for spike-4, spike-9, and 4-9/9-4 MMPI profiles in students at a university mental health center. *Journal of Clinical Psychology, 33*, 718-724.

King, H. (with B. Chambliss) (1972). *Box man.* New York: Harper & Row.

Kipnis, D., & Wagner, W. (1967). Character structure and response to leadership power. *Journal of Experimental Research in Personality, 2*, 16-24.

Kitsuse, J. I., & Dietrick, D. C. (1959). Delinquent boys: A critique. *American Sociological Review, 24*, 208-215.

Kobayashi, Y., Ono, N., Ooe, A., & Sakumichi, S. (1982). Professionalization of violent criminals and characteristics of their criminal situation. *Tohoku Psychologica Folia, 41*, 107-115.

Koriat, A., Melkman, R., Averill, J. R., & Lazarus, R. S. (1972). The self-control of emotional reactions to a stressful film. *Journal of Personality, 40*, 601-618.

Kornhauser, R. (1978). *Social sources of delinquency.* Chicago: University of Chicago Press.

Kraut, R. E. (1976). Deterrent and definitional influences on shoplifting. *Social Problems, 23*, 358-368.

Langan, P. A., & Farrington, D. P. (1983). Two-track or one-track justice? Some evidence from an English longitudinal survey. *Journal of Criminal Law and Criminology, 74*, 519-546.

Langan, P. A., & Greenfeld, L. A. (1983). Career patterns in crime. *Bureau of Justice Statistics: Special Report.* NCJ-88672. Washington, DC: Bureau of Justice Statistics.

Lattimore, P., & Witte, A. (1985). Models of decision making under uncertainty: The criminal choice. In D. Cornish & R. Clarke (Eds.), *The reasoning criminal: Rational choice perspectives on offending* (pp. 129-155). New York: Springer-Verlag.

Leftkowitz, M. M., Eron, L. D., Walder, L. O., & Huesmann, L. R. (1977). *Growing up to be violent: A longitudinal study of the development of aggression.* New York: Pergamon.

Lemert, E. M. (1951). *Social pathology.* New York: McGraw-Hill.

Lemert, E. M. (1972). *Human deviance, social problems and social control* (2nd ed.). Englewood Cliffs, NJ: Prentice-Hall.

Leopold, N. F. (1958). *Life plus 99 years.* Garden City, NY: Doubleday.

Lerner, M. J. (1970). The desire for justice and reactions to victims. In J. Macaulay & L. Berkowitz (Eds.), *Altruism and helping behavior: Social psychological studies of some antecedents and consequences* (pp. 205-229). New York: Academic Press.

Levinson, D., Darrow, C., Klein, E., Levinson, M., & McKee, B. (1978). *The seasons of a man's life*. New York: Knopf.

Linquist, C. A., Smusz, T. D., & Doerner, W. (1985). Causes of conformity: An application of control theory to adult misdemeanant probationers. *International Journal of Offender Therapy and Comparative Criminology, 29,* 1-14.

Lipsey, M. W. (1986). *Research plan: Meta-analysis of juvenile delinquency treatment research*. Unpublished manuscript, Claremont Graduate School, Claremont, CA.

Liska, A. E. (1971). Aspirations, expectations, and delinquency: Stress and additive models. *Sociological Quarterly, 12,* 99-107.

Loeber, R., & Dishion, T. (1983). Early predictors of male delinquency: A review. *Psychological Bulletin, 94,* 68-99.

Loper, R. G., Kammeier, M. L., & Hoffmann, H. (1973). MMPI characteristics of college freshman males who later became alcoholics. *Journal of Abnormal Psychology, 82,* 159-162.

Lubin, B., Larsen, R. M., Matarazzo, J. D., & Seever, M. (1985). Psychological test usage patterns in five professional settings. *American Psychologist, 40,* 857-861.

Luckenbill, D. F. (1977). Criminal homicide as a situated transaction. *Social Problems, 25,* 176-186.

Lykken, D. (1957). A study of anxiety in the sociopathic personality. *Journal of Abnormal and Social Psychology, 55,* 6-10.

Lynch, J., & Cohen, J. L. (1978). The use of subjective expected utility theory as an aid to understanding variables that influence helping behavior. *Journal of Personality and Social Psychology, 36,* 1138-1151.

Maddi, S. A. (1976). *Personality theories: A comparative analysis* (3rd ed.). Homewood, IL: Dorsey Press.

Magid, K., & McKelvey, C. A. (1987). *High risk*. New York: Bantam Books.

Magnusson, D., & Allen, V. L. (1983). *Human development: An interactional perspective*. New York: Academic Press.

Mahoney, A. R. (1974). The effect of labeling upon youths in the juvenile justice system: A review of the evidence. *Law and Society Review, 8,* 583-614.

Mahoney, M. J. (1977). Reflections on the cognitive-learning trend in psychotherapy. *American Psychologist, 32,* 5-13.

Main, M., Kaplan, N., & Cassidy, J. (1985). Security in infancy, childhood, and adulthood: A move to the level of representation. *Monographs of the Society for Research in Child Development, 50* (1-2, Serial No. 209).

Manson, C. (with N. Emmons) (1986). *Manson: In his own words*. New York: Grove Press.

Marks, J., & Glaser, E. (1980). The antecedents of chosen joblessness. *American Journal of Community Psychology, 8,* 173-201.

Marks, P. A., Seeman, W., & Haller, D. L. (1974). *The actuarial use of the MMPI with adolescents and adults*. Baltimore: Williams & Wilkins.

Martinson, R. (1974). What works?—Questions and answers about prison reform. *Public Interest, 10,* 22-54.

Martinson, R. (1979). New findings, new views: A note of caution regarding sentencing reform. *Hofstra Law Review, 7,* 242-258.

Matsueda, R. L. (1982). Testing control theory and differential association: A causal modeling approach. *American Sociological Review, 47,* 489-504.

Matza, D. (1964). *Delinquency and drift*. New York: Wiley.

Maultsby, M. C. (1975). *Help yourself to happiness through rational self-counseling*. New York: Institute of Rational Living.

May, R. (1958). Contributions of existential psychotherapy. In R. May, E. Angel, & H. F. Ellenberger (Eds.), *Existence: A new dimension in psychiatry and psychology* (pp. 61-63). New York: Basic Books.

McClelland, D. C. (1971). *Assessing human motivation.* New York: General Learning Press.

McCord, W., & McCord, J. (1959). *Origins of crime.* New York: Columbia University Press.

McCreary, C. P. (1975). Personality profiles of persons convicted of indecent exposure. *Journal of Clinical Psychology, 31,* 260-262.

McDowell, C. P., & Thygusen, N. (1975). The "loser" and the criminal justice system. *International Journal of Criminology and Penology, 3,* 155-161.

Mednick, S. A. (1987). Introduction. Biological factors in crime causation: The reactions of social scientists. In S. A. Mednick (Ed.), *The causes of crime: New biological approaches* (pp. 1-6). New York: Cambridge University Press.

Megargee, E. I., & Bohn, M. J. (1979). *Classifying criminal offenders: A new system based on the MMPI.* Beverly Hills, CA: Sage.

Megargee, E. I., Cook, P. E., & Mendelsohn, G. A. (1967). Development and validation of an MMPI scale of assaultiveness in overcontrolled individuals. *Journal of Abnormal Psychology, 72,* 519-528.

Meichenbaum, D. (1977). *Cognitive behavior modification.* New York: Plenum.

Meier, R. F. (1983). United States of America. In E. H. Johnson (Ed.), *International handbook of contemporary developments in criminology: General issues and the Americas* (pp. 267-296). Westport, CT: Greenwood Press.

Meisenhelder, T. (1977). An exploratory study of exiting from criminal careers. *Criminology, 15,* 319-334.

Menninger, K. (1968). *The crime of punishment.* New York: Viking.

Merton, R. K. (1957). *Social theory and social structure.* New York: Free Press of Glencoe.

Messner, S. F. (1982). Poverty, inequality, and the urban homicide rate: Some unexpected findings. *Criminology, 20,* 103-114.

Messner, S. F. (1984). The "dark figure" and composite indexes of crime: Some empirical exploration of alternative data sources. *Journal of Criminal Justice, 12,* 435-444.

Mischel, W. (1968). *Personality and assessment.* New York: Wiley.

Mischel, W. (1973). Toward a cognitive social learning conceptualization of personality. *Psychological Review, 80,* 252-283.

Moffitt, T. E., Gabrielli, W. F., Mednick, S. A., & Schulsinger, F. (1981). Socioeconomic status, IQ, and delinquency. *Journal of Abnormal Psychology, 90,* 152-156.

Moncrieff, M., & Pearson, D. (1979). Comparison of MMPI profiles of assaultive and non-assaultive exhibitionists and voyeurs. *Corrective and Social Psychiatry and Journal of Behavioural Technology Methods and Theory, 25,* 91-93.

Moos, R. H. (1975). *Evaluating correctional and community settings.* New York: Wiley.

Mowrer, O. H. (1960). *Learning theory and behavior.* New York: Wiley.

Mowrer, O. H. (1964). *The new group therapy.* Princeton, NJ: Van Nostrand.

Murray. H. A. (1966). *Explorations in personality.* New York: Oxford University Press.

Newman, G. (1982). The implications of tattooing in prisoners. *Journal of Clinical Psychiatry, 43,* 231-234.

Normandeau, A., & Lanciault, R. (1983). The profession of a robber. *Canadian Journal of Criminology, 25,* 33-46.

Novaco, R. (1975). *Anger control: The development and evaluation of an experimental treatment.* Lexington, MA: Heath & Co.

Ono, N. (1980). The characteristic MMPI profile pattern of youthful Japanese delinquents. *Tohoku Psychologica Folia, 39,* 105-112.

Orcutt, J. D. (1987). Differential association and marijuana use: A closer look at Sutherland (with a little help from Becker). *Criminology, 25,* 341-358.

Orsagh, T., & Witte, A. D. (1981). Economic status and crime: Implications for offender rehabilitation. *Journal of Criminal Law and Criminology, 72,* 1055-1071.

Othmer, E., Penick, E. C., & Powell, B. J. (1981). *Psychiatric Diagnostic Interview (PDI) manual.* Los Angeles: Western Psychological Services.

Panton, J. (1958). MMPI profile configurations among crime classification groups. *Journal of Clinical Psychology, 16,* 305-312.

Pankratz, H., Briggs, B., & Robinson, M. (1989, March 24). Madman kills 2 in siege. *Denver Post,* pp. 1-1, 13-A.

Paternoster, R. (1987). The deterrent effect of the perceived certainty and severity of punishment: A review of the evidence and issues. *Justice Quarterly, 4,* 173-217.

Patterson, G. R. (1982). *Coercive family processes.* Eugene, OR: Castalia.

Patterson, G. R. (1986). Performance models for antisocial boys. *American Psychologist, 41,* 432-444.

Paul, G. L. (1969). Outcome of systematic desensitization II: Controlled investigations of individual treatment, technique variations and current status. In C. M. Franks (Ed.), *Behavior therapy: Appraisal and status* (pp. 105-159). New York: McGraw-Hill.

Paulson, M. J., Afifi, A. A., Thomason, M. L., & Chaleff, A. (1974). The MMPI: A descriptive measure of psychopathology in abusive parents. *Journal of Clinical Psychology, 30,* 387-390.

Pearson, F. S., & Weiner, N. A. (1985). Toward an integration of criminological theories. *Journal of Criminal Law and Criminology, 76,* 116-150.

Persons, R. W. (1967). Relationship between psychotherapy with institutionalized boys and subsequent community adjustment. *Journal of Consulting Psychology, 31,* 137-141.

Persons, R. W., & Marks, P. A. (1971). The violent *4-3* MMPI personality type. *Journal of Consulting and Clinical Psychology, 36,* 189-196.

Petersilia, J., Greenwood, P. W., & Lavin, M. (1978). *Criminal careers of habitual felons.* Washington, DC: U.S. Government Printing Office.

Peterson, C. A. (1984). "Hedonism" is no fun: Notes on Burgess's "hedonism" construct. *British Journal of Criminology, 24,* 296-300.

Peterson, M. A., & Braiker, H. B. (1980). *Doing crime: A survey of California prison inmates.* Santa Monica, CA: RAND.

Phillips, L., & Votey, H. L. (1981). *The economics of crime control.* Beverly Hills, CA: Sage.

Piaget, J. (1954). *The construction of reality in the child.* New York: Basic Books.

Piliavin, I., Gartner, R., Thornton, C., & Matsueda, R. L. (1986). Crime, deterrence, and rational choice. *American Sociological Review, 51,* 101-119.

Plummer, K. (1979). Misunderstanding labeling perspectives. In D. Downes & P. Rock (Eds.), *Deviant interpretations.* London: Martin Robertson.

Polk, K., Adler, C., Bazemore, G., Blake, G., Cordray, S., Coventry, G., Galvin, J., & Temple, M. (1981). *Becoming adult: An analysis of maturational development from age 16 to 30 of a cohort of young men* (Final report of the Marion County Youth Study). Eugene, OR: University of Oregon.

Polk, K., & Schafer, W. E. (1972). *School and delinquency.* Englewood Cliff, NJ: Prentice-Hall.

Poole, E. D., & Regoli, R. M. (1979). Parental support, delinquent friends, and delinquency: A test of interactional effects. *Journal of Criminal Law and Criminology, 70,* 188-193.

Porprine, F. J., Doherty, P. D., & Sawatsky, T. (1987). Characteristics of homicide victims and victimization in prison: A Canadian historical perspective. *International Journal of Offender Therapy and Comparative Criminology, 31,* 125-136.

Quay, H. C. (1965). Psychopathic personality as pathological stimulation-seeking. *American Journal of Psychiatry, 122,* 180-183.

Quay, H. C. (1977). Psychopathic behavior: Reflections on its nature, origins, and treatment. In I. Uzgiris & F. Weizman (Eds.), *The structuring of experience.* New York: Plenum.

Quinsey, V. L., Arnold, L. S., Pruesse, M. G. (1980). MMPI profiles of men referred for a pretrial psychiatric assessment as a function of offense types. *Journal of Clinical Psychology, 36,* 410-417.

Rada, R. (1978). *Clinical aspects of the rapist.* New York: Grune & Stratton.

Rader, C. M. (1977). MMPI profile types of exposures, rapists, and assaulters in a court services population. *Journal of Consulting and Clinical Psychology, 45,* 61-69.

Rankin, J. (1977). Investigating the interrelations among social control variables and conformity. *Journal of Criminal Law and Criminology, 67,* 470-480.

Reckless, W. C., Dinitz, S., & Kay, B. (1957). The self component in potential delinquency and potential non-delinquency. *American Sociological Review, 22,* 566-570.

Reckless, W. C., Dinitz, S., & Murray, E. (1956). Self-concept as an insulator against delinquency. *American Sociological Review, 21,* 744-746.

Reiss, A. J., & Rhodes, A. L. (1961). The distribution of juvenile delinquency in the social class structure. *American Sociological Review, 26,* 720-732.

Reiss, A. J., & Rhodes, A. L. (1964). An empirical test of differential association theory. *Journal of Research in Crime and Delinquency, 1,* 5-18.

Rizzo, T. (1989, April 12). Kansas fugitive captured despite cosmetic surgery. *Kansas City Times,* pp. 1, 5.

Robins, L. N., West, P. A., & Herjanic, B. L. (1975). Arrests and delinquency in two generations: A study of black urban families and their children. *Journal of Child Psychology and Psychiatry, 16,* 125-140.

Rogers, C. R. (1951). *Client-centered therapy.* Boston: Houghton Mifflin.

Rosenbaum, J. L. (1987). Social control, gender, and delinquency: An analysis of drug, property and violent offenders. *Justice Quarterly, 4,* 117-132.

Ross, R. R., & Fabiano, E. A. (1985). *Time to think: A cognitive model of delinquency prevention and offender rehabilitation.* Johnson City, TN: Institute of Social Sciences & Arts.

Ross, R. R., Fabiano, E. A., & Ewles, C. D. (1988). Reasoning and rehabilitation. *International Journal of Offender Therapy and Comparative Criminology, 32,* 29-35.

Rotter, J. B. (1966). Generalized expectancies for internal versus external control of reinforcement. *Psychological Monographs, 80* (Whole No. 609).

Rowe, D. C. (1987). Resolving the person-situation debate: Invitation to interdisciplinary dialogue. *American Psychologist, 42,* 218-227.

Ruby, C. T. (1984). Defusing the hostile ex-offender: Rational behavior training. *Emotional First Aid, 1,* 17-22.

Russell, M. (1964). The Irish delinquent in England. *Studies, 53* (Summer 1964).

Rutter, M., & Giller, H. (1984). *Juvenile delinquency: Trends and perspectives.* New York: Guilford Press.

Sampson, R. J., & Castellano, T. C. (1982). Economic inequality and personal victimisation. *British Journal of Criminology, 22,* 363-385.

Satre, J. P. (1956). *Being and nothingness.* New York: Philosophical Library.

Scarpitti, F. R., Murray, E., Dinitz, S., & Reckless, W. C. (1960). The "good" boy in a high delinquency area: Four years later. *American Sociological Review, 25*, 555-558.

Schachter, S., & Singer, J. E. (1962). Cognitive, social, and physiological determinants of emotional state. *Psychological Review, 69*, 379-399.

Schur, E. M. (1971). *Labeling deviant behavior: Its sociological implications.* New York: Harper & Row.

Shaffer, H. R., & Emerson, P. E. (1964). The development of social attachments in infancy. *Monographs of the Society for Research in Child Development, 3*, (Serial No. 94).

Shannon, L. W. (1982). *Assessing the relationship of adult criminal careers to juvenile careers: A summary.* Washington, DC: Office of Juvenile Justice and Delinquency Prevention.

Shavit, Y., & Rattner, A. (1988). Age, crime, and the early life course. *American Journal of Sociology, 93*, 1457-1470.

Short, J. F. (1957). Differential association and delinquency. *Social Problems, 4*, 233-239.

Short, J. F., & Strodtbeck, F. L. (1965). *Group process and gang delinquency.* Chicago: University of Chicago Press.

Shostak, D. A., & McIntyre, C. W. (1978). Stimulation-seeking behavior in three delinquent personality types. *Journal of Consulting and Clinical Psychology, 46*, 582.

Shover, N. (1983). The later stages of ordinary property offender careers. *Social Problems, 31*, 208-218.

Siegel, R. A. (1978). Probability of punishment and suppression of behavior in psychopathic and nonpsychopathic offenders. *Journal of Abnormal Psychology, 87*, 514-522.

Skinner, B. F. (1953). *Science and human behavior.* New York: Macmillan.

Smith, D. A., & Paternoster, R. (1987). The gender gap in theories of deviance: Issues and evidence. *Journal of Research in Crime and Delinquency, 24*, 140-172.

Smith, D. R., Smith, W. R., & Noma, E. (1984). Delinquent career-lines: A conceptual link between theory and juvenile offenses. *Sociological Quarterly, 25*, 155-172.

Snyder, E. C. (1971). The impact of the juvenile court hearing on the child. *Crime and Delinquency, 17*, 180-190.

Spitzer, S. (1975). Toward a Marxian theory of deviance. *Social Problems, 22*, 638-651.

Stack, S. (1982). Social structure and Swedish crime rates. *Criminology, 20*, 499-513.

Stack, S. (1983). Homicide and property crime: The relationships to anomie. *Aggressive Behavior, 9*, 339-344.

Steffensmeier, D. J., & Cobb, M. J. (1981). Sex differences in urban arrest patterns, 1934-1979. *Social Problems, 29*, 37-49.

Steiner, C. (1974). *Scripts people live: Transactional analysis of life scripts.* New York: Bantam Books.

Stewart, C. H. M., & Hemsley, D. R. (1984). Personality factors in the taking of criminal risks. *Personality and Individual Differences, 5*, 119-122.

Stuck, M. F., Ksander, M., Berg, B., Laughlin, J., & Johnson, B. D. (1982). *The consequences of breaking the law: Perceptions of adolescents involved in serious crime.* New York: Interdisciplinary Research Center.

Sutherland, E. H. (1937). *The professional thief.* Chicago: University of Chicago Press.

Sutherland, E. H. (1939). *Principles of criminology* (3rd ed.). Philadelphia: Lippincott.

Sutherland, E. H., & Cressey, D. R. (1978). *Principles of criminology* (10th ed.). New York: Harper & Row.

Sutton, W. (with Q. Reynolds). (1953). *I, Willie Sutton.* New York: Farrar, Straus, & Young.

Sykes, G. M., & Matza, D. (1970). Techniques of delinquency. In W. E. Wolfgang, L. Savitz, & N. Johnston (Eds.), *The sociology of crime and delinquency* (2nd ed., pp. 292-299). New York: Wiley.

Tannenbaum, F. (1938). *Crime and the community.* Boston: Ginn & Company.

Tanner, J. (1987, September 28). The gang that couldn't rob straight. *Newsweek,* p. 30.

Tarde, G. (1912). *Penal philosophy.* Boston: Little, Brown.

Teevan, J. J. (1975). Perceptions of punishment: Current research. In R. L. Henshel & R. A. Silverman (Eds.), *Perceptions in criminology.* New York: Columbia University Press.

Teevan, R. C., & McGhee, P. E. (1972). Childhood development of fear of failure motivation. *Journal of Personality and Social Psychology, 21,* 345-348.

Thomas, C. W. (1977). *The effects of legal sanctions on juvenile delinquency: A comparison of the labeling and deterrent perspectives.* (Final Report, LEAA Grant 75-NI-99-0031 and 76-NI-99-0050). Bowling Green, OH: Bowling Green State University.

Thompson, W. E., Mitchell, J., & Dodder, R. (1984). An empirical test of Hirschi's control theory of delinquency. *Deviant Behavior, 5,* 11-22.

Thornberry, T. P. (1971). *Punishment and crime: The effect of legal dispositions on subsequent criminal behavior.* Unpublished doctoral dissertation, University of Pennsylvania.

Thornberry, T. P. (1987). Toward an interactional theory of delinquency. *Criminology, 25,* 863-892.

Thornberry, T. P., Moore, M., & Christenson, R. L. (1985). The effect of dropping out of high school on subsequent criminal behavior. *Criminology, 23,* 3-18.

Thorsell, B. A., & Klemke, L. W. (1972). The labeling process: Reinforcement or deterrent? *Law and Society Review, 6,* 393-403.

Tillman, R. (1987). The size of the "criminal population": The prevalence and incidence of adult arrest. *Criminology, 25,* 561-579.

Tittle, C. R., Burke, M. J., & Jackson, E. F. (1986). Modeling Sutherland's theory of differential association: Toward an empirical clarification. *Social Forces, 65,* 405-432.

Tittle, C. R., Villemez, W. J., & Smith, D. A. (1978). The myth of social class and criminality: An empirical assessment of the empirical evidence. *American Sociological Review, 43,* 643-656.

Valins, S. (1966). Cognitive effects of false heart-rate feedback. *Journal of Personality and Social Psychology, 4,* 400-408.

Viscusi, W. K. (1983). *Market incentives for criminal behavior.* Unpublished paper, National Bureau of Economic Research.

Vold, G. B. (1979). *Theoretical criminology* (2nd ed.). New York: Oxford University Press.

Voss, H. L. (1964). Differential association and delinquent behavior. *Social Problems, 12,* 78-85.

Wachs, T. D. (1977). The optimal stimulation hypothesis and early development: Anybody got a match? In I. Uzgiris & F. Weizman (Eds.), *The structuring of experience.* New York: Plenum.

Walters, G. D. (1985). Scale *4* (Pd) of the MMPI and the diagnosis antisocial personality. *Journal of Personality Assessment, 49,* 474-476.

Walters, G. D. (1989). Predicting the disciplinary adjustment of maximum and minimum security prison inmates using the Lifestyle Criminality Screening Form. Unpublished manuscript.

Walters, G. D., Greene, R. L., & Solomon, G. S. (1982). Empirical correlates of the over-controlled-hostility scale and the MMPI *4-3* high-point pair. *Journal of Consulting and Clinical Psychology, 50,* 213-218.

Walters, G. D., Revella, L., & Baltrusaitis, W. J. (1990). Predicting parole/probation outcome with the aid of the Lifestyle Criminality Screening Form. *Psychological Assessment: A Journal of Consulting and Clinical Psychology, 2.*

Walters, G. D., Solomon, G. S., & Greene, R. L. (1982). The relationship between the overcontrolled-hostility scale and the MMPI 4-3 high-point pair. *Journal of Clinical Psychology, 38,* 613-615.

Walters, G. D., & White, T. W. (1987). *Examining lifestyle criminality: The Leavenworth 500.* Unpublished manuscript, United States Penitentiary, Leavenworth, KS.

Walters, G. D., & White, T. W. (1988). Crime, popular mythology, and personal responsibility. *Federal Probation, 52,* 18-26.

Walters, G. D., & White, T. W. (1989a). Heredity and crime: Bad genes or bad research? *Criminology, 27,* 455-485.

Walters, G. D., & White, T. W. (1989b). Lifestyle criminality from a developmental standpoint. *American Journal of Criminal Justice, 13,* 257-278.

Walters, G. D., & White, T. W. (1989c). The thinking criminal: A cognitive model of lifestyle criminality. *Criminal Justice Research Bulletin, 4,* No. 4.

Walters, G. D., & White, T. W. (in press). Therapeutic interventions with the lifestyle criminal. *Journal of Offender Counseling, Services and Rehabilitation.*

Walters, G. D., & White, T. W., & Denney, D. (in press). The Lifestyle Criminality Screening Form: Preliminary data. *Criminal Justice and Behavior.*

Ward, D. A., Jackson, M., & Ward, R. E. (1969). Crimes of violence by women. In D. J. Mulvihill & M. M. Tumin (Eds.), *Crimes of violence* (pp. 843-909). Washington, DC: U.S. Government Printing Office.

Warren, C. (1974). The use of stigmatizing social labels in conventionaling deviant behavior. *Sociology and Social Research, 58,* 303-311.

Warren, M. Q. (1983). Applications of interpersonal-maturity theory to offender populations. In W. S. Laufer & J. M. Day (Eds.), *Personality theory, moral development, and criminal behavior* (pp. 23-50). Lexington, MA: Lexington Books.

Warren, M. Q., & Rosenbaum, J. L. (1986). Criminal careers of female offenders. *Criminal Justice and Behavior, 13,* 393-418.

Waters, L. K., & Kirk, W. E. (1968). Stimulus-seeking motivation and risk-taking behavior in a gambling situation. *Educational and Psychological Measurement, 28,* 549-550.

Weaver, F. M., & Carroll, J. S. (1985). Crime perceptions in a natural setting by expert and novice shoplifters. *Social Psychology Quarterly, 48,* 349-359.

Wells, L. E. (1978). Theories of deviance and the self-concept. *Social Psychology, 41,* 189-204.

Werner, H. (1957). The concept of development from a comparative and organismic point of view. In D. Harris (Ed.), *The concept of development.* Minneapolis: University of Minnesota Press.

West, D. J., & Farrington, D. P. (1977). *The delinquent way of life: Third report of the Cambridge study in delinquent development.* London: Heinemann Educational Books.

Wiatrowski, M. D., Griswold, D. B., & Roberts, M. K. (1981). Social control theory and delinquency. *American Sociological Review, 46,* 525-541.

Wilkins, L. T. (1965). *Social deviance: Social policy, action, and research.* Englewood Cliffs, NJ: Prentice-Hall.

Williams, F. P. (1984). The demise of the criminological imagination: A critique of recent criminology. *Justice Quarterly, 1,* 91-106.

Wilson, J. Q., & Herrnstein, R. J. (1985). *Crime and human nature.* New York: Simon & Schuster.

Witte, A. D. (1980). Estimating the economic model of crime with individual data. *Quarterly Journal of Economics, 94,* 57-84.

Wolfgang, M., Figlio, R. F., & Sellin, T. (1972). *Delinquency in a birth cohort.* Chicago: University of Chicago Press.

Wolfgarth, A. (1976). Perceptual and cognitive factors in therapy with antisocial individuals. *Ontario Psychologist, 8,* 26-35.

Wollersheim, J. P. (1970). Effectiveness of group therapy based on learning principles in the treatment of overweight women. *Journal of Abnormal Psychology, 76,* 462-474.

Wrightsman, L. S. (1974). Measures of philosophies of human nature. *Psychological Reports, 14,* 743-751.

Yamamoto, J., Seeman, W., & Lester, B. K. (1963). The tattooed man. *Journal of Nervous and Mental Diseases, 136,* 365-367.

Yochelson, S., & Samenow, S. E. (1976). *The criminal personality: Vol. I. A profile for change.* New York: Jason Aronson.

Yochelson, S., & Samenow, S. E. (1985). *The criminal personality: Vol. II. The change process* (rev. ed.). New York: Jason Aronson.

Yochelson, S., & Samenow, S. E. (1986). *The criminal personality: Vol. III. The drug user.* New York: Jason Aronson.

Zivan, M. (1966). *Youth in trouble: A vocational approach* (Final Report of a Research and Demonstration Project, May 31, 1961 to August 31, 1966). Dobbs Ferry, NY: Children's Village.

Zuckerman, M. (1975). *Manual and research report for the Sensation Seeking Scale.* Newark, DE: University of Delaware.

Zuckerman, M., Neary, R. S., & Brustman, B. A. (1970, August). Sensation-Seeking Scale correlates in experience (smoking, drugs, alcohol, "hallucinations," and sex) and preference for complexity (designs). *Proceedings of the 78th Annual Convention of the American Psychological Association.* Washington, DC: American Psychological Association.

Zuckerman, M., Tushup, R., & Finner, S. (1976). Sexual attitudes and experience: Attitude and personality correlates and changes produced by a course in sexuality. *Journal of Consulting and Clinical Psychology, 44,* 7-19.

Author Index

*table or figure

Subject Index

Aspirations, working class, 29
Assessment, criticisms of, 156-157
Assessment, lifestyle model, 165-167
  cognitive profiling, 166-167 (Problem Oriented Survey, 163-165*; single pill dilemma, 166-167)
  developmental assessment, 166
  lifestyle analysis, 165-166 (Lifestyle Criminality Screening Form, 160-163*, 165, 192)
Assessment, Minnesota Multiphasic Personality Inventory (MMPI)
  development of, 157
  high-point combinations: *4-3* pattern, 159; *4-8/8-4* pattern, 159-160; *4-9/9-4* pattern, 160; spike *4* pattern, 158-159
  special scales: Overcontrolled-Hostility Scale (*O-H*), 159
  standard scale elevations: scale *4*, 158
Attribution Theory, 34

Career criminal, 16-17, 53-57, 100
  age and the, 57
  concept: criticisms of, 57
  gender and the, 57
  methodologies: cohort, 54; longitudinal criminal history, 55; survey, 54; target sample, 54-55
  race and the, 57
Causes/Correlates of crime
  age, 14, 57-58, 114*
  biological and genetic factors, 12, 14, 42, 43
  choice, 13, 14, 16, 18, 60-61, 80-81
  drugs, 14
  economic status, 45-46
  family, 14, 42, 101
  guilt, 39-40
  intelligence, 14, 101

media violence, 14
peers, 13, 23, 31, 101, 115-116
physical traits, 12
school, 27, 32
social class, 14, 27
temperament, 14
Choice, importance of, 13, 15, 44-46, 80-81, 107-108; *see also* Causes/Correlates of crime *and* Criminal lifestyle
Cognition
  criminal-noncriminal differences, 130
  development of, 16, 18-19, 60-61
  differentiation of, 148-149
  irrational, 128-129
  magical thinking, 146
  see also Criminal lifestyle
Comprehensive Crime Control Act, 53-54
Conditions, 14-15, 18-19, 79-80, 101-106
  action of: exacerbating/mitigating function, 80, 107-108; risk/protective function, 80, 107-108
  types of: interactive variables, 15; person variables, 14; situation variables, 14
Control
  importance of in criminal thinking, 119, 139, 140, 141
  locus of, 104
Crime
  desistance from, 58-59, 60-61, 96, 116, 118, 119, 123
  severity of, 118-119
  specialization, 23, 55-56
  statistics and data: aggregate-level, 30, 45; official, 17; self-report, 17; victimization, 17
  white-collar, 53
Criminal lifestyle
  alcohol & drug abuse, 74-75, 102
  anger, 91, 113

About the Author

Glenn D. Walters has spent the past six years serving as a staff psychologist with the Federal Bureau of Prisons at the United States Penitentiary in Leavenworth, Kansas. He received a B.A. in psychology from Lebanon Valley College in 1976, an M.A. from Indiana University of Pennsylvania in clinical psychology in 1978, and a Ph.D. in counseling psychology from Texas Tech University in 1982. He took his internship training at Dwight David Eisenhower Army Medical Center, Fort Gordon, Georgia, where he had his first exposure to incarcerated offenders. After completing his internship, Dr. Walters served as chief psychologist at the United States Disciplinary Barracks, Fort Leavenworth, Kansas, from whence he transferred to the United States Penitentiary after twenty months. In addition to developing a theory of lifestyle criminality, recent publications have dealt with the use of psychometric data to predict criminal outcomes, the genetic correlates of crime, and inmate classification.